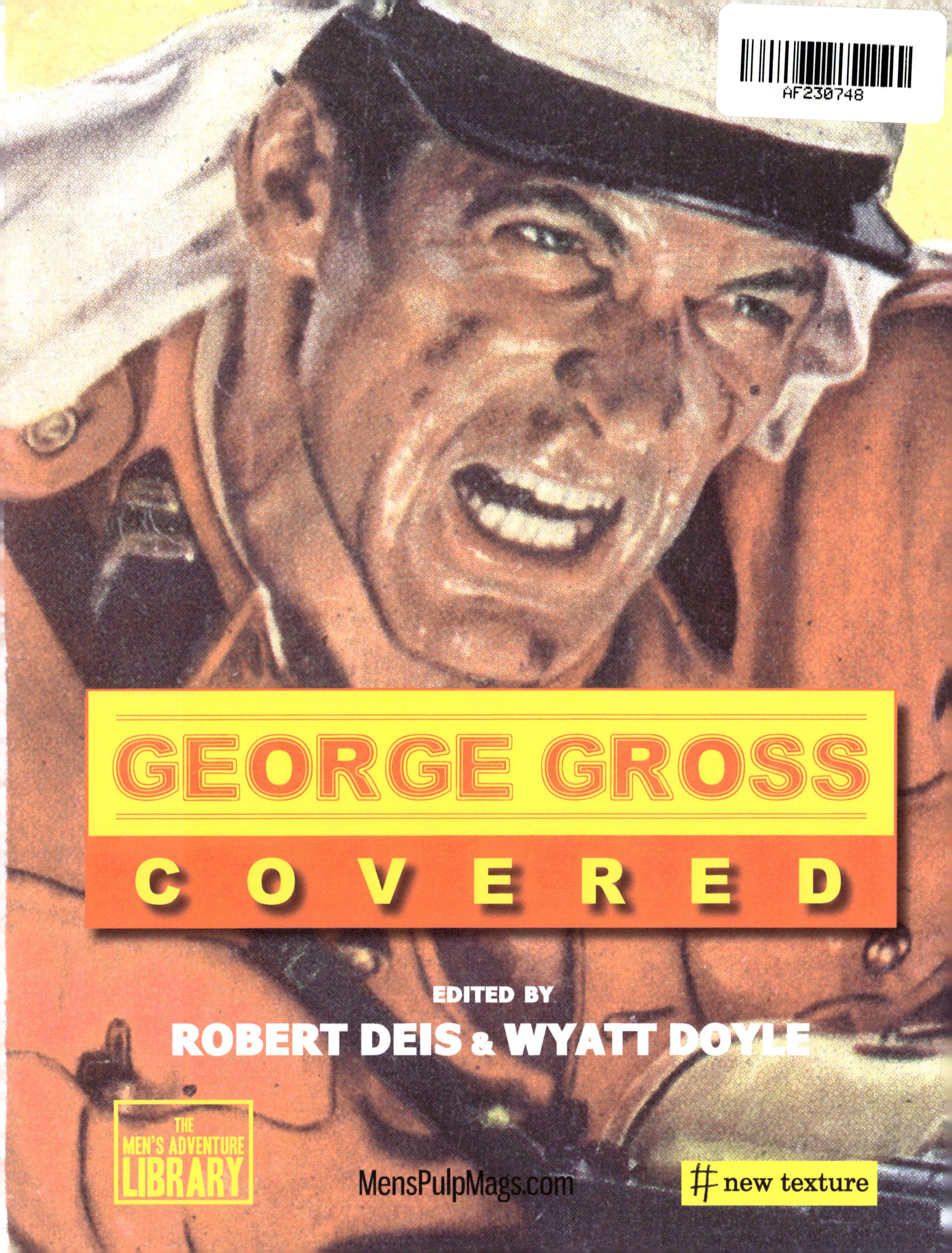

GEORGE GROSS

COVERED

EDITED BY

ROBERT DEIS & WYATT DOYLE

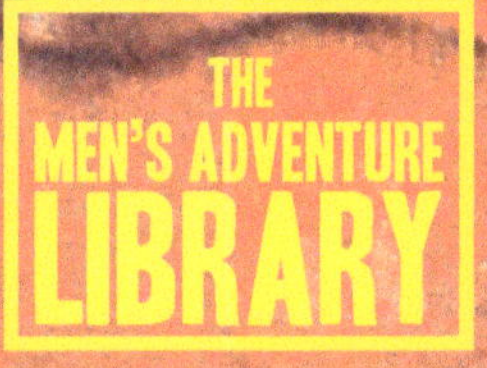

MensPulpMags.com

new texture

A New Texture book

Designed by Wyatt Doyle for The Men's Adventure Library

Archival materials supplied by The Robert Deis Archive
Additional materials courtesy Mort Künstler.

With thanks to David Saunders, Mort Künstler, Jane Künstler, Linda Swanson, and Rich Oberg

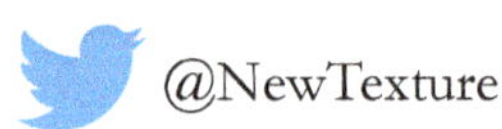 @NewTexture 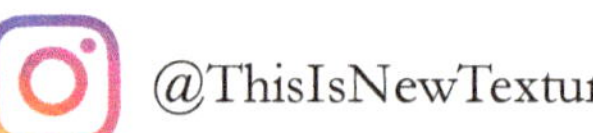 @ThisIsNewTexture   MensPulpMags.com   NewTexture.com

Booksellers: *George Gross: Covered* and other New Texture books are available through Ingram Book Co.

ISBN 978-1-943444-04-5

First New Texture softcover edition: August 2022

Also available as a deluxe expanded hardcover with additional content.

Printed in the United States of America

10 9 8 7 6 5 4 3 2 1

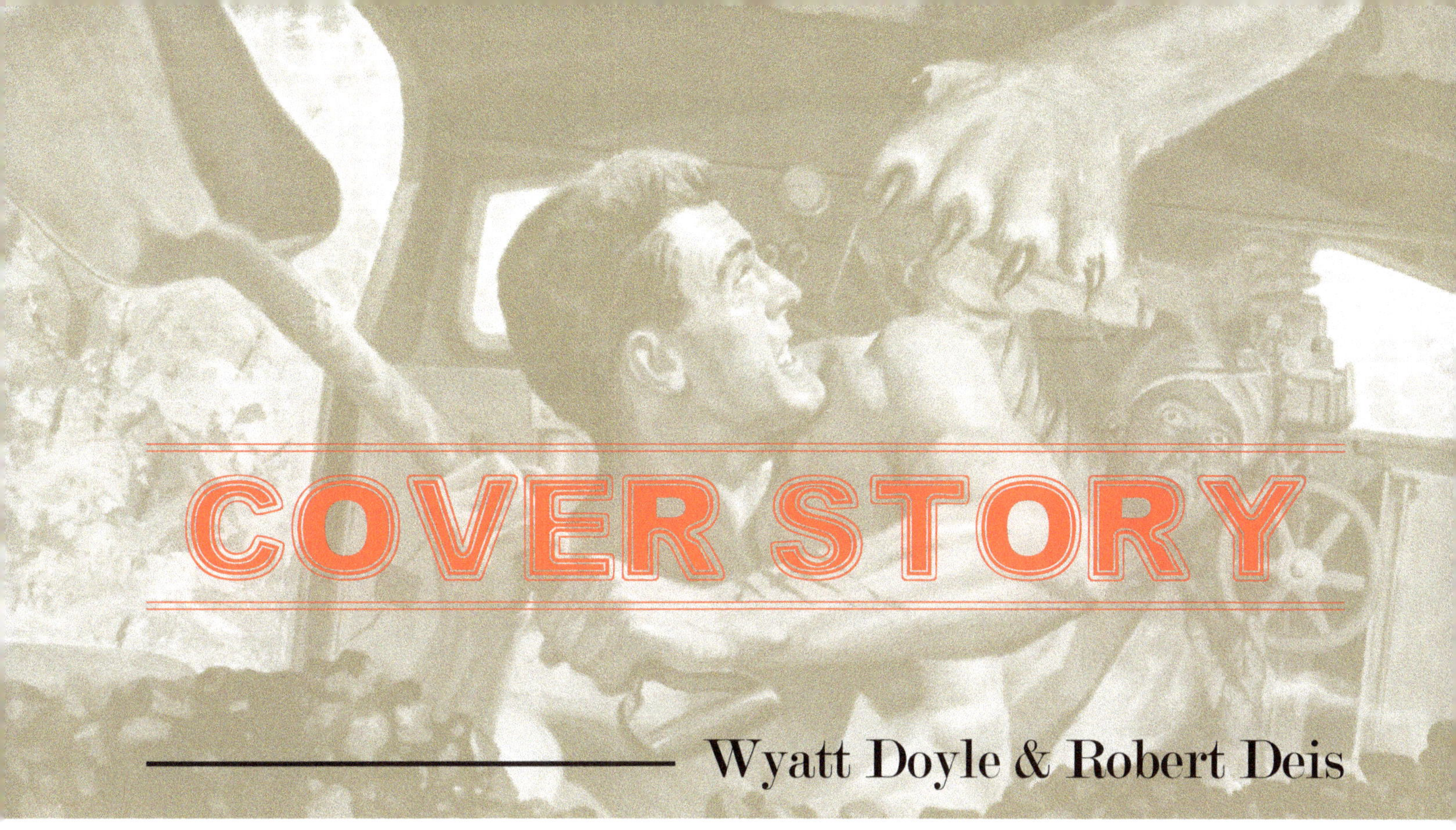

The unapologetic thrills, excitement, and escape provided by action/adventure fiction cemented its popularity as one of the leading diversions of the 20th century (and beyond). The genre as we know it grew out of and was defined by three key print formats: Pulp magazines, which emerged at the end of the 19th century, continued through the 1950s, and existed in a variety of genres, including crime, mystery, Western, and outdoor and exotic adventure. Those subjects, along with popular themes such as *shudder pulp* (often emphasizing sexual threat, terror, and torment) and stories drawing on fears of foreign and adversarial cultures and antisocial fringe groups, clearly informed the next stage of adventure fiction: the tough, terse storytelling in men's adventure magazines, or MAMs. MAMs, an outgrowth and expansion of the pulps, emerged as pulps were fading to become a crucial part of the lowbrow landscape into the 1970s.

Action/adventure paperbacks followed a parallel course, exploding in the 1950s with the introduction of *paperback originals* (books first printed as paperbacks). Frequently intersecting with MAMs, action-focused paperbacks would reignite interest in vintage pulp fiction in the 1960s by repackaging old pulps as mass market reprints. By the 1970s, paperbacks further emulated pulps with serial adventure novels built around recurring characters—a concept pulps popularized with heroes like Doc Savage and The Shadow.

Today, paperbacks are the last format standing, and vintage paperback series of the 1960s and '70s are becoming as hotly collected as original pulp mags and MAMs.

The no-nonsense, heightened strain of adventure fiction those formats shaped and cultivated has antecedents in the work of respected writers from Jules Verne to Robert Louis Stevenson to Kipling to Conrad to Hemingway to Mailer, and those iconic names occasionally saw print in those publications via reprints of their work.

Pulps and MAMs and action/adventure paperbacks adopted a direct and populist approach, building readerships on their own terms. Practical considerations such as the need to fill pages on deadline helped define the emerging genre's style, leaving little room for literary refinement.

It was not missed. Readers responded to the intensity and lack of pretense shared by all three formats. While there are clear differences in the approaches of each, and further distinctions arise when exploring individual publishers and publications, a common current ran through them: Brass-tacks, aggressively action-focused writing. Thrills for the sake of thrills, with no loftier purpose. Authors didn't waste time getting to the good stuff, and the good stuff could be bigger than life, and wild. These formats and their unpretentious, meat-and-potatoes writing were literary fast food—*junk* food, to snobs and bluenoses who dismissed them.

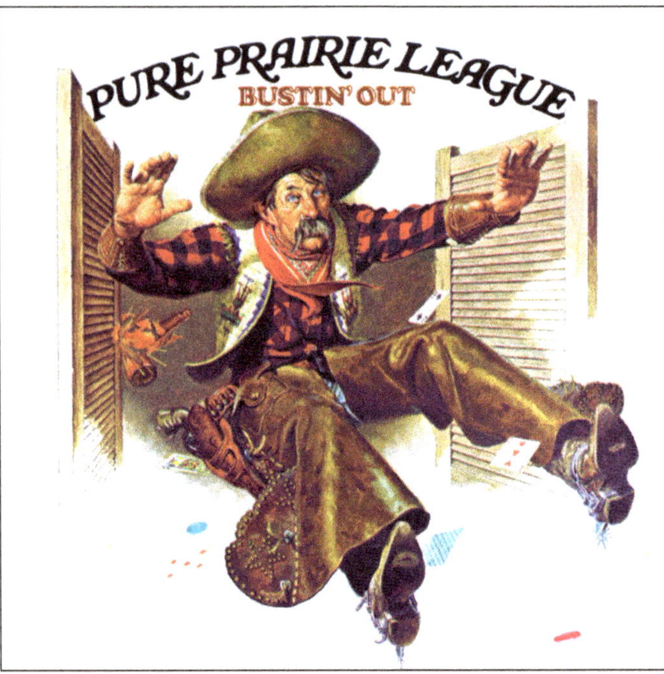

Gross's pulp roots informed his work throughout his career. In 1972, Pure Prairie League turned to Gross for cover art in a vintage style equally inspired by Norman Rockwell for their hit LP, *Bustin' Out*.

This spicy, caffeinated approach was similar yet different from adventure fiction that had gone before; it scratched a slightly different itch. The tremendous popularity of each of these formats in their time suggests this was an itch shared by a sizable portion of the reading public.

Common threads and strands of shared influence among the formats are evident, owing to their shared point of origin: Pulp magazine publishers were often paperback publishers, and by the '50s, many were publishing MAMs, too.

The average MAM offered more than solely action fiction, including other kinds of fiction. The formula was broad, open to any subject thought of interest to men. Non-fiction included features on history, travel, sexuality, celebrities, pin-up photography, scandals and exposés, even straight-shooting cultural critique and commentary.

But while those subjects might appear as headlines on covers,[1] for most of the MAM era, cover art meant action illustrations, frequently over-the-top and outrageous. It was that violent, sweaty promise

of action, of adventure, of excess…and ultimately, the promise of *escape* that sold magazines. Cover subjects at times are strange and often extreme, but were in fact tested, tried-and-true approaches known to sell magazines. Competition on newsstands was fierce, and the entire table of contents was for naught if the cover didn't shut out the other mags and open the reader's wallet. That's a lot of pressure on the cover, but pressure can create diamonds.

George Gross's work on those MAM covers is the focus of this collection, and there are diamonds here. As lifelong friend and colleague Mort Künstler relates in his reminiscences (pg. 9), these pieces sat high among the work Gross was proudest of.

Gross shines in the more contained scenarios, and in his frequent use of close-up portraits. A master at rendering facial expressions, he recognized the drama inherent in the human face, and many of his most memorable pieces reflect that, with skilled, detailed depictions of tension, terror, anxiety, agony, rage.

We've included covers credited to Gross, and those bearing his painted signature. There are examples of reuses and repurposing of his images by other MAM titles, as was common practice.

He lived to see a revival of the pulps when they were reconfigured as paperbacks, then he painted the covers for those, too. His many series included The Avenger (initially pulp reprints, followed by pastiches), Operator 5 (pulp reprints), the first ten books in Don Pendleton's Mack Bolan/Executioner series (no pulp origins, but MAM fiction-adjacent), and the Nick Carter Killmaster books (a reinvention of a character with pulp roots).

He did little artwork for major mainstream magazines, but he was one of a small number of illustration artists who made memorable contributions to pulp magazines, MAMs, *and* action/ adventure paperbacks. His covers bridge all three.

The strain of action/adventure these formats hatched demanded a functional visual vocabulary. It needed images and iconography to help illuminate and define it. With direction from their publishers' art directors, artists like George Gross created those images and helped establish that iconography, so effectively that much of it is now taken for granted.

His covers attracted millions who were drawn to tough, masculine subject matter. His arresting paintings converted browsers to buyers, transporting them before they'd read a word. His art sold books and magazines for decades, to generations of readers.

Too little documented before now, George Gross is among the greats of 20th century illustration art. The covers collected here, only a segment of a long career, are ample testament.

---

1   MAM cover headlines speak volumes, not only about the magazines' contents, but also the presumed attitudes, interests, and curiosities of their readers. If you can't lay hands on the magazines, read the covers.

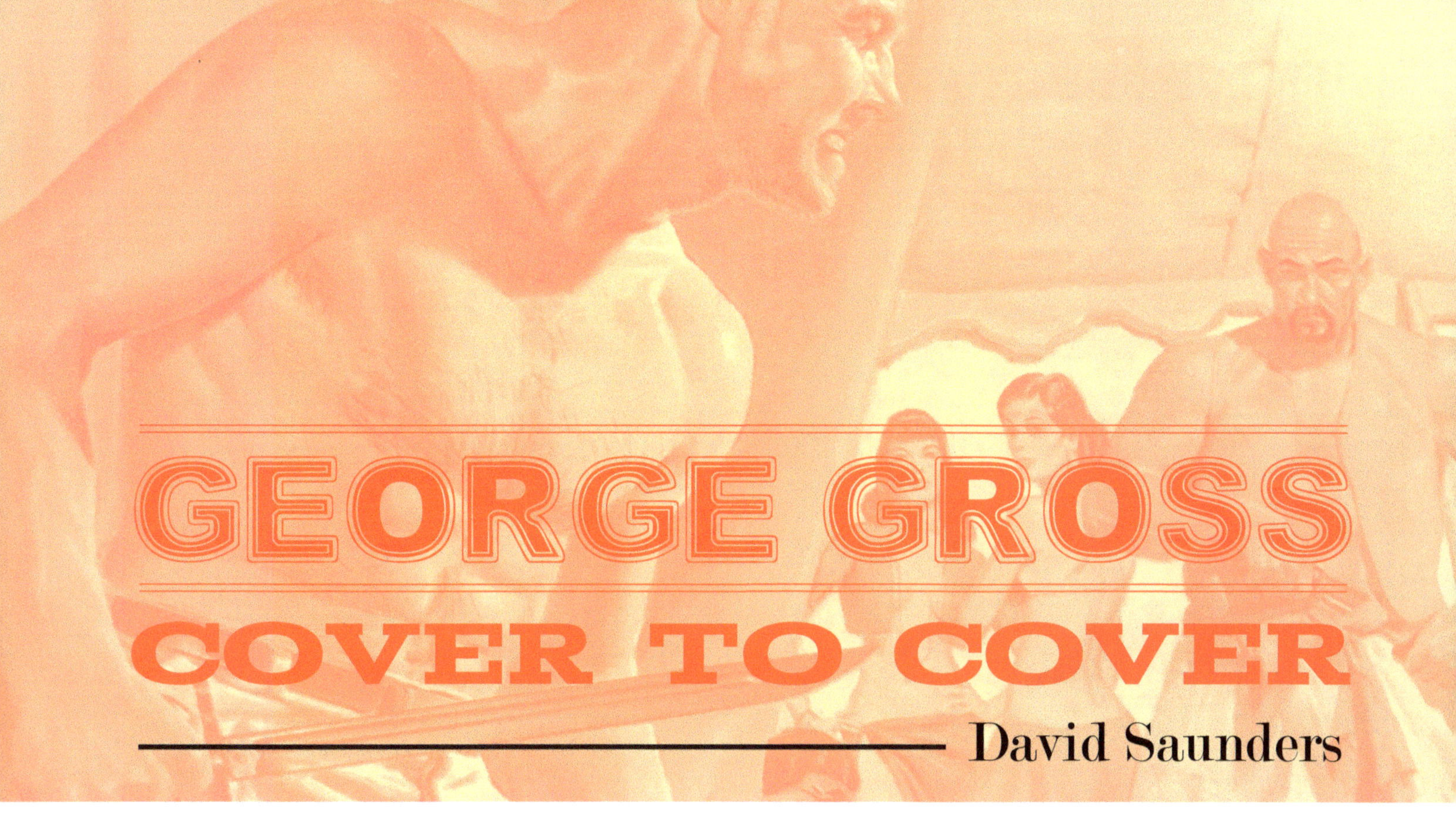

George Gross was born of Hungarian-Jewish ancestry on February 16, 1909 in New York City. His father, Deszo "Dave" Gross, was born in 1887 in the city of Szeged, Hungary, and in 1891, at the age of eight, came to America with his family and settled in NYC. George's mother, Serena Krauss, was born in 1891 in Hungary, and in 1906, at the age of sixteen, moved to America with her family. The Grosses married in 1908, and had three children, George (b.1909), Arthur (b. 1910), and their little sister, Beatrice (b.1913). At first the family lived in an apartment at 466 East Tenth Street in Manhattan's Lower East Side, but after the arrival of their third child, the family moved to a larger apartment in Brooklyn at 2365 83rd Street.

Dave Gross had studied art at Pratt Institute of Brooklyn, and enjoyed a successful career as an illustrator in the NYC fashion industry. He owned and operated a midtown art studio called Fashion Paper. One of his biggest clients was Montgomery Ward, a dry goods mail-order business of Chicago. At that time it was too expensive to reproduce photographs by Rotogravure, so all of the illustrations in the company catalog were drawn by hand and reproduced by steel engraving.

By 1918, the father's commercial art studio was prosperous enough for the Gross family to buy a private home at 105 Bay 29th Street in Brooklyn.

The 1926 and 1927 editions of Lee & Kirby's annual directory of Advertising Arts & Crafts listed the Dave Gross Art Studio at 229 Fourth Avenue in Manhattan.

On December 2, 1926, all Brooklyn newspapers carried the heartwarming story of Arthur Gross, a sixteen-year-old sophomore at New Utrecht High School, who was awarded a $25 first prize for designing the best poster for Christmas Seals, which were displayed throughout the city's trolley cars, subways, buses, and elevated trains.

One month later, in January of 1927, George Gross graduated from Jefferson High School, which was located in Brooklyn at the corner of Pennsylvania and Dumont Avenues.

In September of 1928, George Gross followed in his father's and brother's footsteps and began to study art at Pratt Institute of Brooklyn. His drawing teacher was Rudolph Belarski (1900–1983), his advertising instructor was Frederick Blakeslee (1898–1973), his painting instructor was Nicholas Riley (1900–1944), and he studied illustration with Harold Winfield Scott (1897–1977). Two of his classmates were Frank Volp (1912–1980) and Howard Sherman (1909–1993), both of whom were native New Yorkers. Volp, Sherman, and Gross went on to become best friends, studio mates, and fellow pulp artists.

In June of 1931 George Gross graduated from Pratt. Even before graduation he had begun to work at his father's commercial art studio in NYC. He was soon joined by both of his younger siblings,

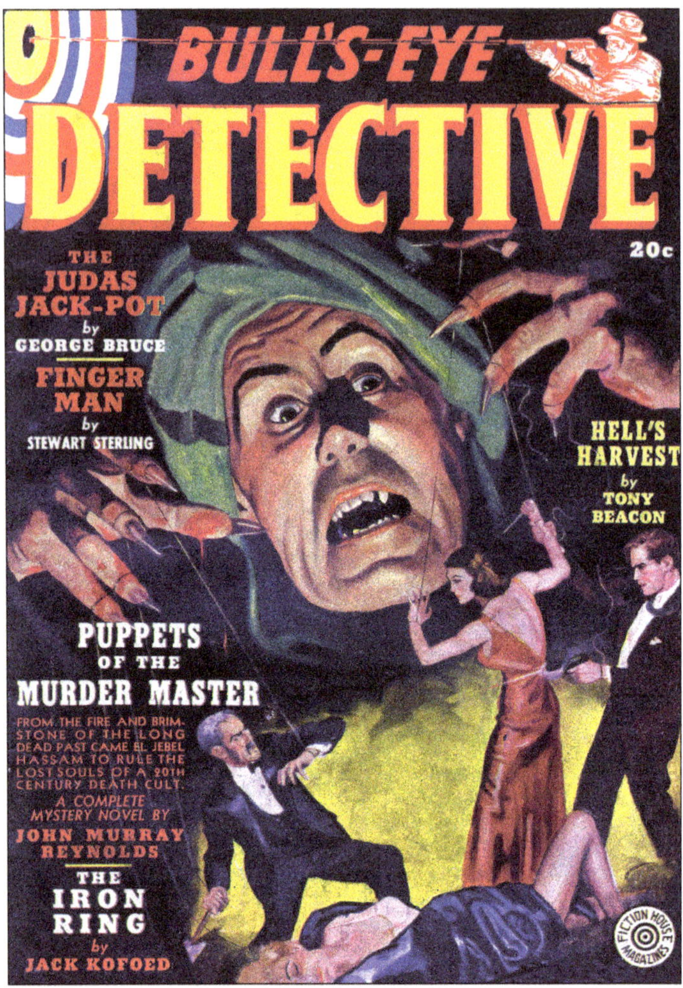

Gross donned turban and claws to model as the villain in his cover for the Fall 1938 issue of *Bulls-Eye Detective*.

Arthur and Beatrice Gross, who had also graduated from Pratt. The Dave Gross commercial art studio provided all three young artists with a uniquely business-like approach to commercial illustration.

In 1934, George Gross painted his first pulp painting, which appeared on the cover of *Double Action Western* from Louis Silberkleit's Winford Publications. The artist next found work at Thurmon Scott's Fiction House, and sold pulp covers to Street & Smith's *Western Story* and *Sport Story*, as well as A. A. Wyn's Ace Magazines, which used his covers for *Ace Sports*, *Romance Round-Up*, *Western Aces*, and *Western Trails*.

In 1936, the artist's father, Dave Gross, formed a new art agency, called the Nangro Ferrod Studios, located at 15 West 38th Street in Manhattan. George Gross shared his studio space at these offices with his brother and sister. He produced all of his pre-war pulp covers in the moonlight hours, while working as a full-time employee at his father's studio. His brother, Arthur Gross, drew pen-and-ink story illustrations for pulps produced by Fiction House, Popular Publications, Winford, and Ace Publications. He also painted two pulp covers that appeared on *Western Action Novels Magazine*. Arthur Gross also drew story illustrations for slick magazines, such as *Collier's* and *Boy's Life*.

In 1938, the five members of the Gross family —father Dave (age fifty-one), mother Serena (age forty-seven), and three grown children, George (age twenty-nine), Arthur (age twenty-eight), and Beatrice (age twenty-five)—all still lived together in their Brooklyn home at 105 Bay 29th Street.

On June 1, 1939 George Gross (age thirty) married Dora Weitzman (age thirty-three) in her hometown of Parkway, New Jersey, where she was born of Russian-Jewish ancestry on February 1, 1906. She had attended public school up to the eighth grade, and then entered the workforce. She worked as a salesgirl at a millenary shop in Essex, NJ. The married couple moved into an apartment building at 309 West 14th Street, near Eighth Avenue, in Manhattan.

In 1942, George Gross reported to his draft board for military service in WWII. Although he was still young enough to serve (age thirty-three), he was disqualified from military service because of a lifelong impairment of vision in his right eye, which effected his depth perception and required corrective glasses. So instead of disappearing from pulp publishing for the duration, he was one of the few artists who continued to work for NYC pulp publishers during the war.

This advantage helped him to become one of the top pulp cover artists. He painted dozens of freelance covers for Fiction House magazines, such as *Action Stories*, *Air Stories*, *All-American Football*, *Baseball Stories*, *Complete Northwest*, *Detective Book Magazine*, *Fight Stories*, *Football Action*, *Lariat Story*, *Jungle Stories*, *North West Romances*, *Planet Stories*, and *Wings*.

According to the pulp author William Robert Cox (1901–1988), "George Gross could do exciting paintings even when there were no scantily clad damsels around, and what's more amazing, Fiction House let him!"

After the war, George Gross began to sell freelance illustrations to paperback books from such publishers as Dell, Star Books, Lion Books, Bantam, Berkley Books, Cameo Books, and Ace Publications.

In 1946, the artist and his wife left Manhattan and moved to a rented home in Flushing, Queens, from which he would commute by subway to his art studio on White Street in the warehouse section of

Lower Manhattan, known as Tribeca.

In 1950, George Gross and his wife got away from the bustling city to spend their summer in a rented apartment of the garage building at the residence of Miss Fannie Kipp, an art teacher of Milford, Pennsylvania. George and Dora continued to enjoy this annual vacation for the next four years, until 1954, when they bought their own summer home in Milford.

On March 18, 1955, the artist's father, Dave Gross, died at the age of sixty-eight in Brooklyn.

By that time the pulp magazine industry had dried up. Since most of the pulps had folded, the pulp artists had to find other sources of income. George Gross soon found freelance assignments at men's adventure magazines, such as *Action For Men*, *Argosy*, *Adventure*, *Bluebook For Men*, *Cavalcade*, *Male*, *Man's Conquest*, *Man's Illustrated*, *Man's World*, *Real*, *Saga*,

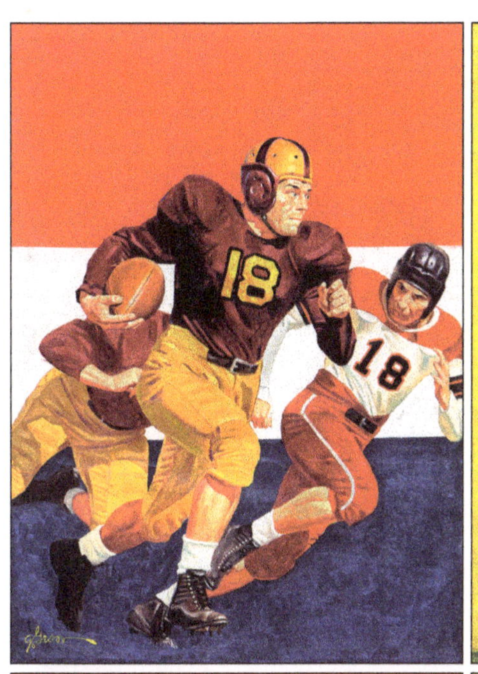
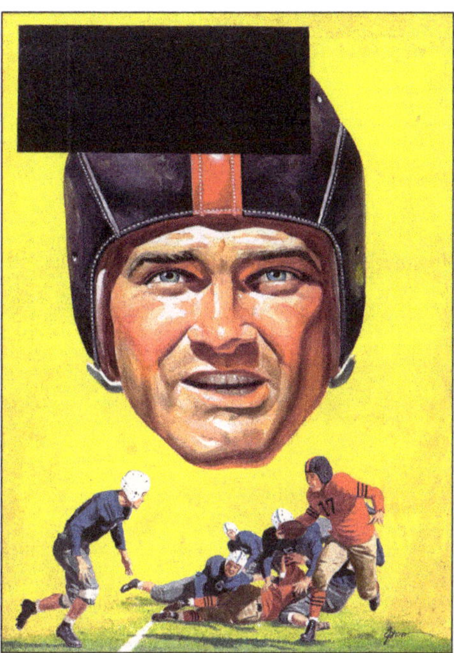
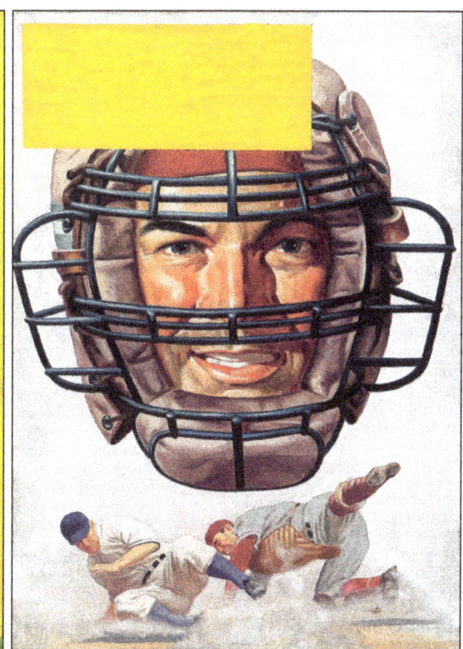
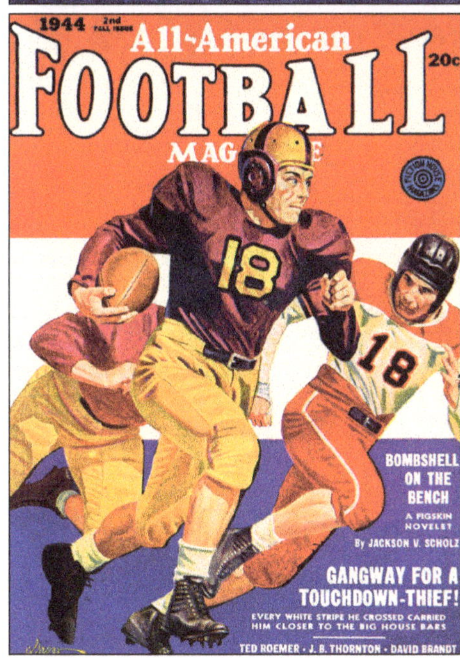

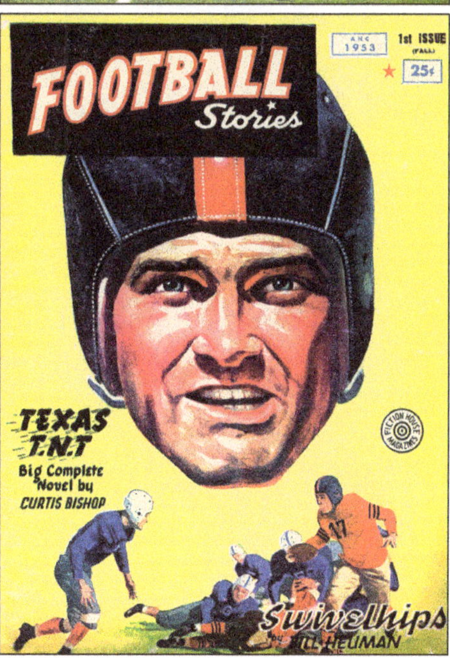

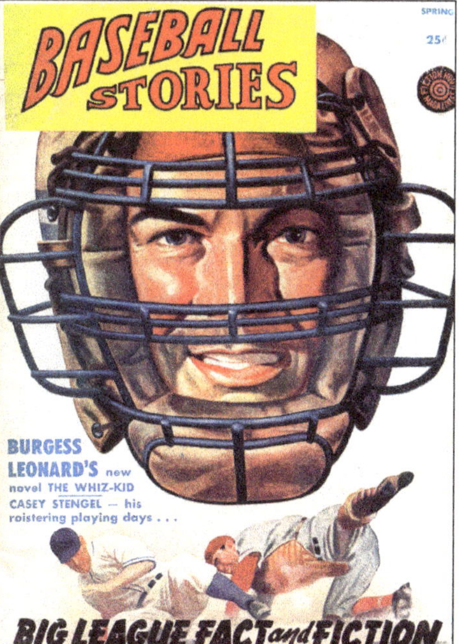

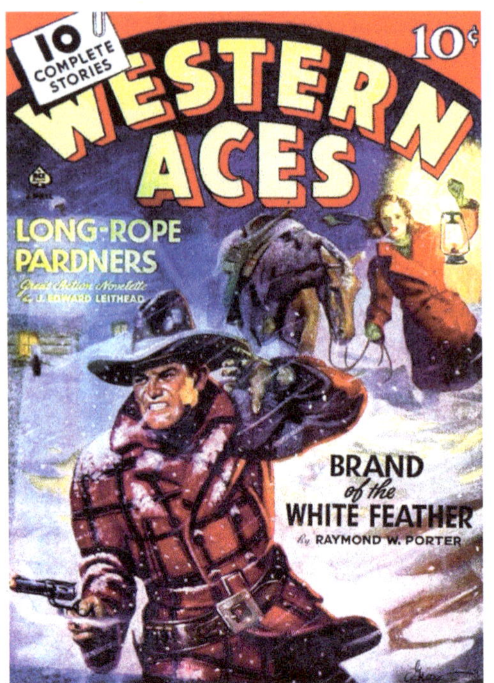
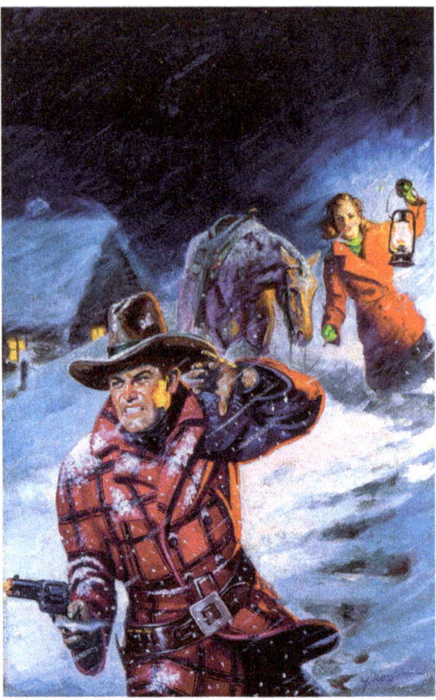
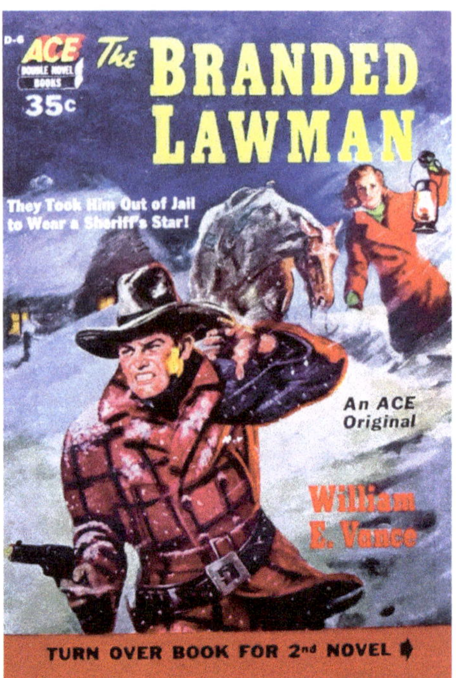

A 1941 Gross cover for the pulp *Western Aces* reappears a decade later on the cover of the Ace paperback *The Branded Lawman* in 1952. Whether the artist was consulted, credited, or paid for such re-uses varied by publisher.

Images courtesy David Saunders

See, Stag, and *True Adventures.*

At the same time, he began to share his Tribeca art studio with an up-and-coming young illustrator, Mort Kunstler (b.1927), who had just graduated from Pratt. According to Kunstler, "My father had known his father. I used to call him Uncle George. He was twenty-two years older than me, and his own father had been a successful artist. So it really made me feel like I wasn't just a kid working out of my parents' house anymore! I chose him as my mentor. George sort of took me under his wing, and he taught me whatever he knew. It was a wonderful thing for me."

On April 12, 1965 the artist's mother, Serena Krauss Gross, died at the age of seventy-four.

In the 1970s, George Gross painted covers for The Avenger series of paperback books, published by Warner Paperbacks.

On August 22, 1972 the artist's wife, Dora (Weitzman) Gross, died at the age of sixty-six in Milford, PA. They had no children.

In 1979 George Gross married his second wife, Gidget Buchberg. She was born on April 16, 1913 in Polish-Jewish ancestry, and had come to America in 1921. She was a graduate of Columbia University's School of Pharmacy (Class of 1935), where she was one of very few female students. She worked as a pharmacist until her marriage in 1937 to Irving Horowitz, who played woodwind instruments as a staff musician with the CBS, ABC, and NBC broadcasting companies. The Horowitzes had three children, Susan (b.1937), David (b.1938), and Frances (b.1940). When Irving Horowitz died at the age of sixty in 1971, he had been an oboist with the orchestra of *The Dick Cavett Show*. At the time of her second marriage, all of her kids were full-grown and married, so George Gross and Gidget Buchberg Horowitz Gross bought a new home in Rockaway, New Jersey, where they lived by themselves.

In the 1980s, the artist painted covers for the popular Nick Carter series of paperbacks for Ace Publications.

In 1984, at the age of seventy-five, the artist retired from commercial illustration. He and his wife enjoyed their final years together in Rockaway, NJ.

George Gross died at the age of ninety-four on February 23, 2003. He is buried at King Solomon Memorial Park in Clifton, NJ, where his bronze plaque reads, *"George Gross, beloved husband, father and friend,"* with a brief quote from the 12th century Sephardic Jewish philosopher, Maimonides: *"I believe."*

DAVID SAUNDERS *is a pulp art historian who created the website* www.pulpartists.com, *with biographical profiles on hundreds of artists that worked for the pulp magazine industry. He is the son of the legendary artist, Norman Saunders (1907–1989).*

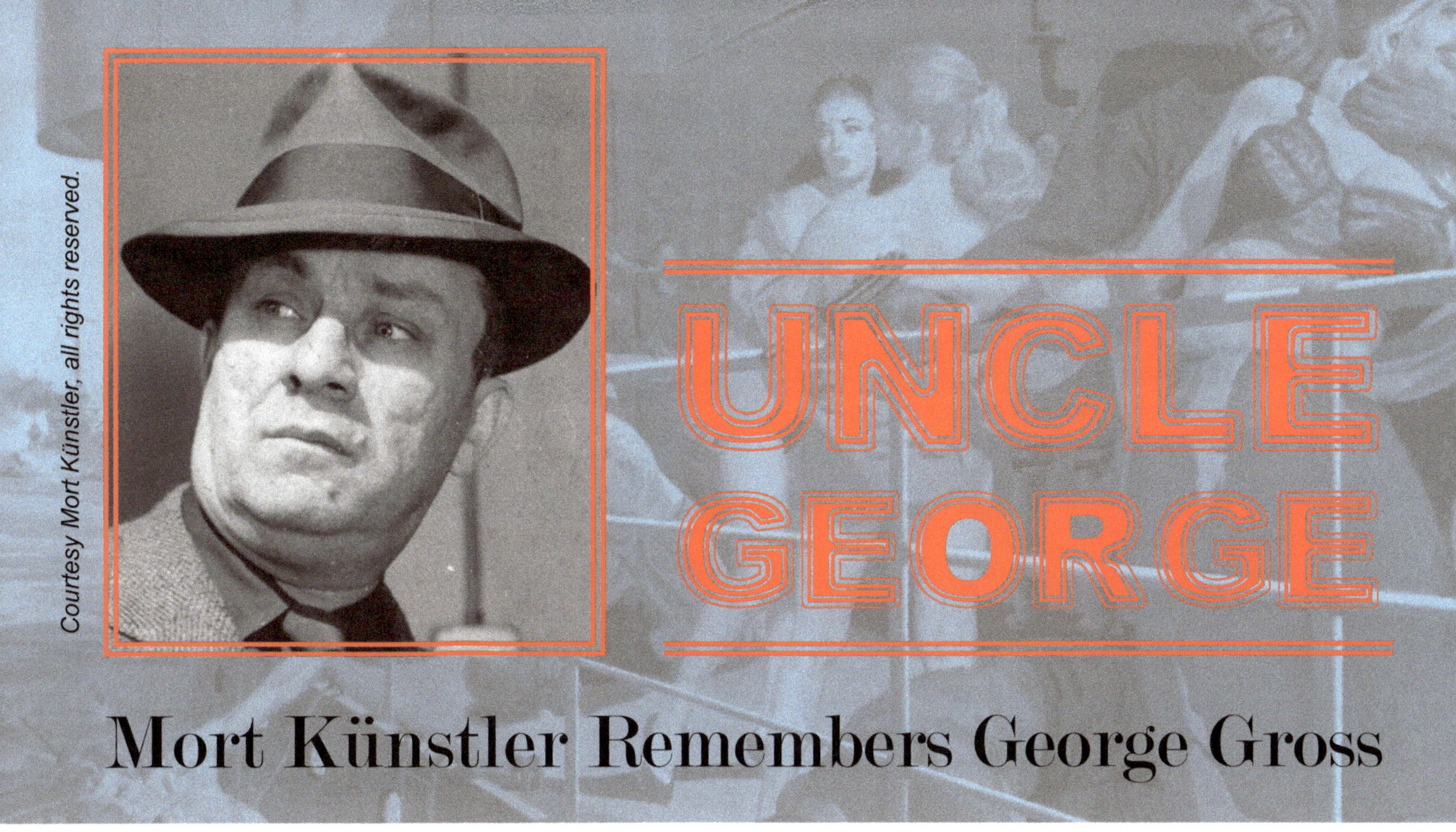

Mort Künstler Remembers George Gross

Mort *Künstler (b.1927), a recognized master of illustration art, is one of the most prolific and admired American artists, known for his extensive research and artistic mastery of US historical subjects. His paintings are in over 50 museum collections and have been the subject of more than 60 one-man shows. Künstler has chronicled American history from before the Europeans arrived, through 21ˢᵗ century military experiences and popular culture. His prolific body of work began with his early illustrations for men's adventure magazines (MAMs) of the 1950s and 1960s, which helped define an era in publishing. His captivating and sometimes provocative images adorned the covers and illustrated the stories in magazines such as* Male, Stag, For Men Only, *and* True Adventure.

Less discussed is his lifelong friendship and professional association with one of the greatest names in vintage pulp illustration (and beyond): George Gross (1909–2003). Here Künstler recalls his lifelong friend and mentor.

GEORGE Gross was a fabulous person, one of my favorite people. He helped me in every possible way. I knew George from practically the time I was an infant. His father, Dave, and my father were very close. His father was older than my father, as George was older than me. I used to call him *Uncle George.* (He was 15, 20 years older than me.)

Dave Gross made a very good living as an illustrator. He was a fashion artist. You have to realize, there were no color photos in those days.

Montgomery Ward catalogs, Sears Roebuck catalogs, etc. were all using full-color paintings of men's suits or women's clothing, and it had to be done by artists. Well, Dave was very good at it, and he ended up with this vast company of 75 artists working for him.

My father, Tom, was a salesman and an amateur artist, coached by Dave. Every Saturday they got together at Dave Gross's studio, just to schmooze, you know? In the '30s, men didn't work a five-day week; they worked a *five-and-a-half-day* week. A lot of men would work their half-day on Saturday, and a regular group met up in Dave Gross's studio after. These weren't all artists, just old friends. They'd go out to lunch together, or bring food in and have lunch in the studio.

The studio was shared by Dave and his kids: George, Arthur, and Beatrice. My father started taking me up there with him when I was about 8 or 10. They'd kibbitz and fool around and talk about the old days.

But they'd set me up with a pad and pencil or charcoal and a still life to keep me quiet, then they'd give me critiques on it afterward. Their instructions were always: "Put down what you see." And I did.

They kept me doing still lifes and drawings from the time I was a little kid. It was a great way to grow up, because I enjoyed doing it and they gave good criticism. I certainly learned to draw there. Of course, I carried that off at home too. You can't do just it on a Saturday afternoon, you know?

It was a very exciting thing for me to go on a Saturday and see real artists painting with oils on easels, then seeing reproductions in print of what they had painted the week or month before. They were professionals, and I was a kid. I had a sort of an inside track. It was very, very exciting for me at the time. I saw how pictures were done by professionals; that was a big thing! I had an advantage over any of the kids I went to school with.

Of course, George started out in the pulps in the '30s, and he became a very popular pulp artist. He did the original pulps, like *Doc Savage* and things of that sort. But initially, Artie sort of got the applause of the family, because he was getting advertising work. This was during World War II. Color photography hadn't come in yet, so there was great demand for color artwork. In retrospect, Artie's work was not nearly as good as George's, but he was getting advertising, and George was doing pulp covers. So instead of $500, $700, or even $1000 for a picture, George was getting $150. But Artie didn't work that often, while George had one cover to do after another. George just kept getting better and better at it, and he never went a day without work. There were always companies that wanted to give him covers to do.

But in fact, he thought so little of them—and this is not a lie or made up—he would very often give me his old canvases on stretcher bars! He would say, "Turn them upside down and paint over them; you'll have free canvas." So I'd bring them into art school to re-use, where everyone was astounded by them. I painted on these wonderful pulp cover masterpieces, so help me. I wish I had them now! They'd probably be worth a pile of money. But that's the way George treated his pulp stuff.

I graduated from Pratt [Institute] in 1950. I did samples like other artists, and I didn't really know what to do with them. I lived in Brooklyn with my parents, and it was quite a thing to drag your big, heavy portfolio into the city and walk around in July, looking for work, showing your samples. George had a studio in downtown Manhattan, where I'd stop by all the time. He'd give me criticism of my samples, and suggest who to go see [for work], and that sort of thing.

He used to give me very practical lessons. I got the best lesson in my life very early on. I remember one time I said, "I was just at [publisher] Dodd, Mead, and they promised me a painting [commission]. I'll have one next week." I was so excited! I hadn't gotten an assignment from anyone yet.

George said to me, "Let me tell you something,

Mutz." (My nickname was Mutz; still is.) "It's not a job when someone *likes* your work. It's not a job when they *say* they're going to give you work. It's not a job when they *give* you the work. It's not a job when you *deliver* the painting. It's not a job when it's *approved*, not even when the *boss* approves it. It's a *job* when you get the check—and the check doesn't bounce." Now that's Depression-era talk: *"It's a job when the check doesn't bounce."* In Depression days, I'm sure checks *did* bounce, you know? That was his first business lesson for me. Right from the start, he always kept me levelheaded. He was just about the best influence that anyone could have had. He was my mentor.

Eventually, he spoke to the guy who ran the studio. He said, "Hey, you've got an unused drawing board over there. Give the kid the drawing board, let him come in, sit in the city like he's a pro. He can run errands for you. He can clean up, cut mattes, and he'll be available to do a little touch-up if an artist's unavailable. And it'll save him running back and forth from Brooklyn." Because I was always stopping off; every day, practically. The guy said, "Fine," and they gave me a drawing table next to George, which was a delight, of course. So there was very little I did that George didn't see and give me a comment on. That lasted for a couple of years, and it made such a big difference in my career at that time. It gave me a home base in the city, with a New York City phone number. I wasn't just a student operating out of his house, you know? He gave me hints on where to go,

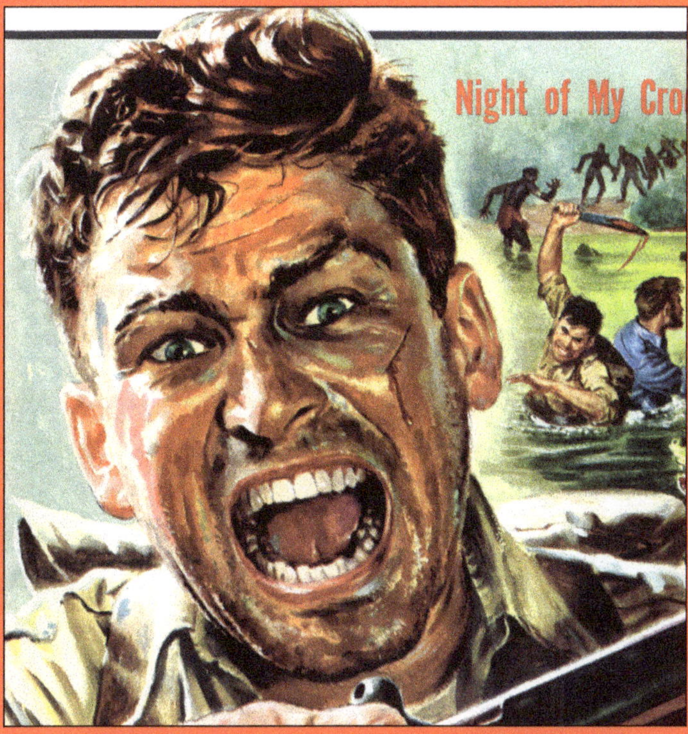

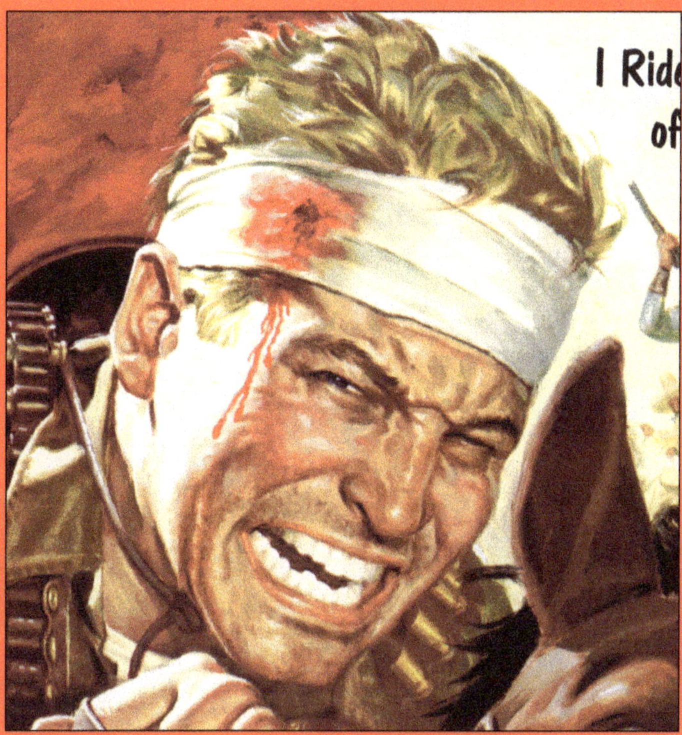

he gave me critiques on everything I did.

He had a darkroom there, he showed me how to do photography. He showed me how to pose models, how to book models…. I really learned from that. My classmates got jobs at ad agencies and were being paid two and three times what I was being paid, but they never went any further; they became sketch artists at ad agencies, finally.

I started to get work from the low end of the business. I think they were book jackets at the time, hardcover books. And then, paperbacks paid better, and I started getting really good work by the mid-'50s.

At the time, pulp covers were low-level art, so to speak. George was still doing pulp covers, but the field was changing. The pulps were dying, and paperbacks were coming in. George graduated to digest-size books, a format like paperbacks, larger paperbacks. And he went eventually to paperbacks. Color photography was not a factor there; they all needed painted covers. So that was a lot of artwork, and it kept a lot of artists busy, working away.

George's basic career was pulps, digest-size, and then paperbacks. He did a little magazine work, not very much. I got to that men's adventure stuff very early on, some of them very complicated, which was the best training I could have had. George got into it roughly the same time I did. (We worked for the same people at times, but we each ended up building up a completely different clientele after a while.) He got a

handful of jobs doing men's adventure illustrations, and he was most proud of those. But he did more in paperbacks. He was very well suited for paperbacks, because the demands were similar in many ways to the pulps.

He was very conscious of light. It was very important, because he was pretty much blind in one eye, and he needed good light. That was the most important thing, he had to have a big north light window. Whenever he was looking for a studio, he'd go with a light meter to measure the light, because it was so important to him.

We shared studio space on White Street in the late '50s. I would get into work at, say 9:00, 9:30, and he'd start usually at 8:00. The radio was on from the time he came in 'til the time he went home. He used to listen to Harlem stations, nutritionist Colton Fredericks's talk show, he used to listen to every kind of show. I'd paint at my drawing table, which was next to his. We'd talk, the radio would be on…. George was always funny, had funny remarks all the time. He had a great sense of humor.

We'd work until one o'clock, then we'd take off and have lunch. We'd get back to the studio, and we'd be painting again until 5:00. George quit earlier in the winter, because the light wasn't good. (He never could really work in artificial light. I don't know whether it was fear of straining his eyes, or that he had trouble seeing in artificial light; I know I can't see color as well in artificial light as I can in

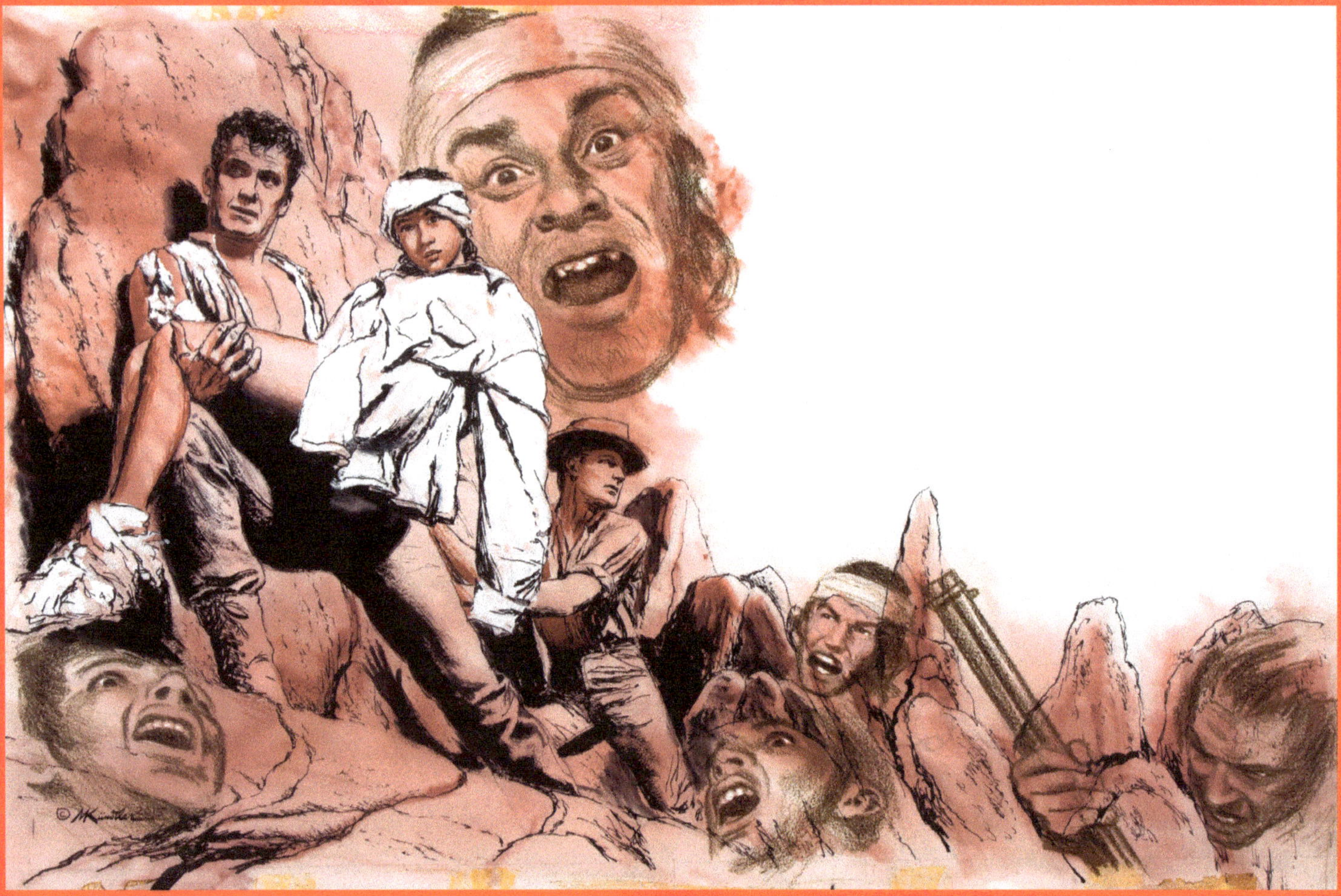

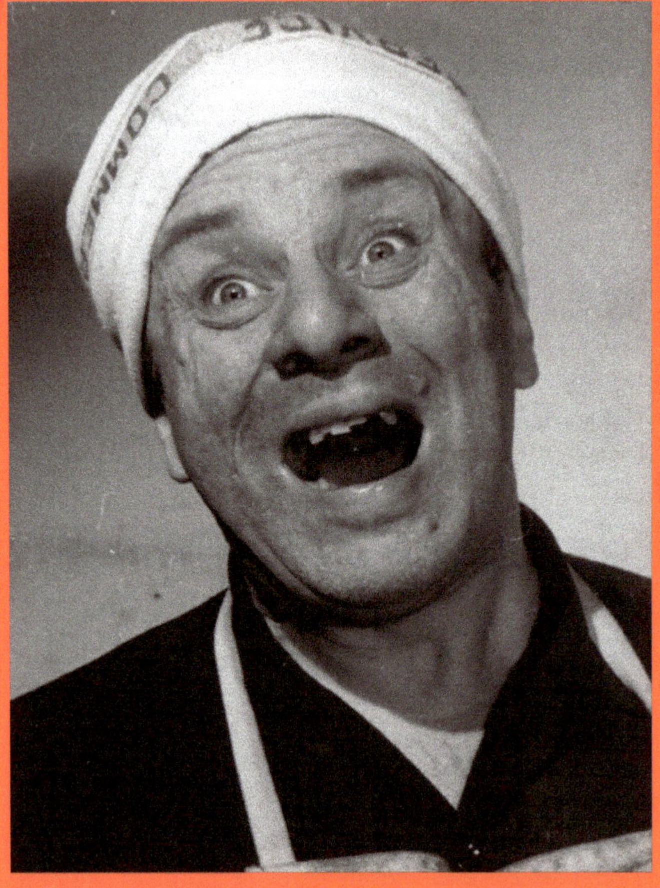

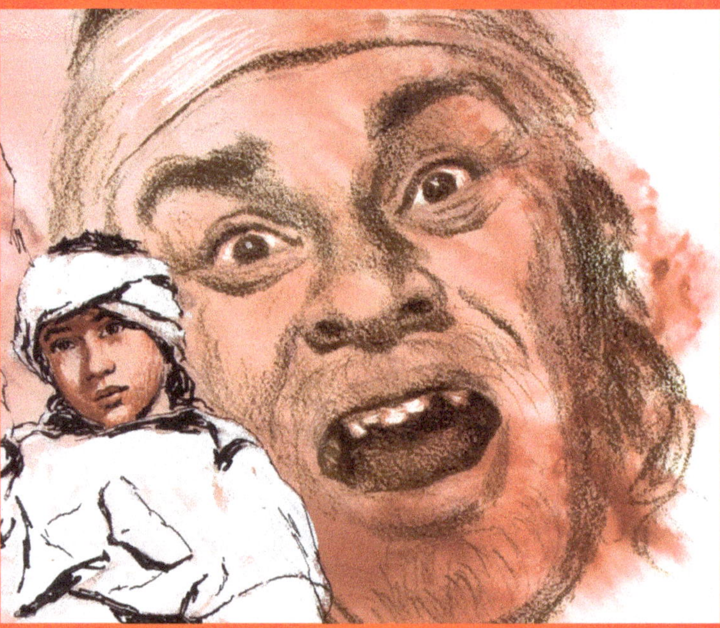

Künstler renders Gross: George models for Mort's illustration for the story "Yaqui Devil," in the March 1956 issue of _Men_. Reference photo of Gross by Künstler.

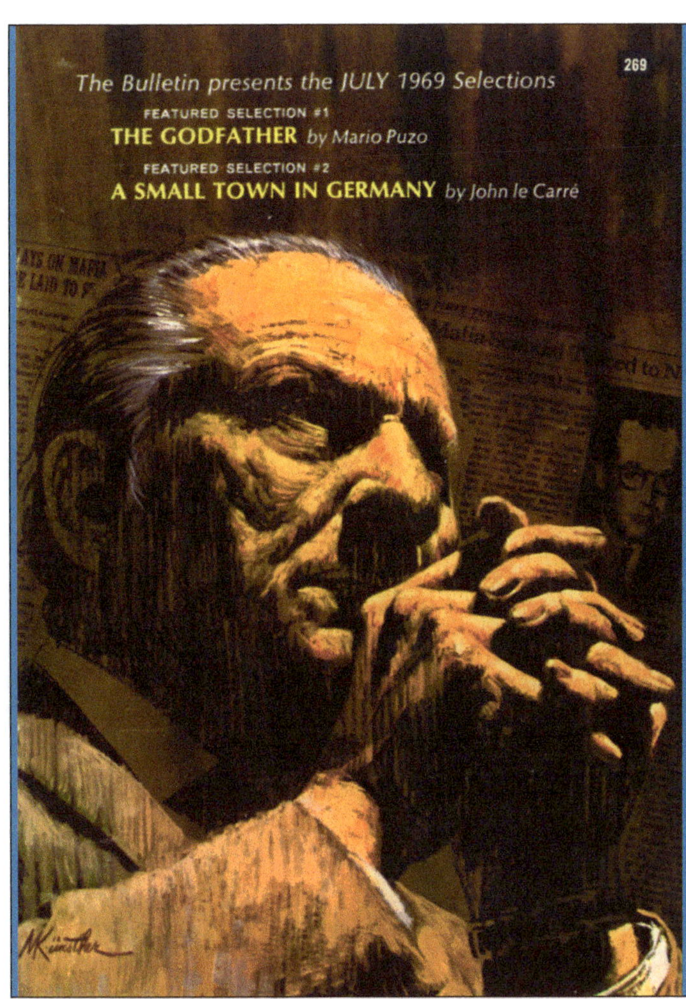

In 1969, *The Literary Guild Bulletin* commissioned illustrations by Mort Künstler to publicize a new novel by MAM writer/editor Mario Puzo, and Künstler asked Gross to model the title figure. These were the first depictions anywhere of characters from *The Godfather*. So, for the record, the first person to portray Don Corleone was…George Gross.

daylight.) And that was our day. He'd go home, take the subway back to Queens—Flushing, I guess, at that time. And then same thing the next day. He would work Saturdays, too, and very often Sundays.

I don't know if perspective was a great strength of his. He was not a great composer. He always had decent compositions, but they did not come naturally. It took a lot of work and a lot of studying of other compositions to figure out what he wanted to do. His greatest strength, however, was his ability to paint very realistically. His *painting* was his strength. He drew well, so the hands looked like hands, etc. Things were…*proper*.

He was certainly a very capable paperback artist. He painted paperbacks for years and years, and did them well, better than almost anyone else. And basically, those covers were never that complex, so you wouldn't have to worry too much about perspective, you didn't have to worry too much about composition.

I guess I surpassed him eventually, by doing the most expensive kind of advertising art. George never clicked with advertising work. He was not fast; he was methodical. A paperback cover that would take me a day, two days maximum, would take him a week. He kept busy at paperbacks, and he was very good at it—one of the best. He worked for the best companies: Bantam, Dell, Avon.

He'd make suggestions to me, showing me good points about a Dean Cornwell painting, or a Rockwell. And I used to say, "Well, why don't you do this? Why don't you [work like] that?" And he'd say, "I can *see* what's good. I *know* what's good. But I can't do it in my own work."

He used to copy a lot of compositions, then photograph them so they were different. And he really depended a lot on what he *saw*, whereas a lot of mine came out my head, from the text descriptions the art director gave me.

All he did was encourage me. There was never an ounce of jealousy, never once. I always worried about it. But he was just proud of me, that he had that influence on me. George, as I say, was *Uncle George*; my dear friend, mentor, and guide. He made life a lot easier.

In retrospect, I think I had a lot of talent, I think I would've had a good career. But he made those early years so much easier—and shorter. The first five years can be torment for an artist! And he took those five years and condensed them into two, and made them an *easy* two.

I think you learn by doing, more than anything. I can walk you through the details of what George would do to create a picture, but that doesn't teach you to do it. I think the way you get good is by *doing*. I mean, George worked and worked and worked, and *I* worked and worked and worked…it's a tough business to make a living at, but we both did all right.

As told to Wyatt Doyle

MortKunstler.com *welcomes inquiries about purchasing Mort Künstler's original paintings, limited edition prints and products, and licensing his images, as well as general questions and comments. The Men's Adventure Library's* **Mort Künstler: The Godfather of Pulp Fiction Illustrators** *is available wherever books are sold.*

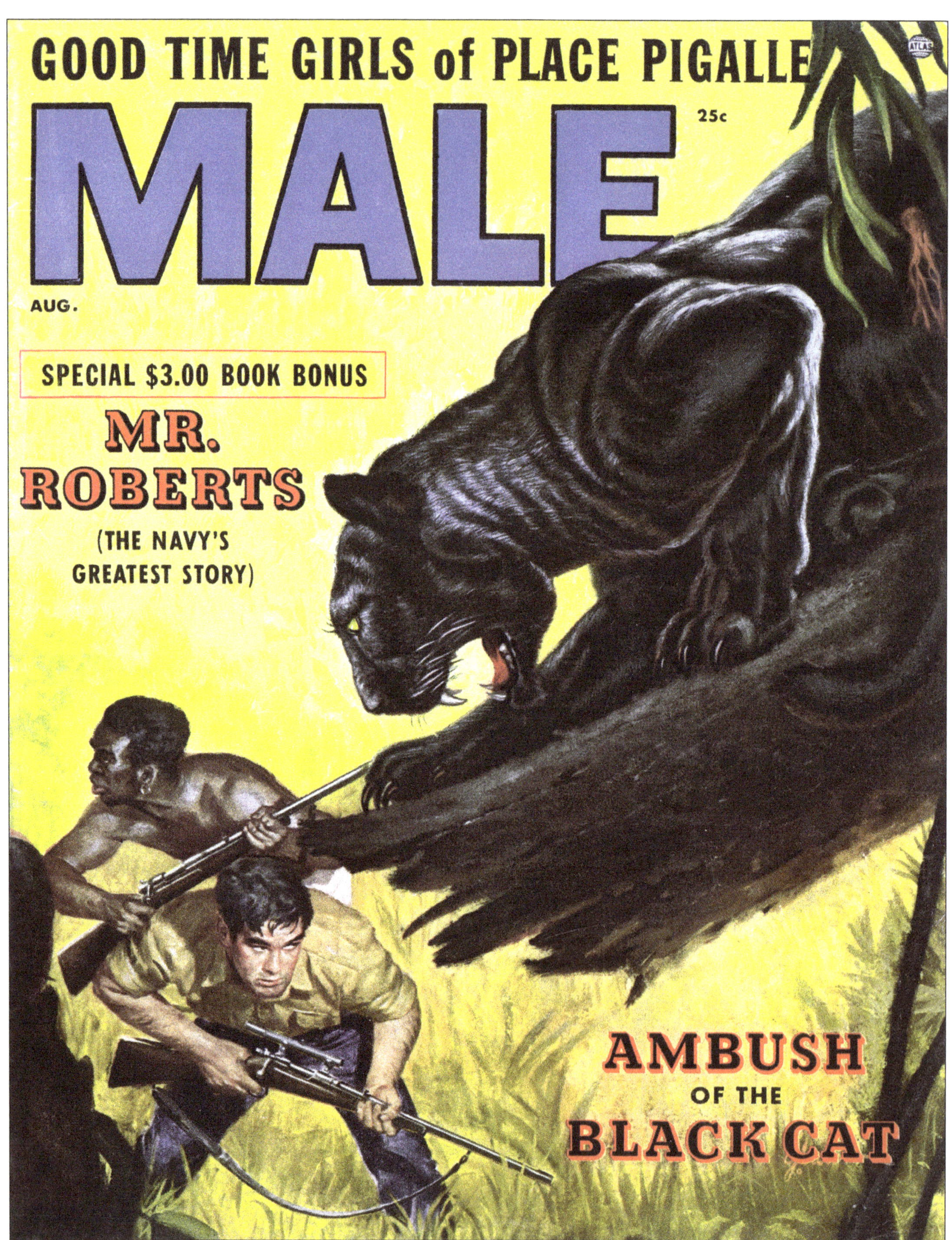

GOOD TIME GIRLS of PLACE PIGALLE
MALE
25c
AUG.
SPECIAL $3.00 BOOK BONUS
MR. ROBERTS
(THE NAVY'S GREATEST STORY)
AMBUSH
OF THE
BLACK CAT
ATLAS

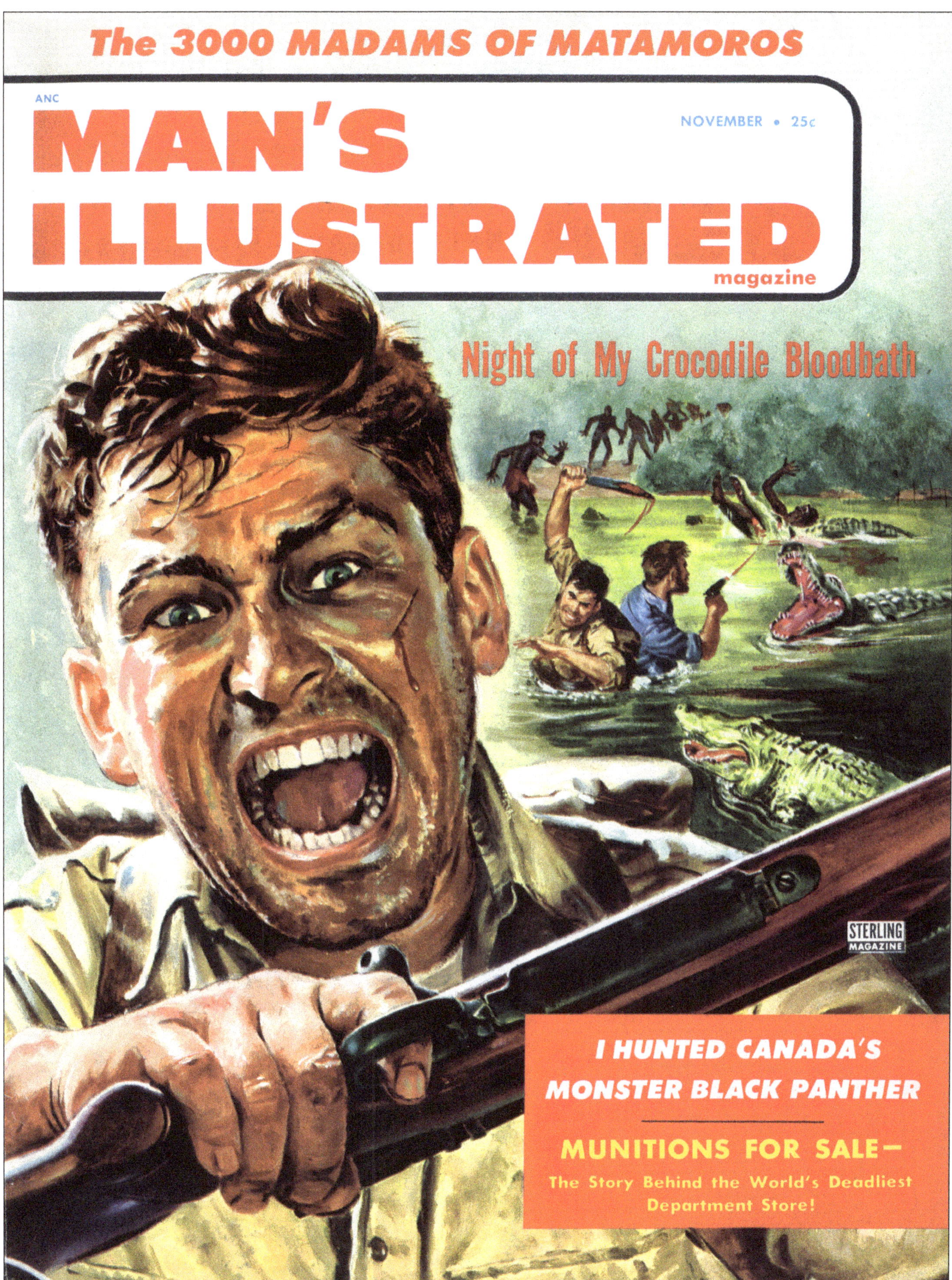

November 1955

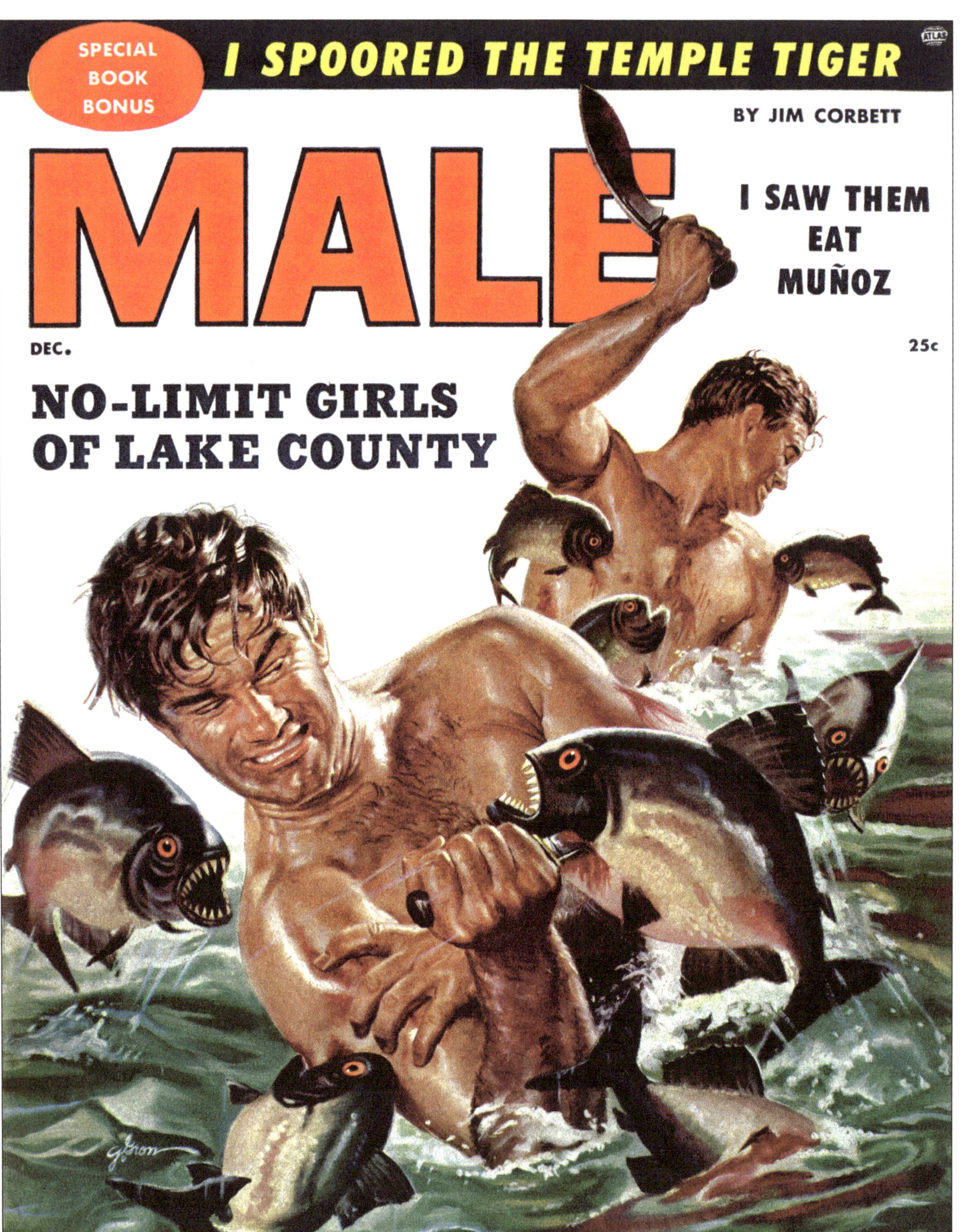

SPECIAL BOOK BONUS
I SPOORED THE TEMPLE TIGER
BY JIM CORBETT
MALE
I SAW THEM EAT MUÑOZ
DEC.
25c
NO-LIMIT GIRLS OF LAKE COUNTY
December 1955

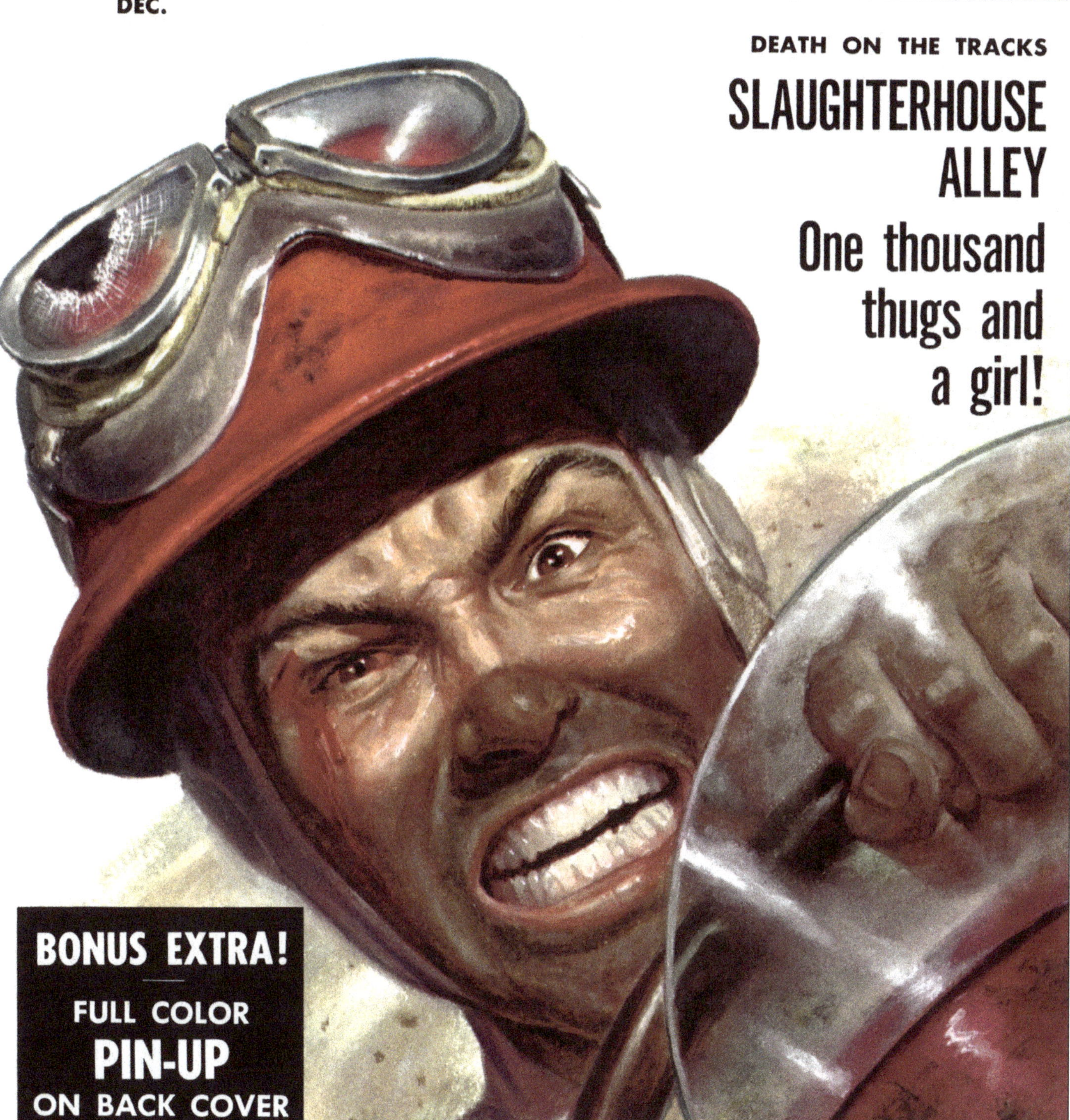

December 1955

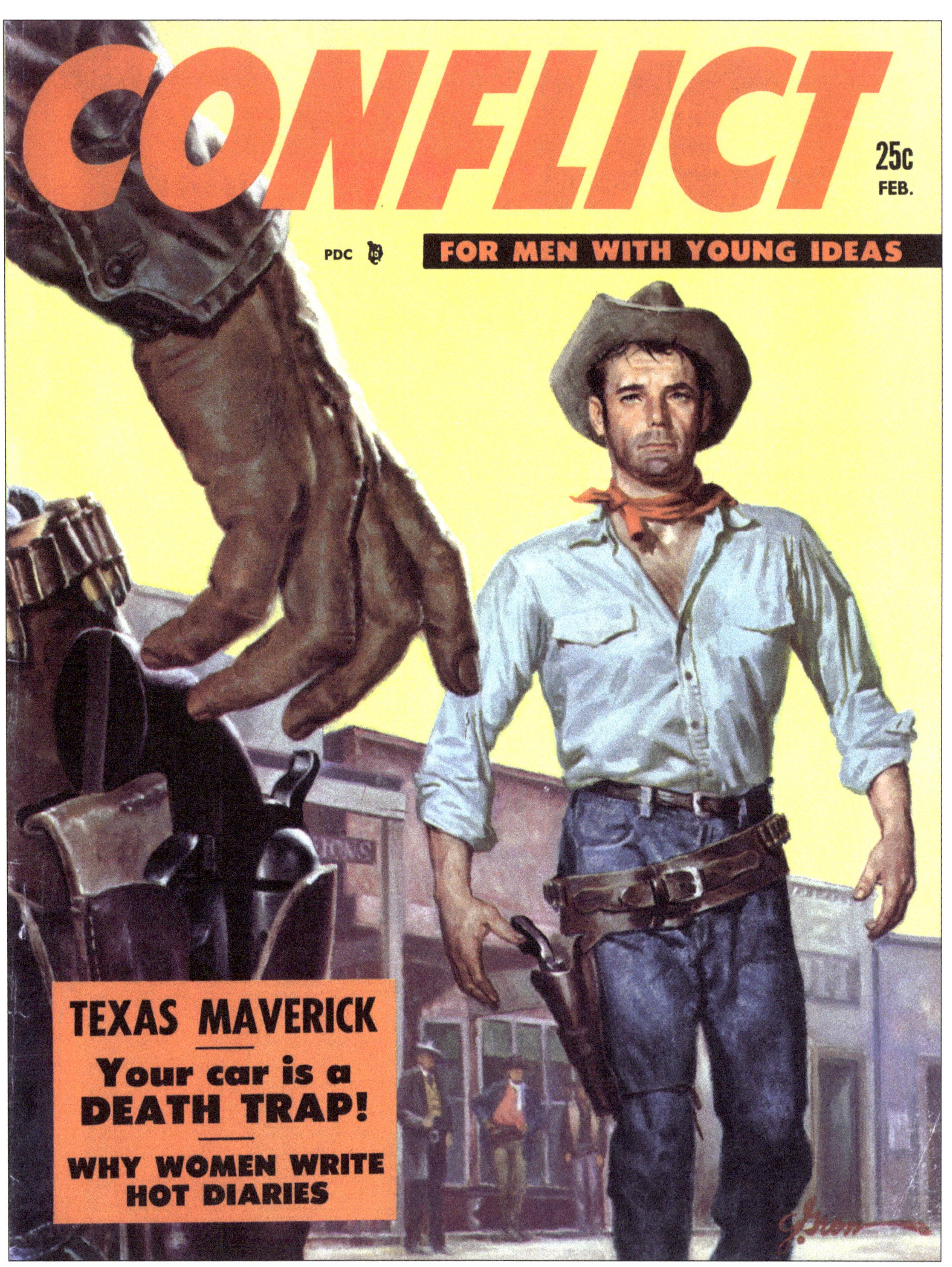

February 1956

HOW HIDDEN FEARS RUIN YOUR SEX LIFE
STERLING MAGAZINE
ANC
APRIL 25c
MAN'S ILLUSTRATED
Charge of the Killer Baboons
REVENGE OF THE FRENCH FOREIGN LEGION —
Massacre in Blood Alley

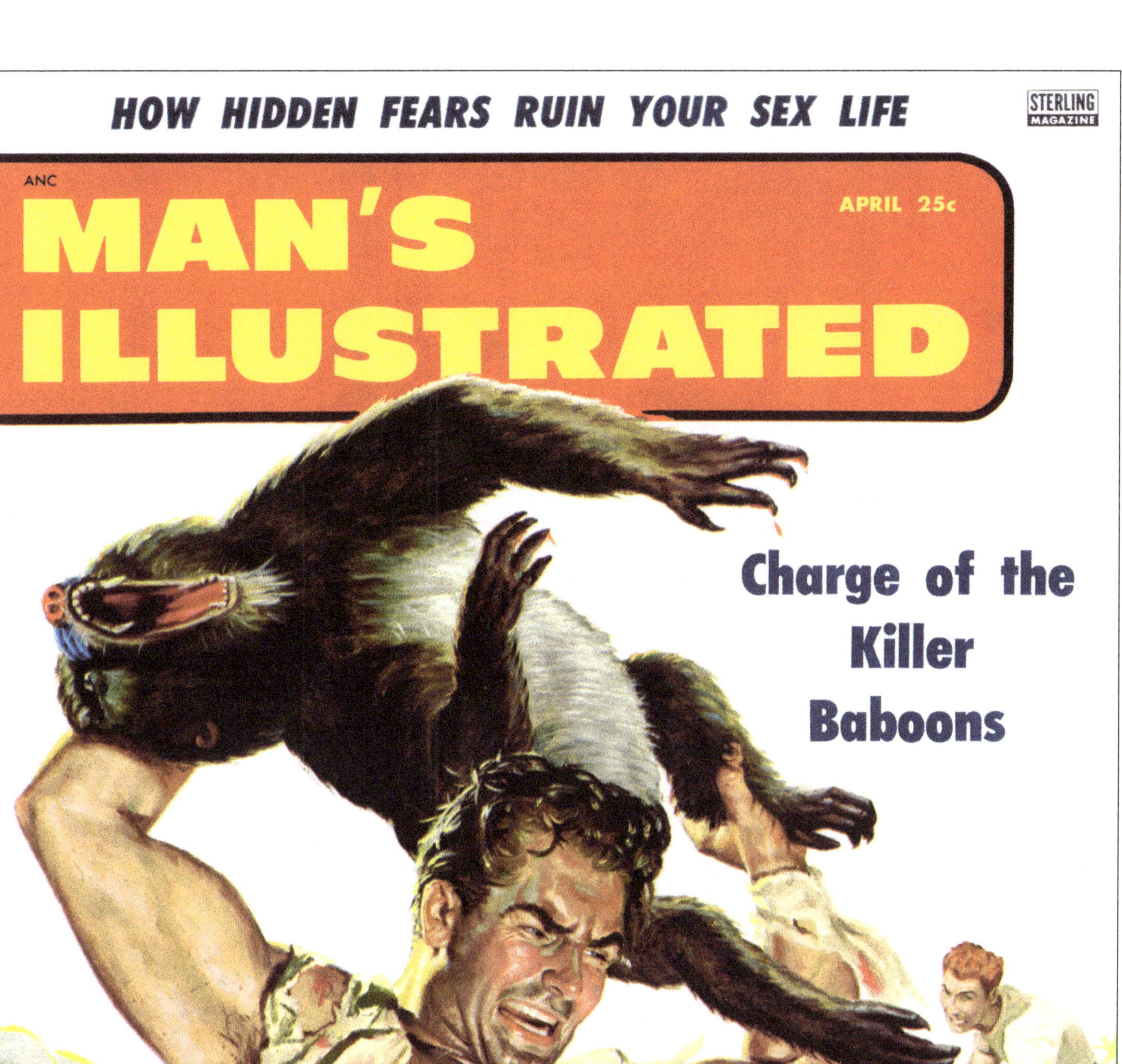

April 1956

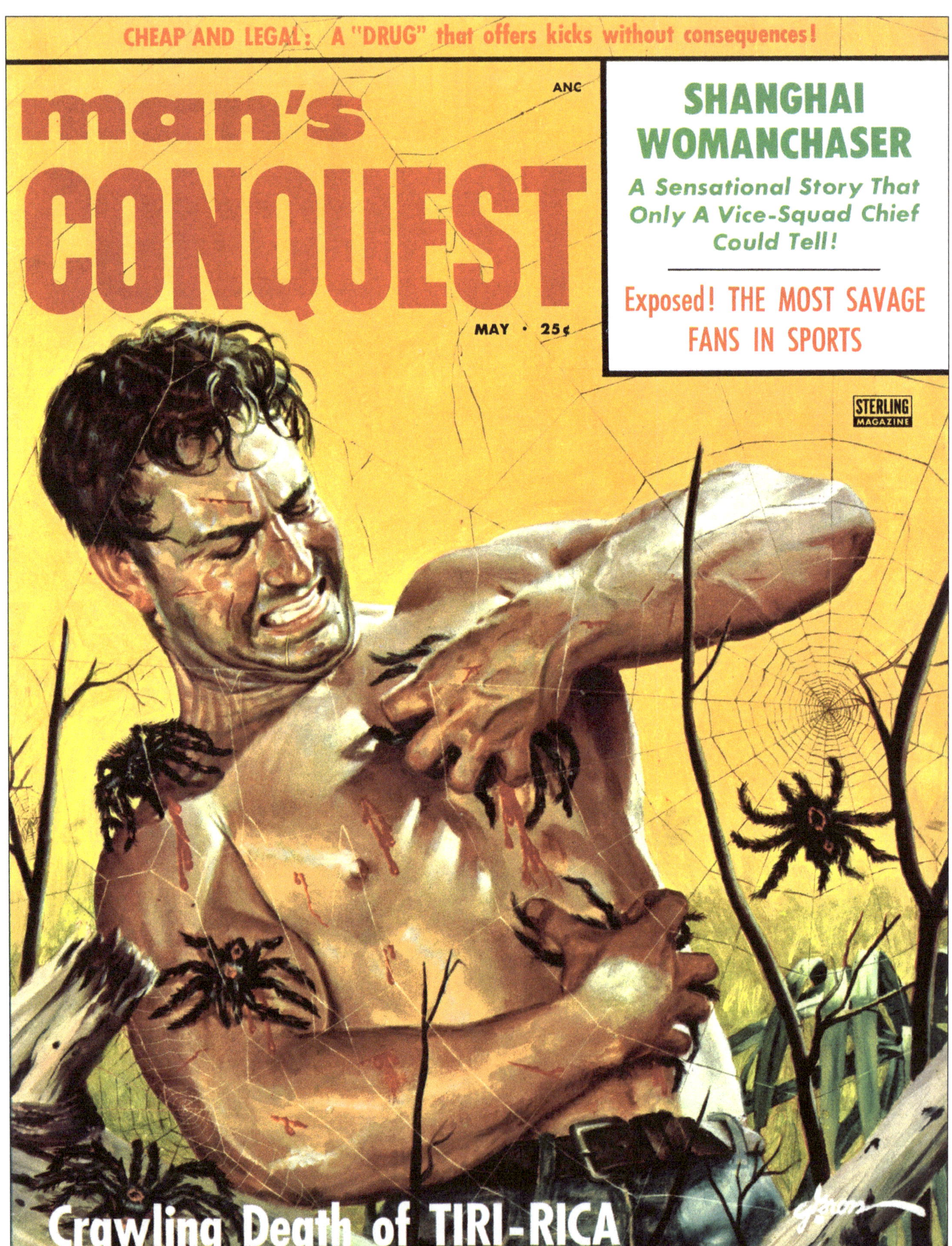

CHEAP AND LEGAL: A "DRUG" that offers kicks without consequences!
man's CONQUEST
ANC
MAY · 25¢
STERLING MAGAZINE
SHANGHAI WOMANCHASER
A Sensational Story That Only A Vice-Squad Chief Could Tell!
Exposed! THE MOST SAVAGE FANS IN SPORTS
Crawling Death of TIRI-RICA

May 1956

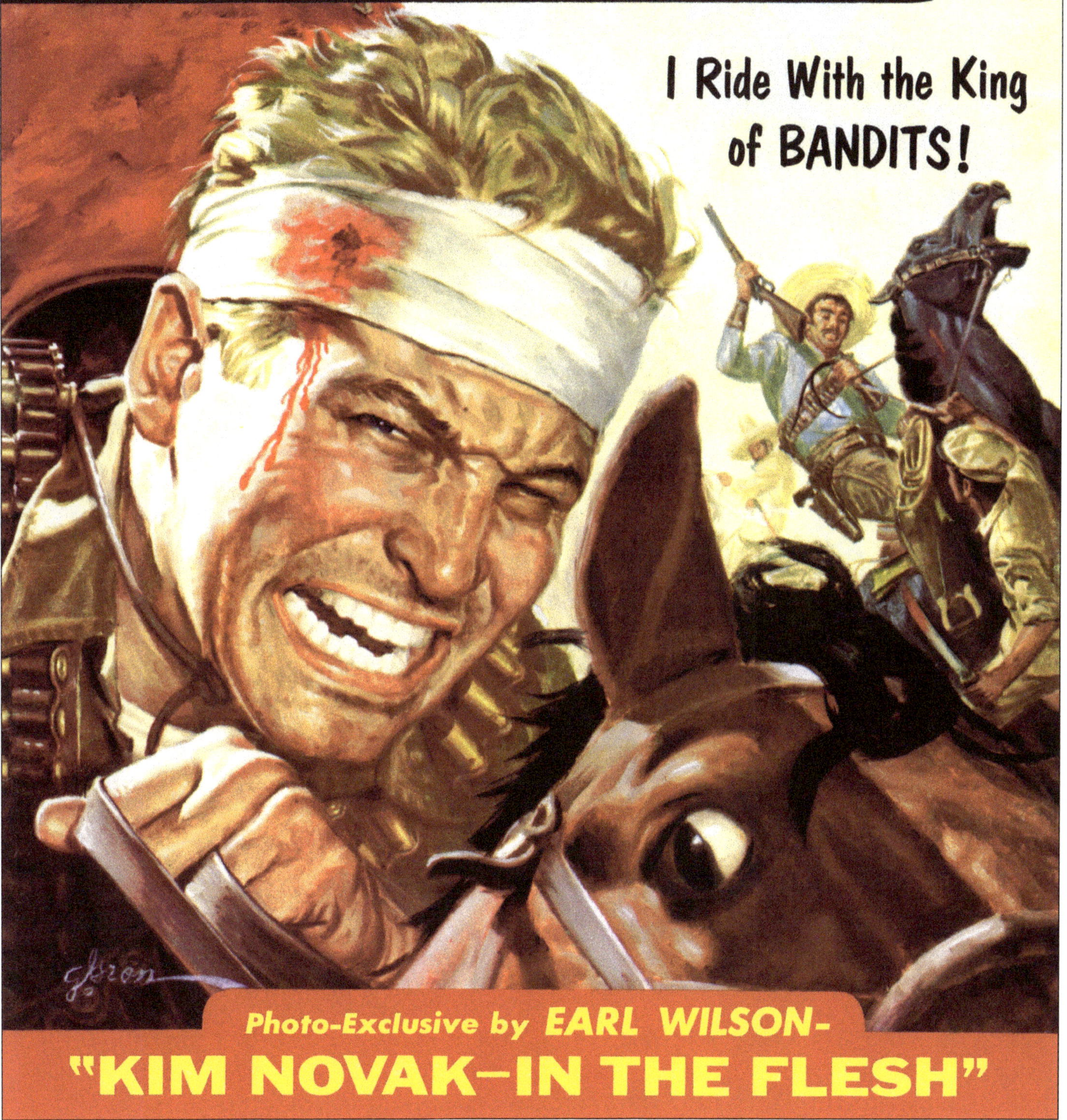

BETTER YOUR SEX LIFE WITH A NEW DIET
STERLING MAGAZINE
ANC
MAN'S ILLUSTRATED
JUNE • 25¢
I Ride With the King of BANDITS!
Photo-Exclusive by EARL WILSON—
"KIM NOVAK—IN THE FLESH"

June 1956

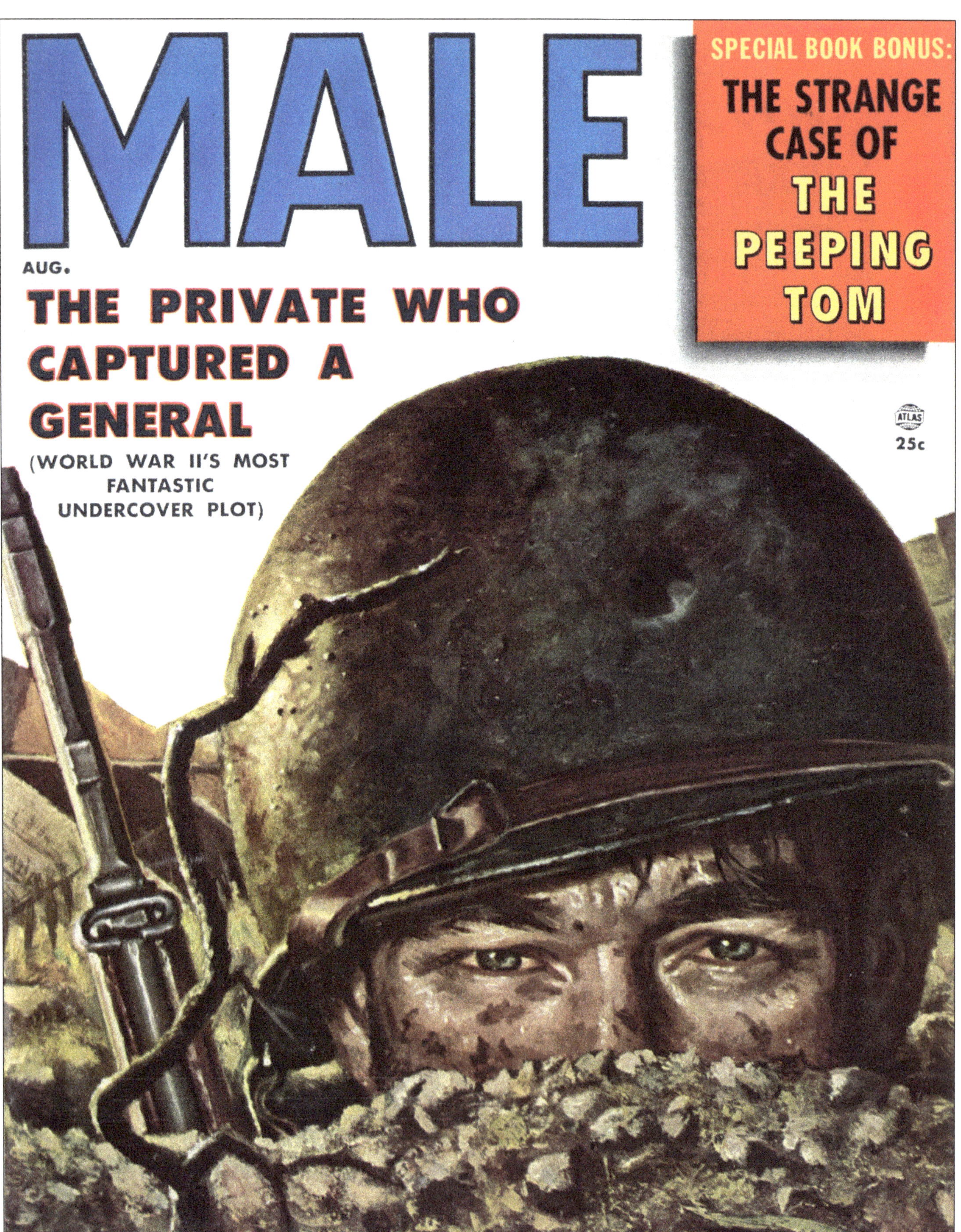

MALE
AUG.
THE PRIVATE WHO CAPTURED A GENERAL
(WORLD WAR II'S MOST FANTASTIC UNDERCOVER PLOT)
SPECIAL BOOK BONUS:
THE STRANGE CASE OF THE PEEPING TOM
ATLAS
25c

August 1956

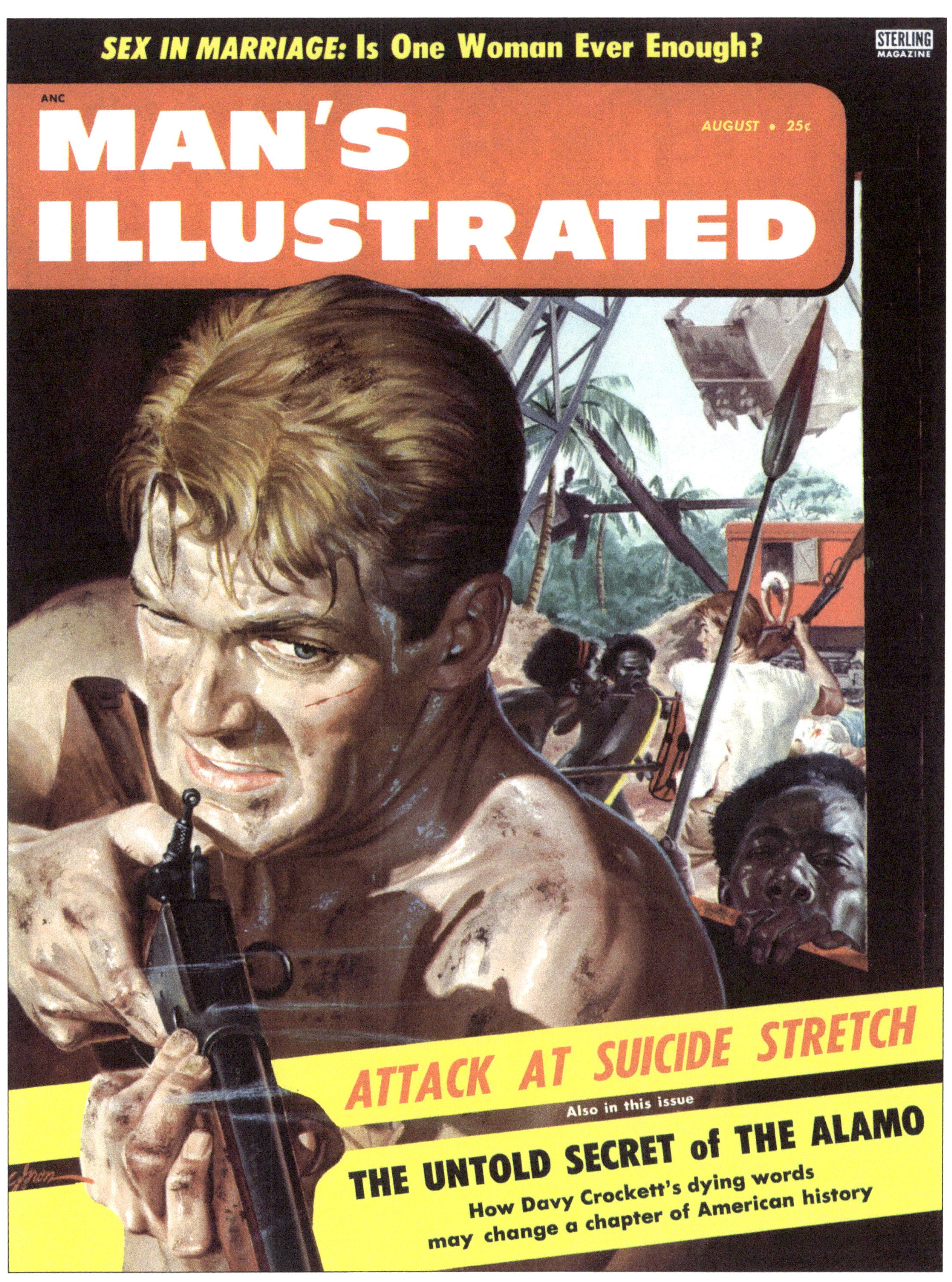
SEX IN MARRIAGE: Is One Woman Ever Enough?
STERLING MAGAZINE
ANC
MAN'S ILLUSTRATED
AUGUST • 25¢
ATTACK AT SUICIDE STRETCH
Also in this issue
THE UNTOLD SECRET of THE ALAMO
How Davy Crockett's dying words
may change a chapter of American history

August 1956

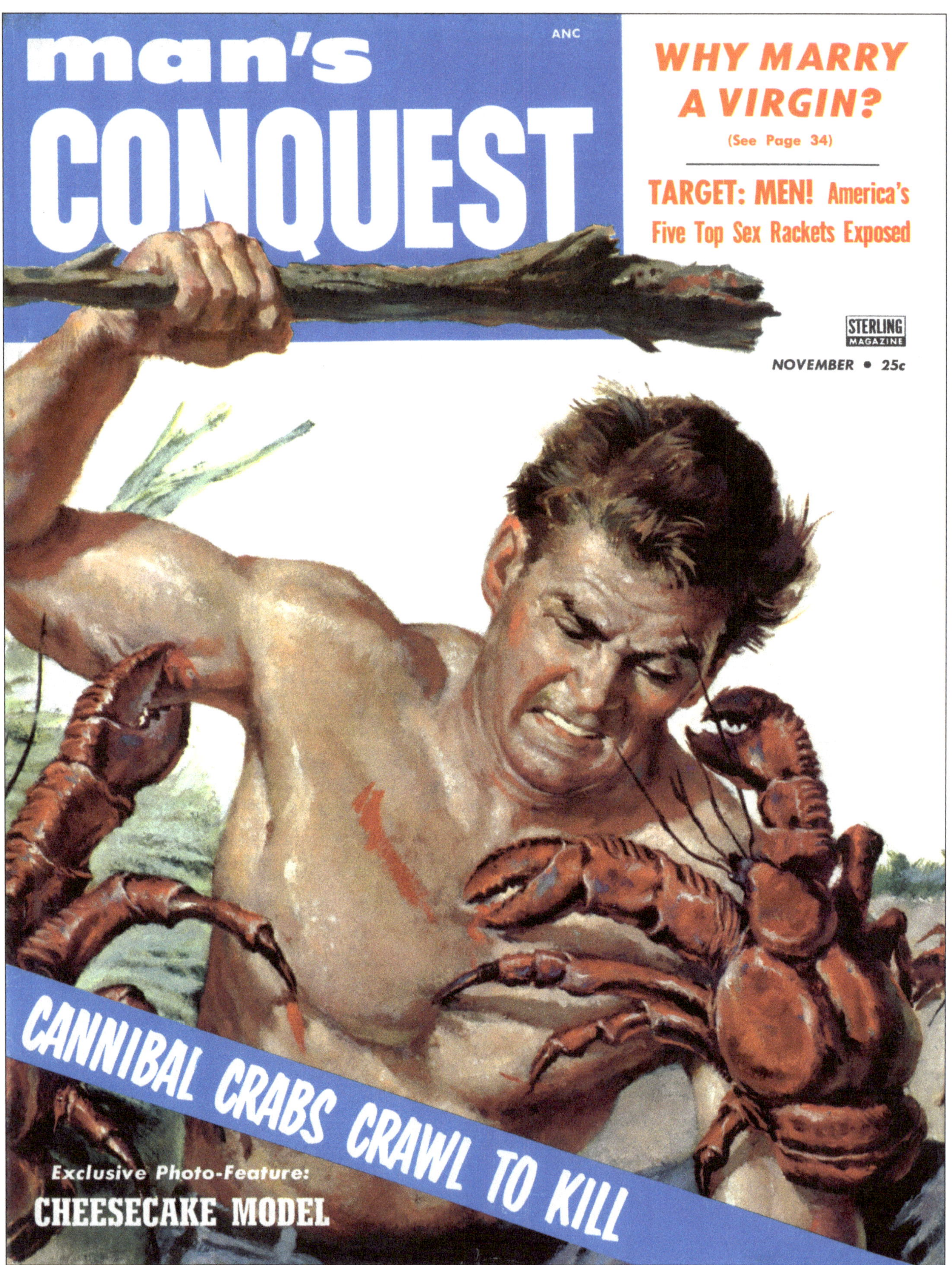

November 1956

24

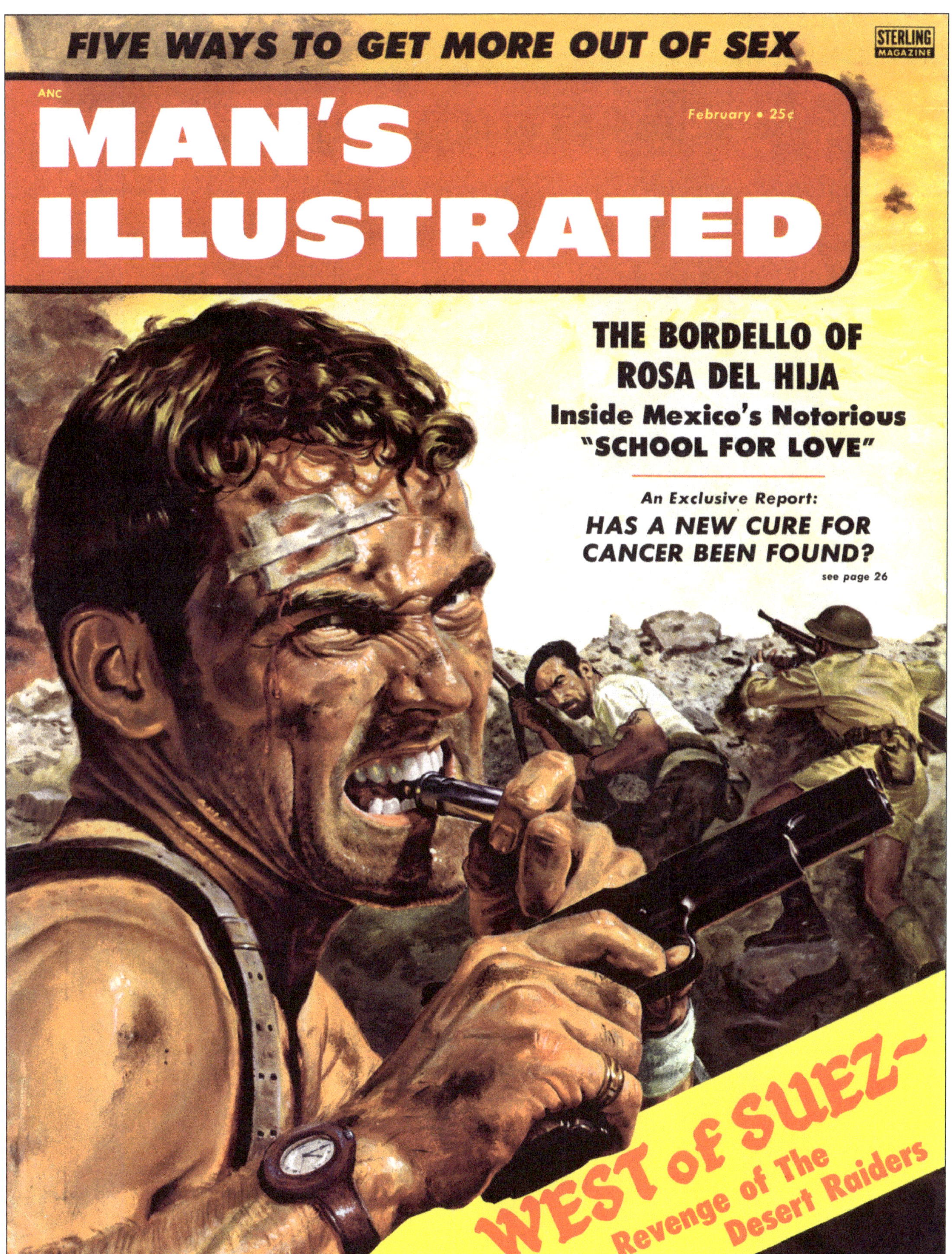

February 1957

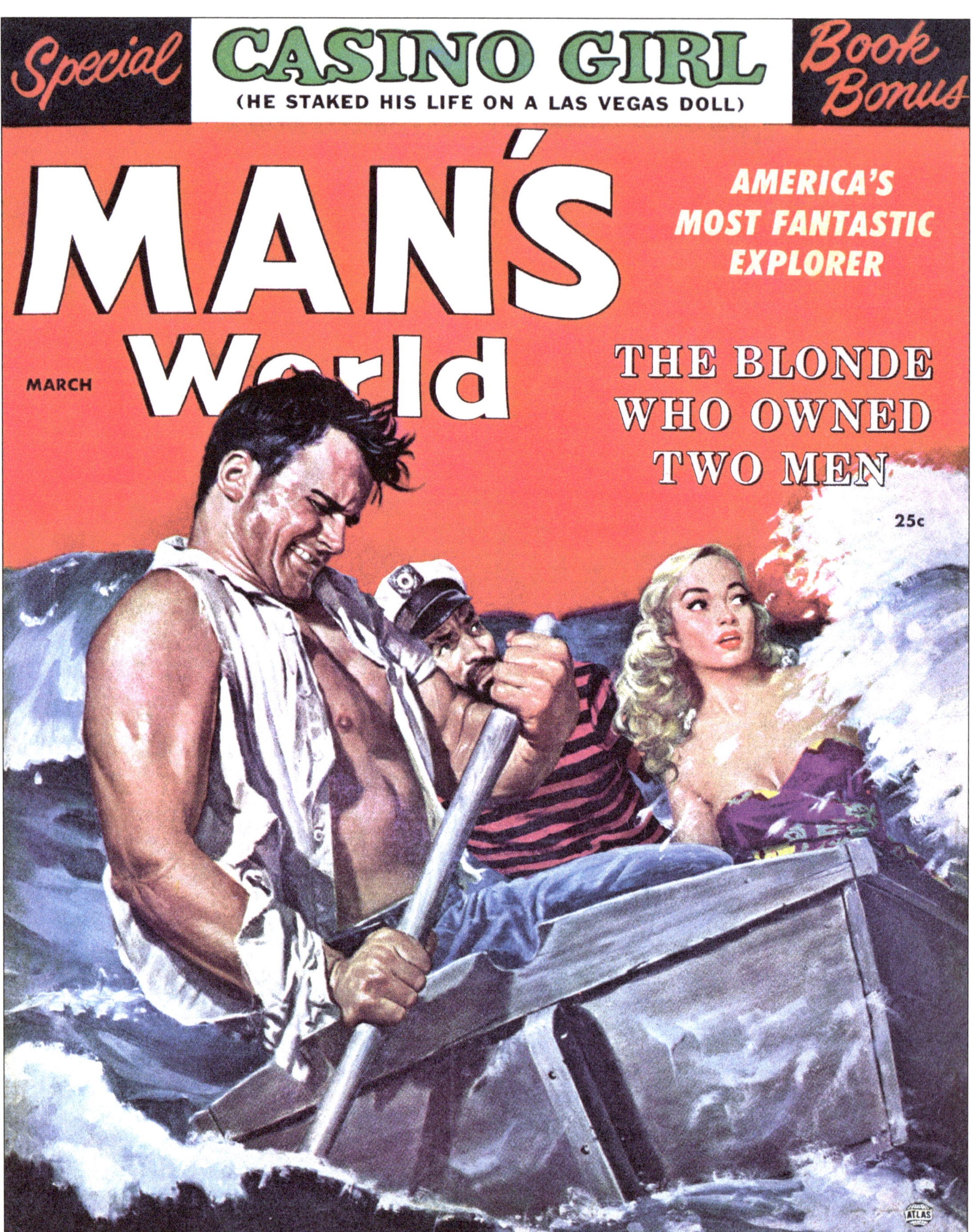

Special
CASINO GIRL
(HE STAKED HIS LIFE ON A LAS VEGAS DOLL)
Book Bonus
MARCH
MAN'S World
AMERICA'S MOST FANTASTIC EXPLORER
THE BLONDE WHO OWNED TWO MEN
25c
ATLAS

March 1957

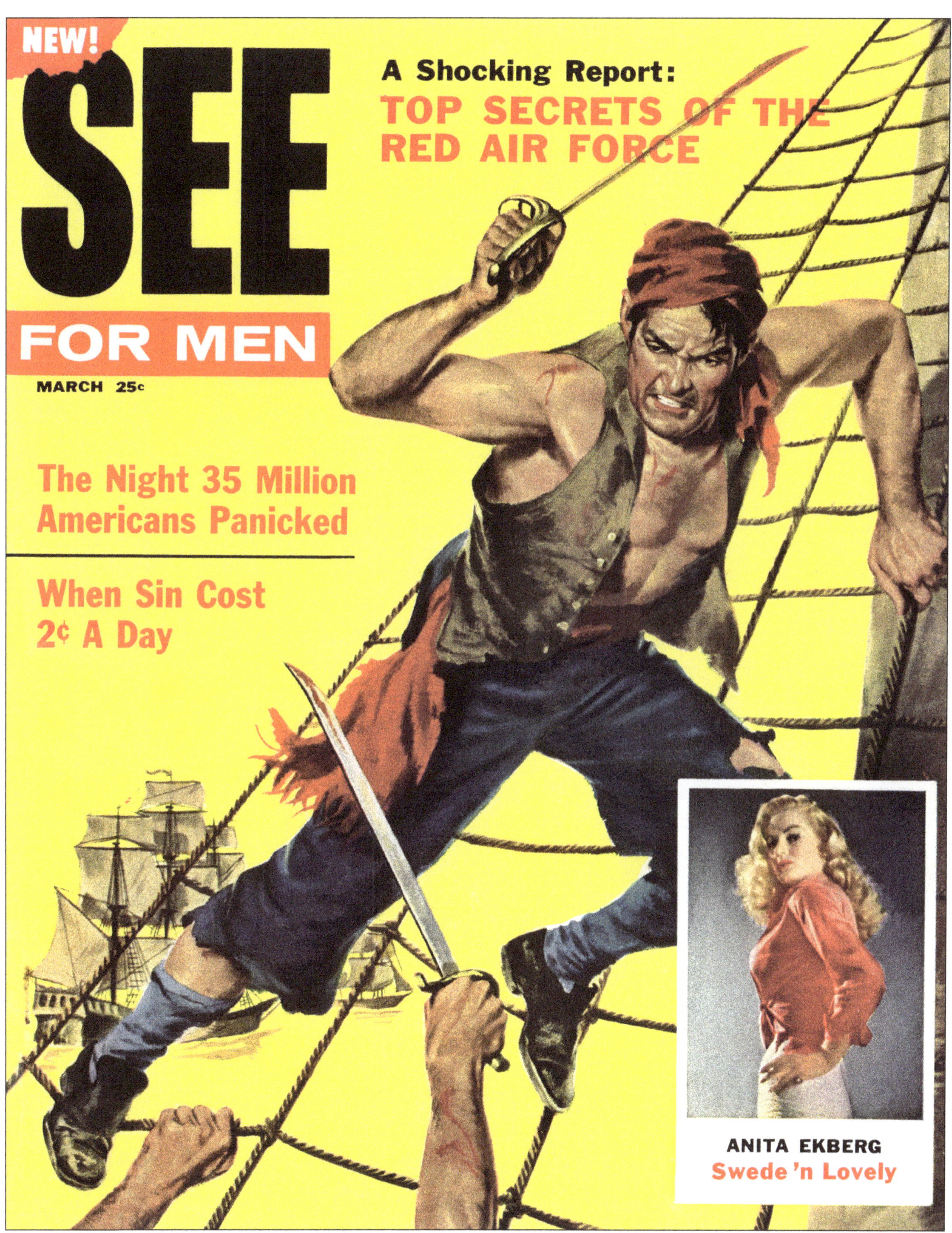

NEW!
SEE
FOR MEN
MARCH 25¢
A Shocking Report:
TOP SECRETS OF THE RED AIR FORCE
The Night 35 Million Americans Panicked
When Sin Cost 2¢ A Day
ANITA EKBERG
Swede 'n Lovely

March 1957

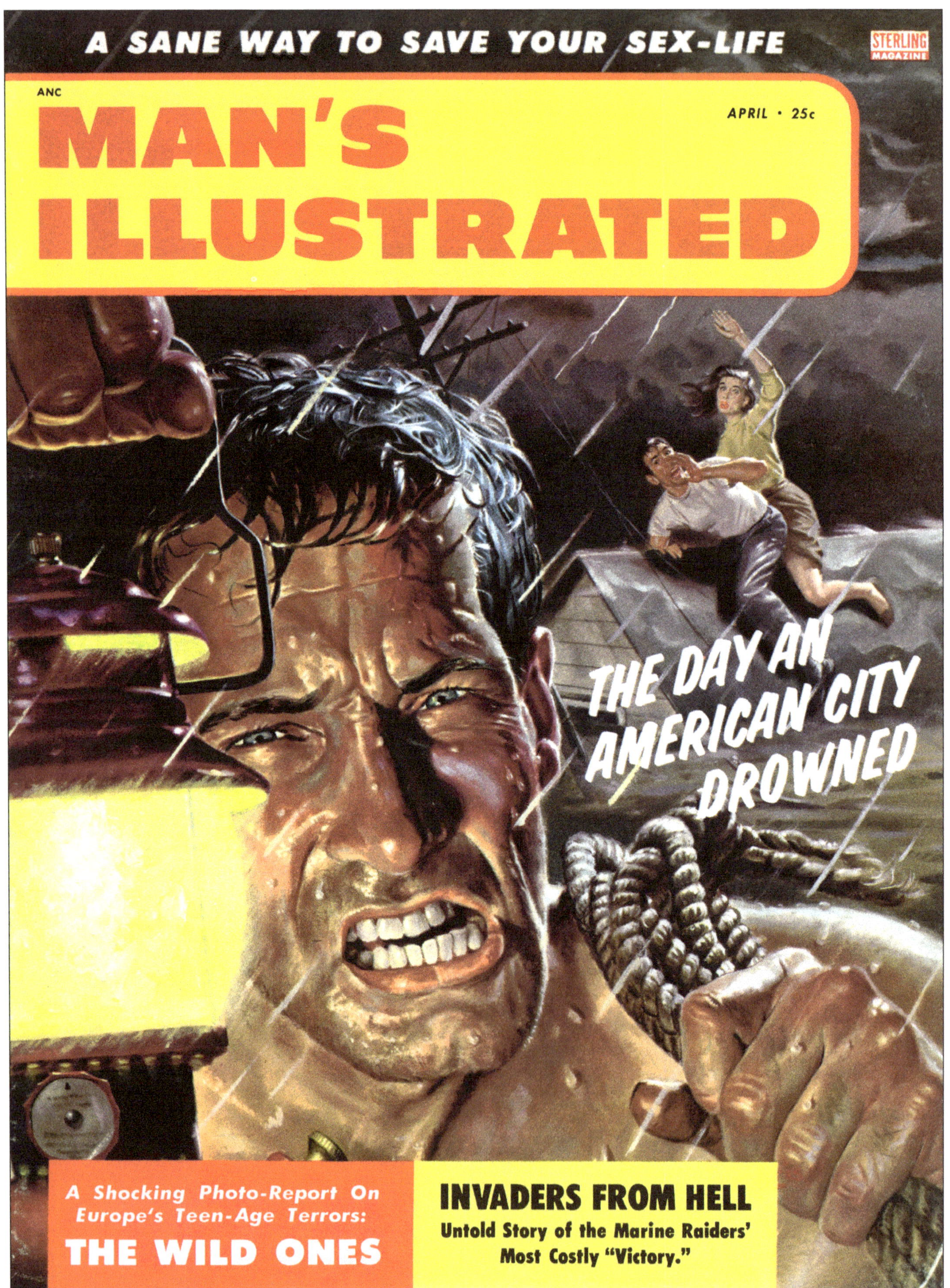

A SANE WAY TO SAVE YOUR SEX-LIFE
STERLING MAGAZINE
ANC
MAN'S ILLUSTRATED
APRIL · 25c
THE DAY AN AMERICAN CITY DROWNED
A Shocking Photo-Report On Europe's Teen-Age Terrors:
THE WILD ONES
INVADERS FROM HELL
Untold Story of the Marine Raiders' Most Costly "Victory."

April 1957

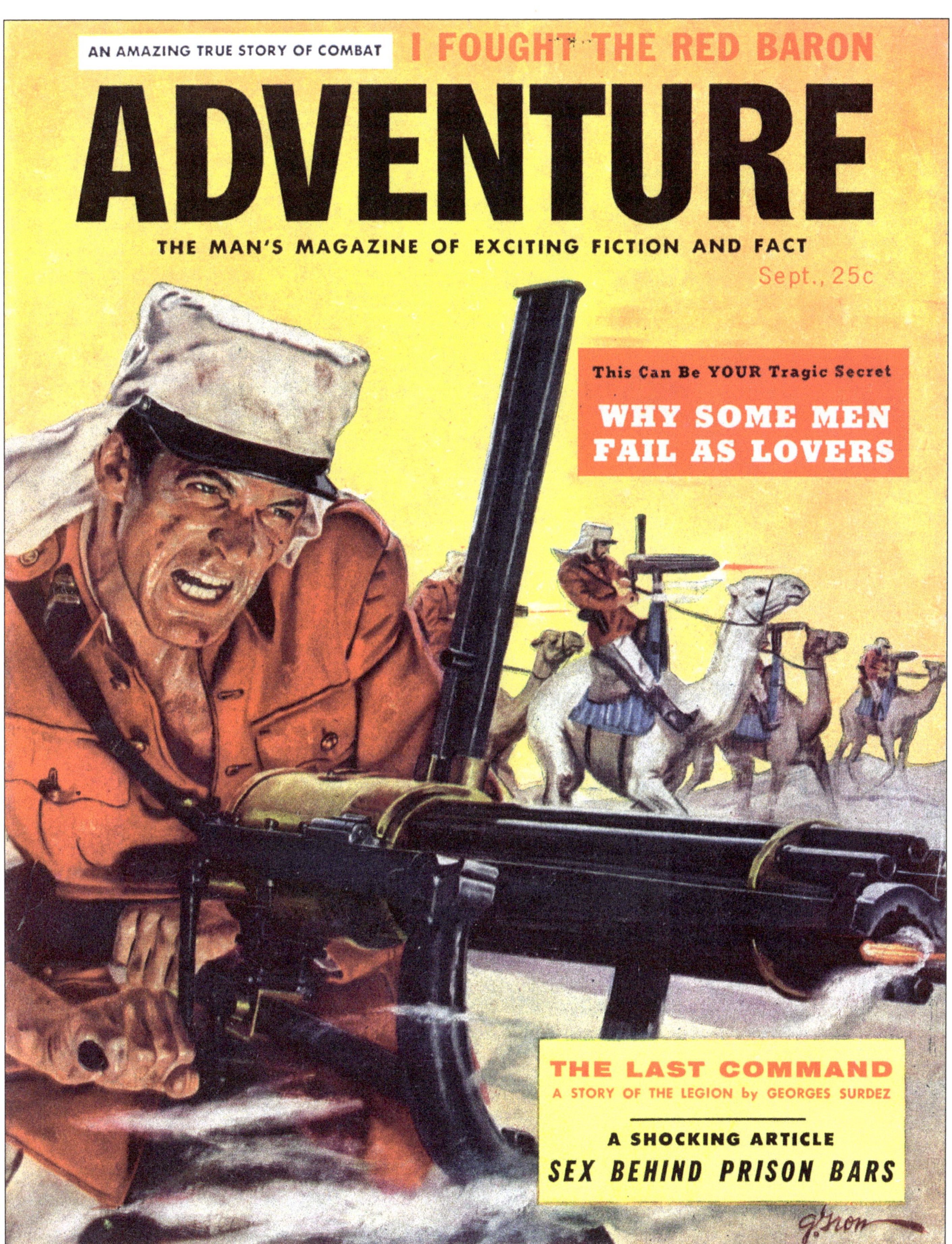

September 1957

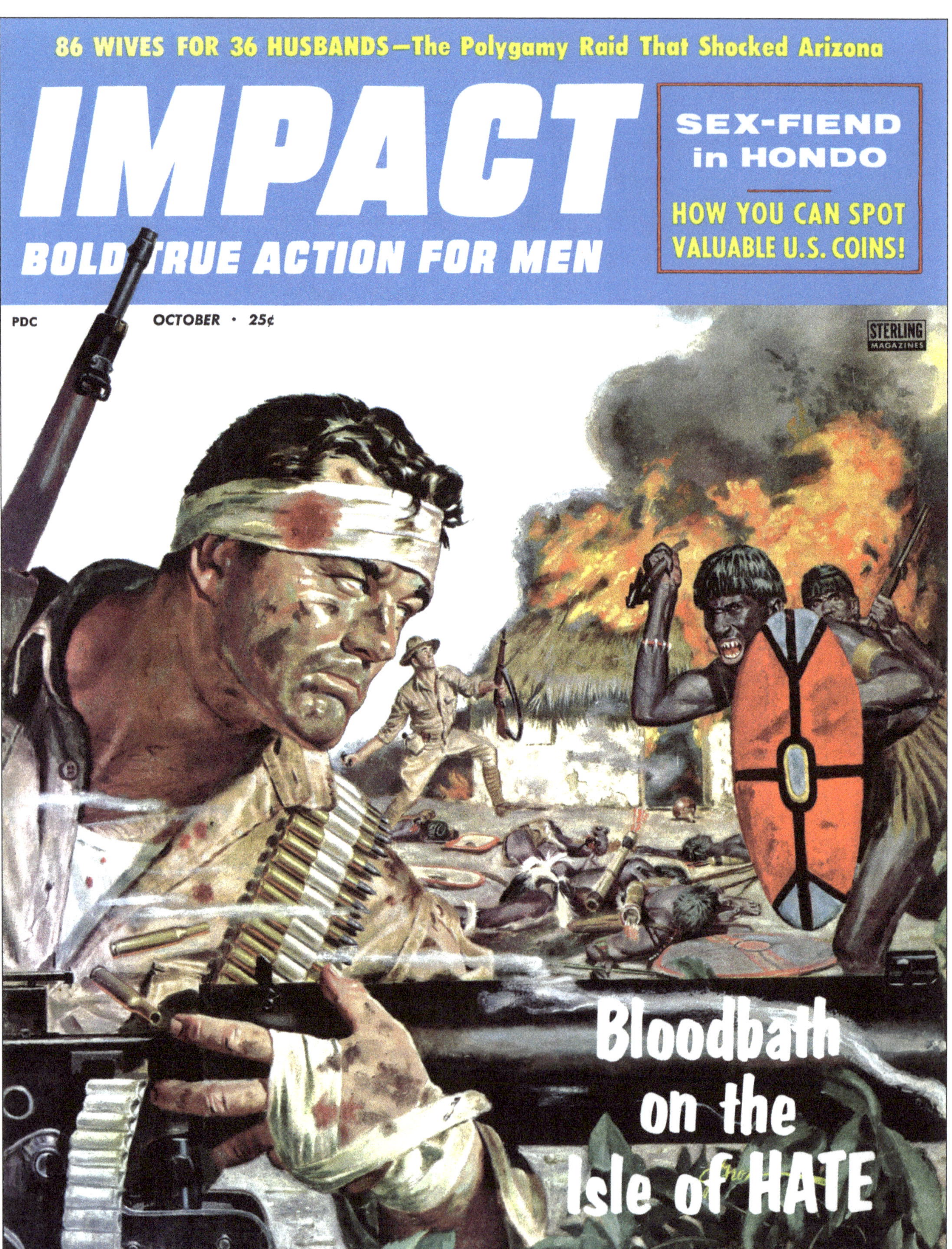

October 1957

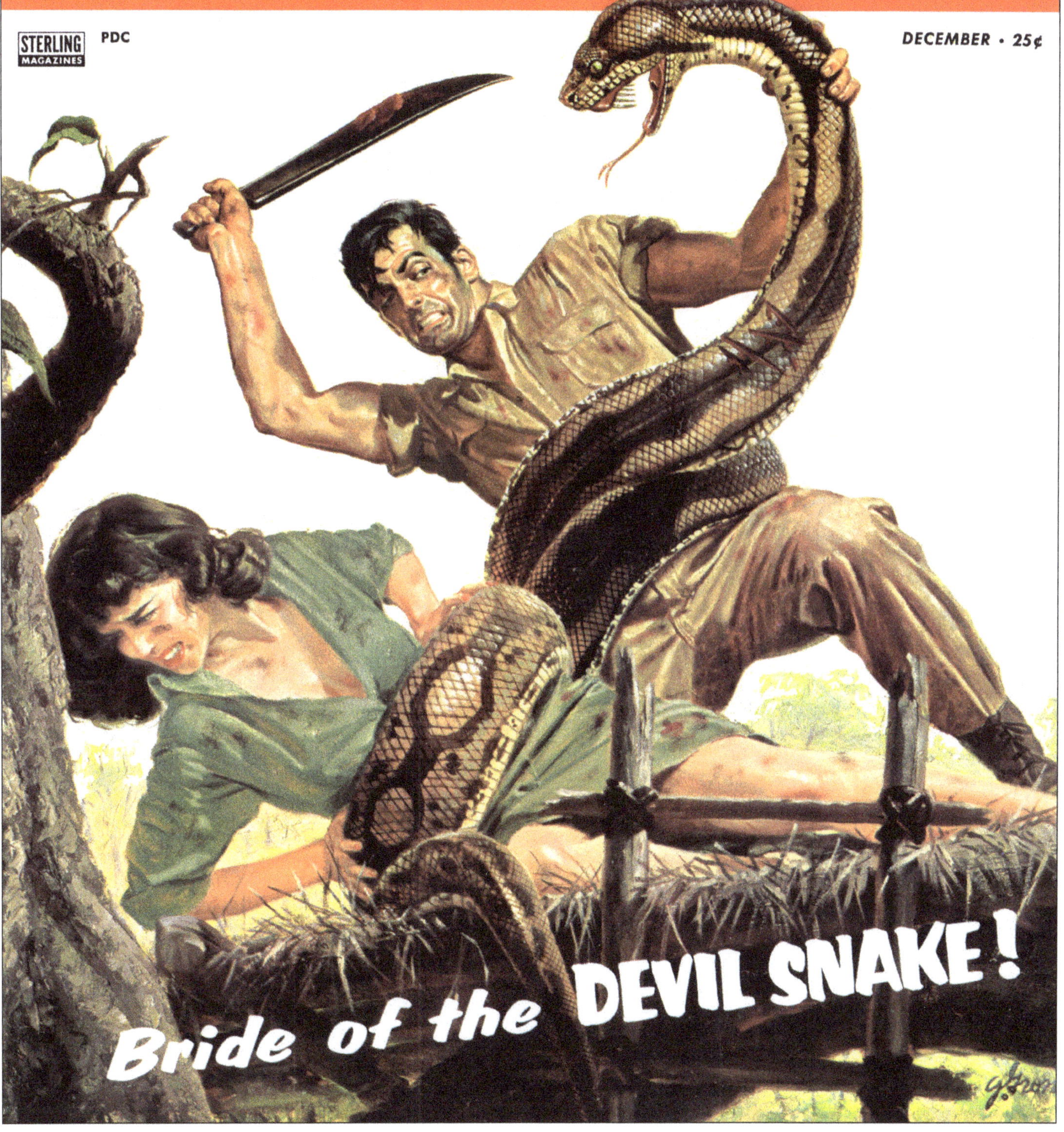

December 1957

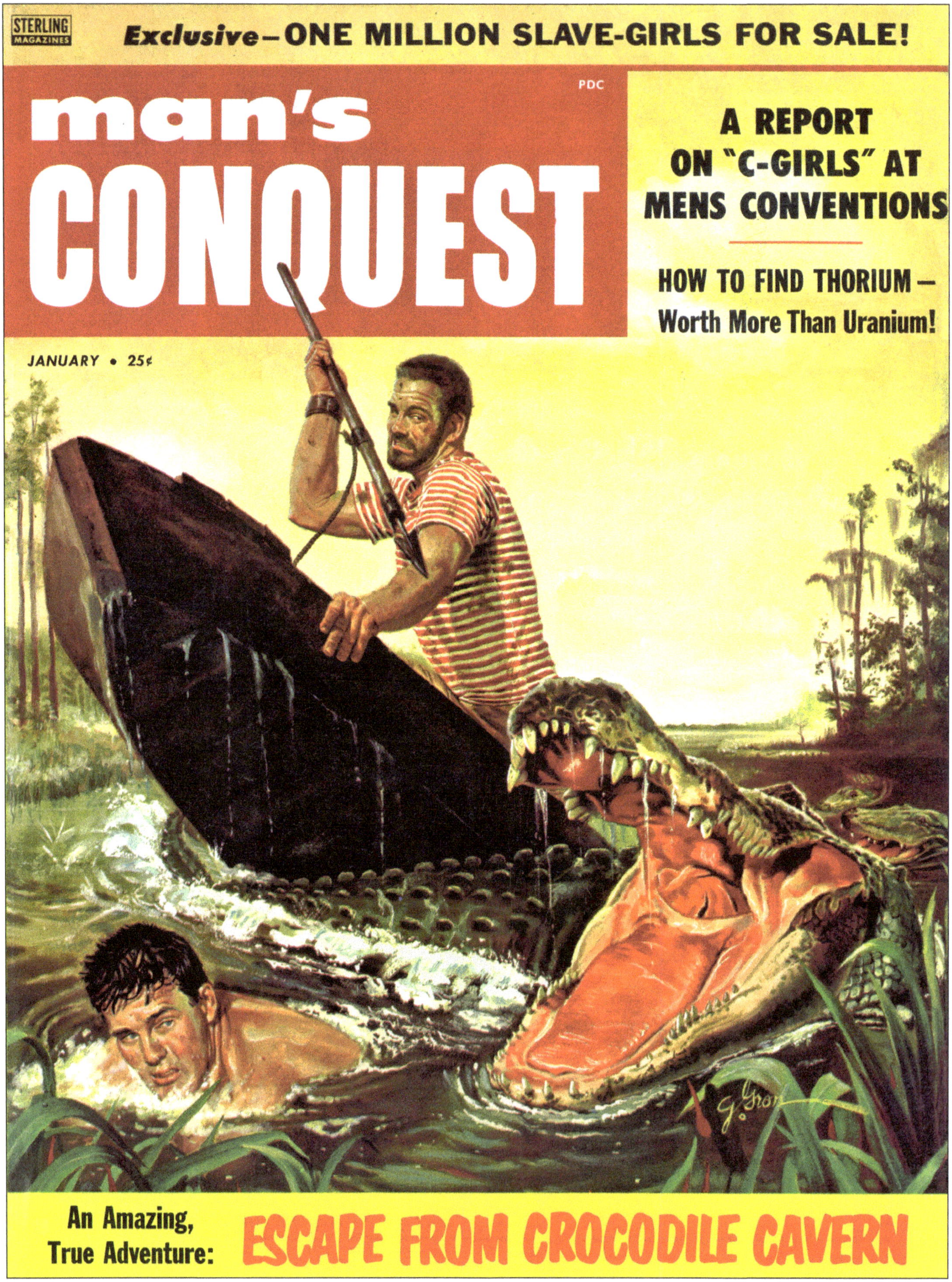

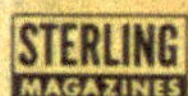

January 1958

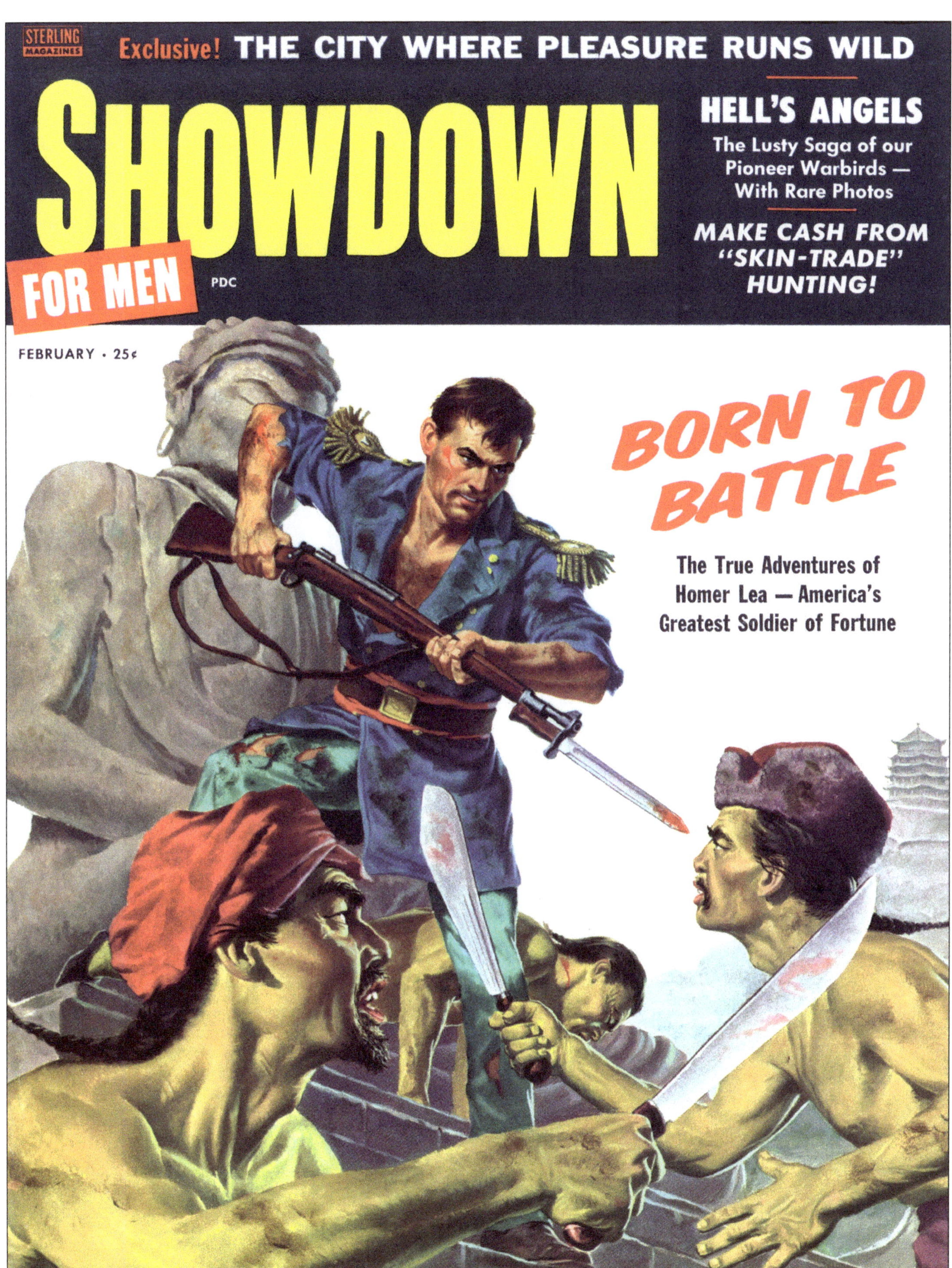

February 1958

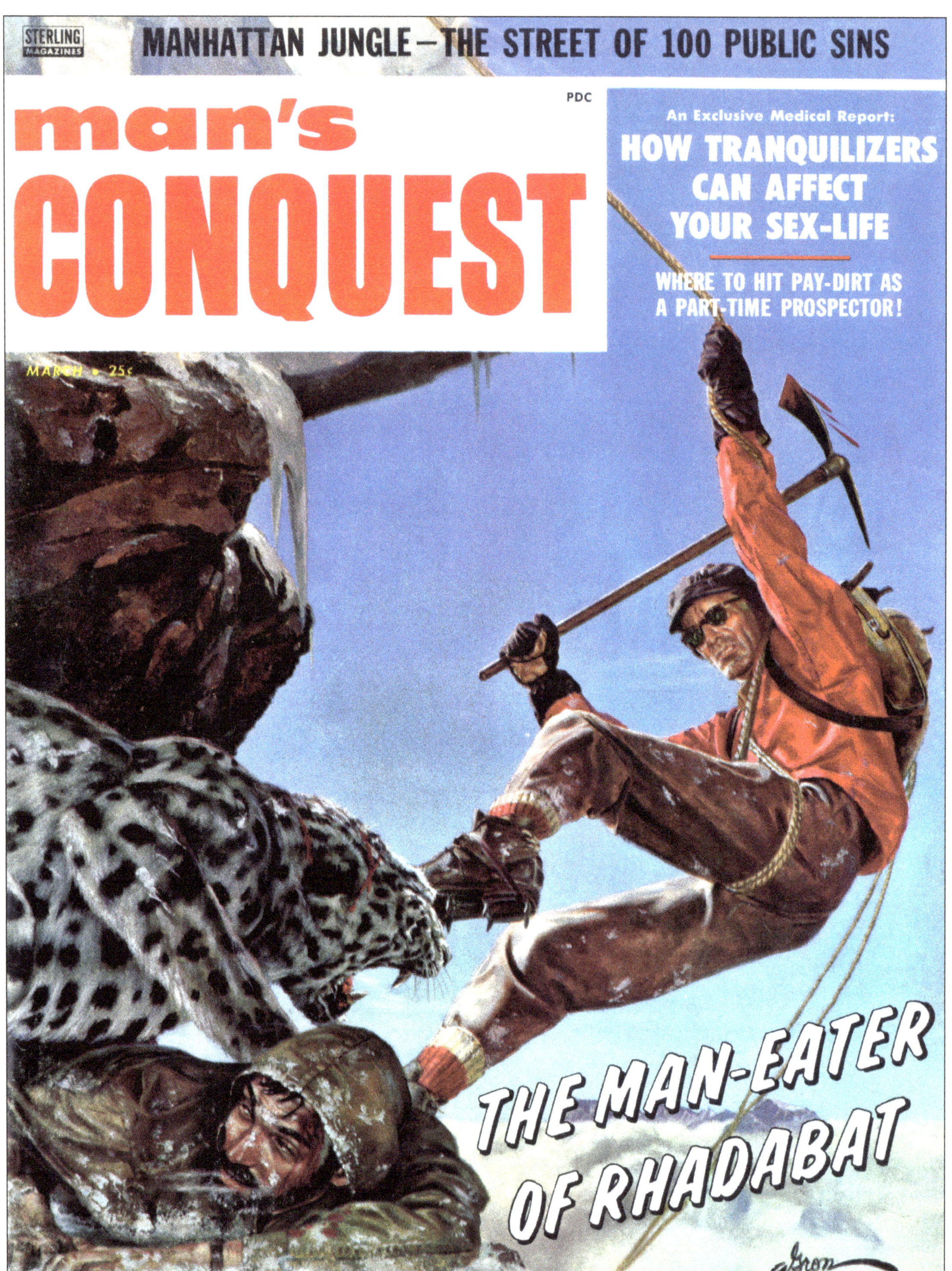

STERLING MAGAZINES
MANHATTAN JUNGLE—THE STREET OF 100 PUBLIC SINS
PDC
man's CONQUEST
MARCH • 25¢
An Exclusive Medical Report:
HOW TRANQUILIZERS CAN AFFECT YOUR SEX-LIFE
WHERE TO HIT PAY-DIRT AS A PART-TIME PROSPECTOR!
THE MAN-EATER OF RHADABAT

March 1958

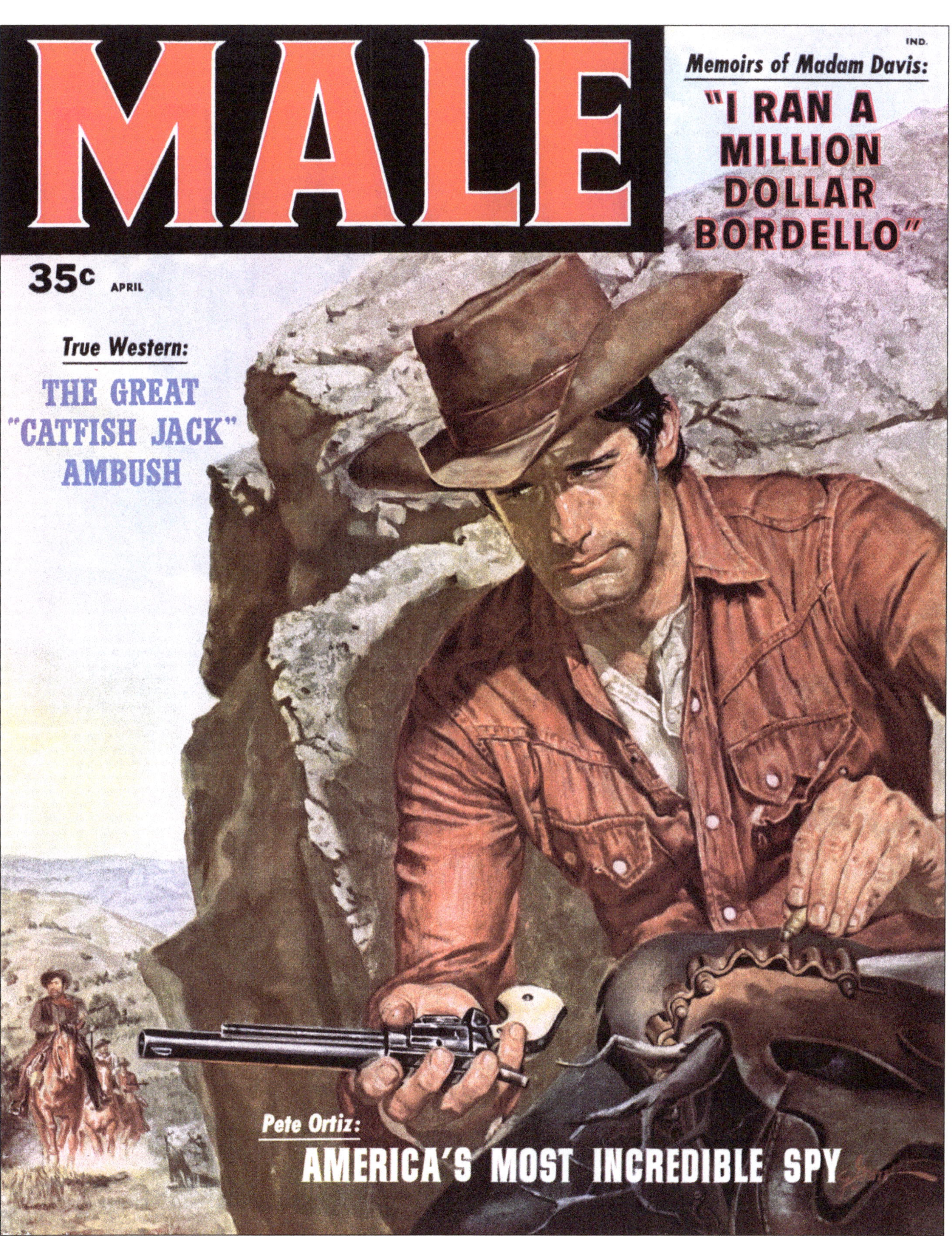

MALE
IND.
Memoirs of Madam Davis:
"I RAN A MILLION DOLLAR BORDELLO"
35c APRIL
True Western:
THE GREAT "CATFISH JACK" AMBUSH
Pete Ortiz:
AMERICA'S MOST INCREDIBLE SPY

April 1958

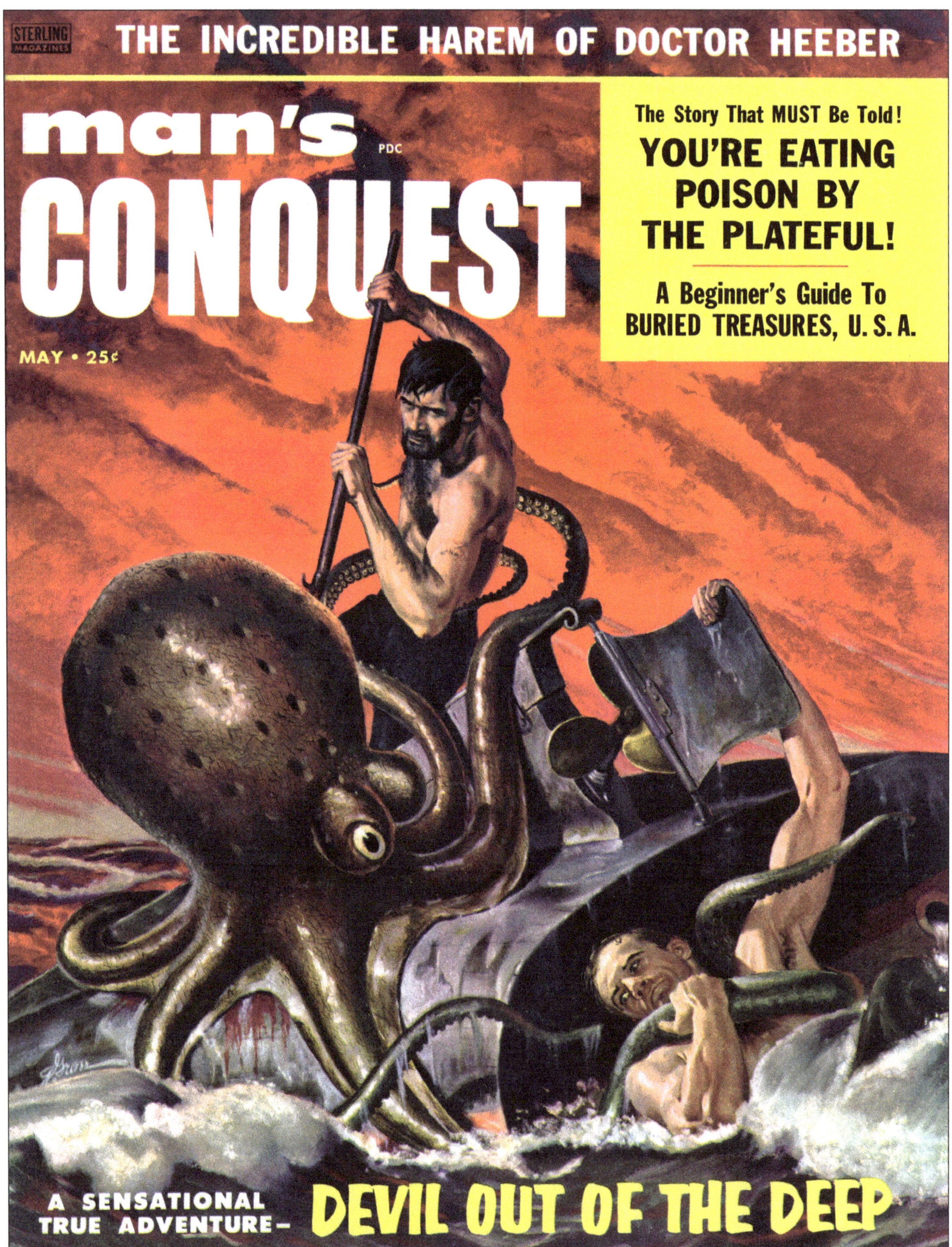
STERLING MAGAZINES
THE INCREDIBLE HAREM OF DOCTOR HEEBER
man's PDC
CONQUEST
MAY • 25¢
The Story That MUST Be Told!
YOU'RE EATING POISON BY THE PLATEFUL!
A Beginner's Guide To BURIED TREASURES, U. S. A.
A SENSATIONAL TRUE ADVENTURE—
DEVIL OUT OF THE DEEP

May 1958

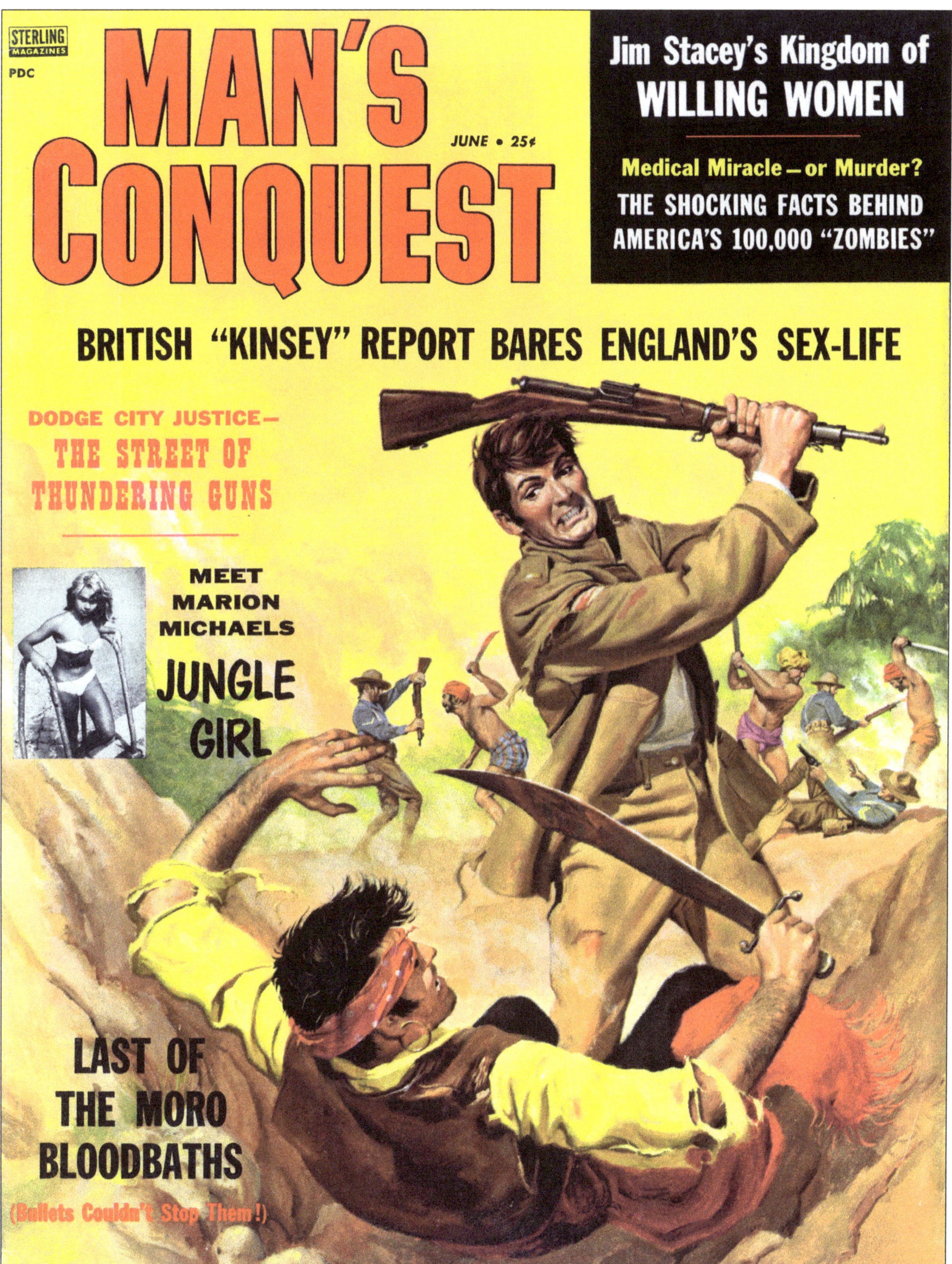

STERLING MAGAZINES
PDC
MAN'S CONQUEST
JUNE • 25¢
Jim Stacey's Kingdom of WILLING WOMEN
Medical Miracle—or Murder?
THE SHOCKING FACTS BEHIND AMERICA'S 100,000 "ZOMBIES"
BRITISH "KINSEY" REPORT BARES ENGLAND'S SEX-LIFE
DODGE CITY JUSTICE—
THE STREET OF THUNDERING GUNS
MEET MARION MICHAELS
JUNGLE GIRL
LAST OF THE MORO BLOODBATHS
(Bullets Couldn't Stop Them!)

June 1958

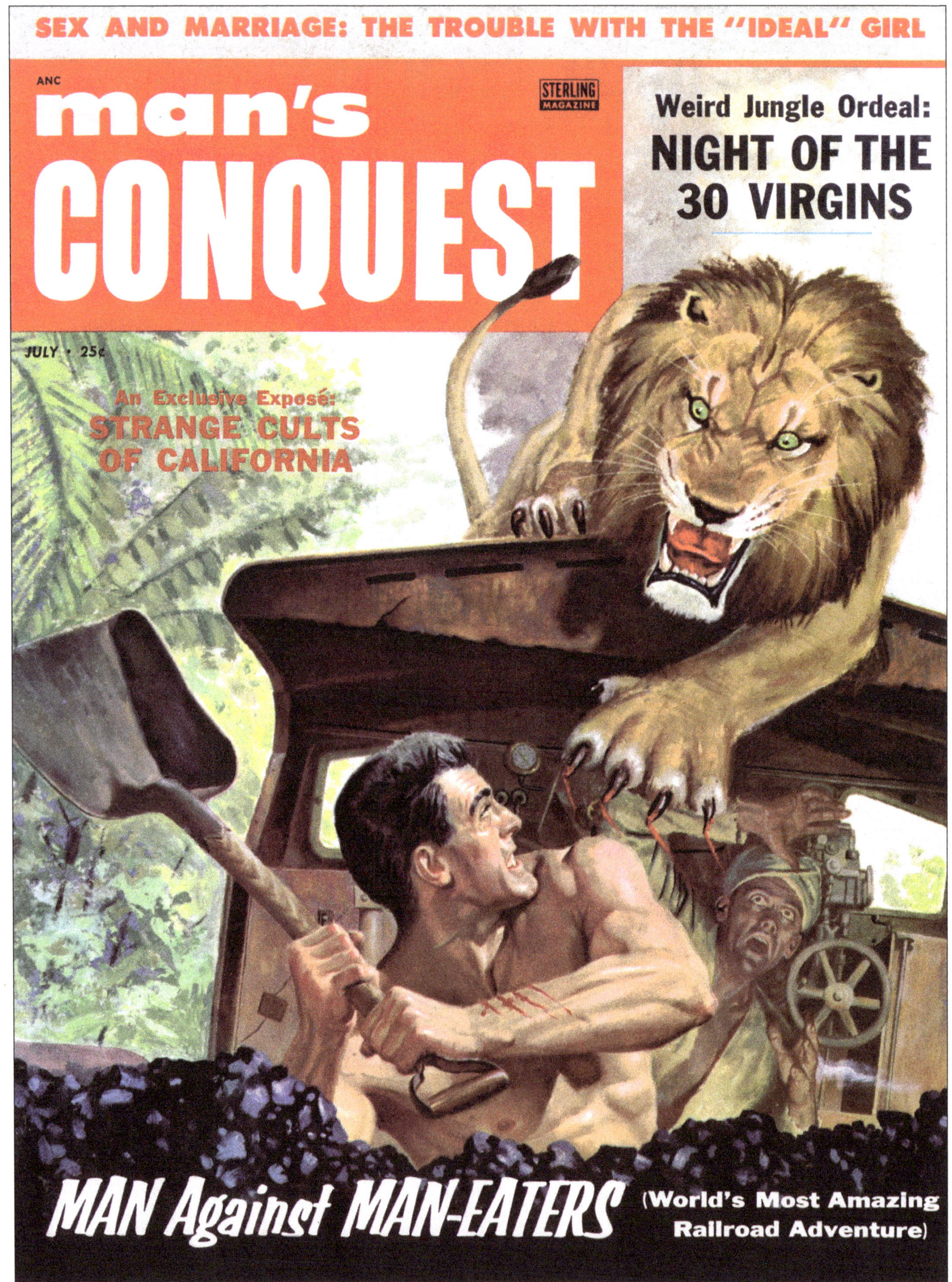

SEX AND MARRIAGE: THE TROUBLE WITH THE "IDEAL" GIRL
ANC
STERLING MAGAZINE
man's CONQUEST
JULY · 25¢
Weird Jungle Ordeal:
NIGHT OF THE 30 VIRGINS
An Exclusive Exposé:
STRANGE CULTS OF CALIFORNIA
MAN Against MAN-EATERS (World's Most Amazing Railroad Adventure)

July 1958

38

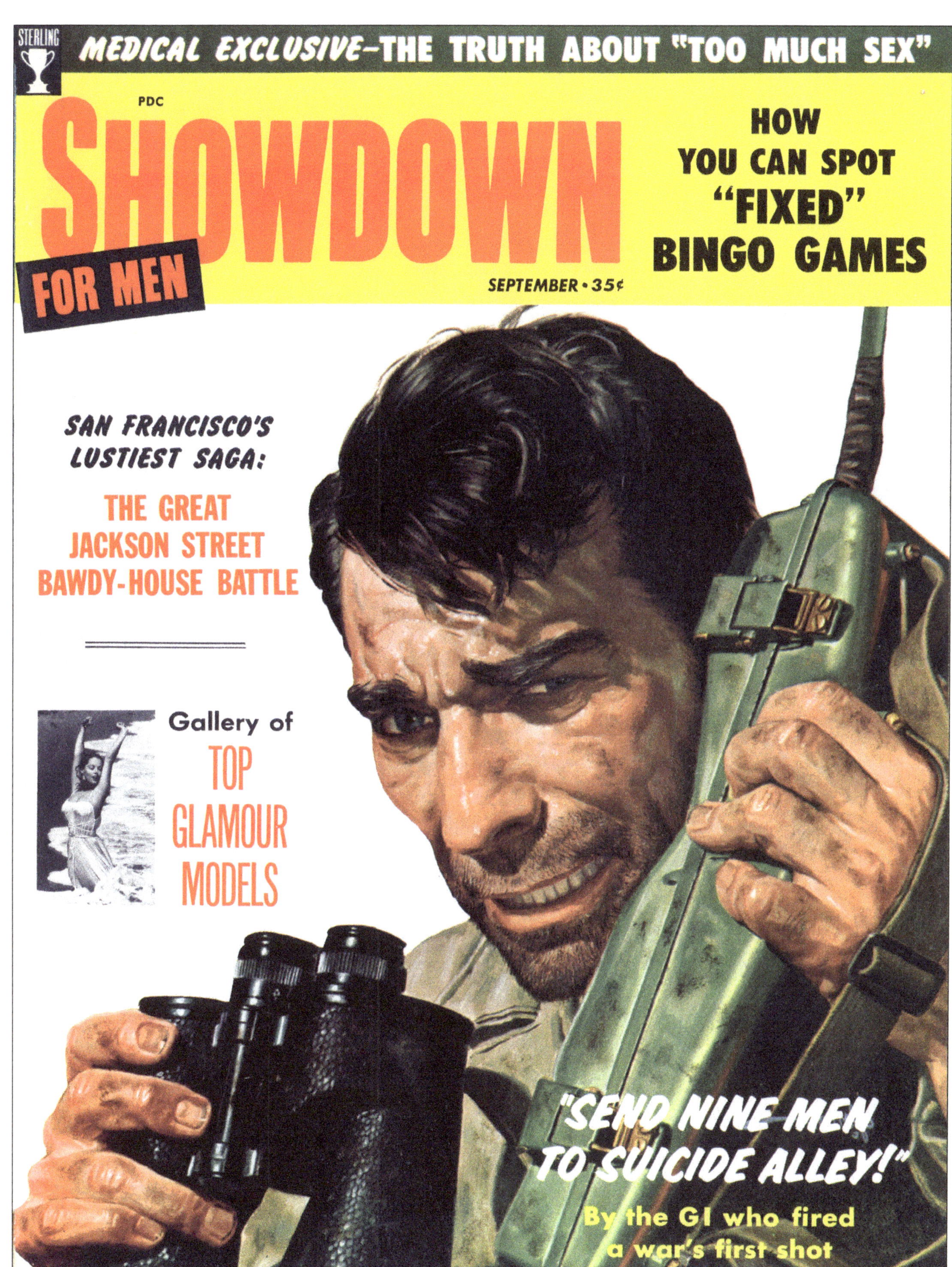

September 1958

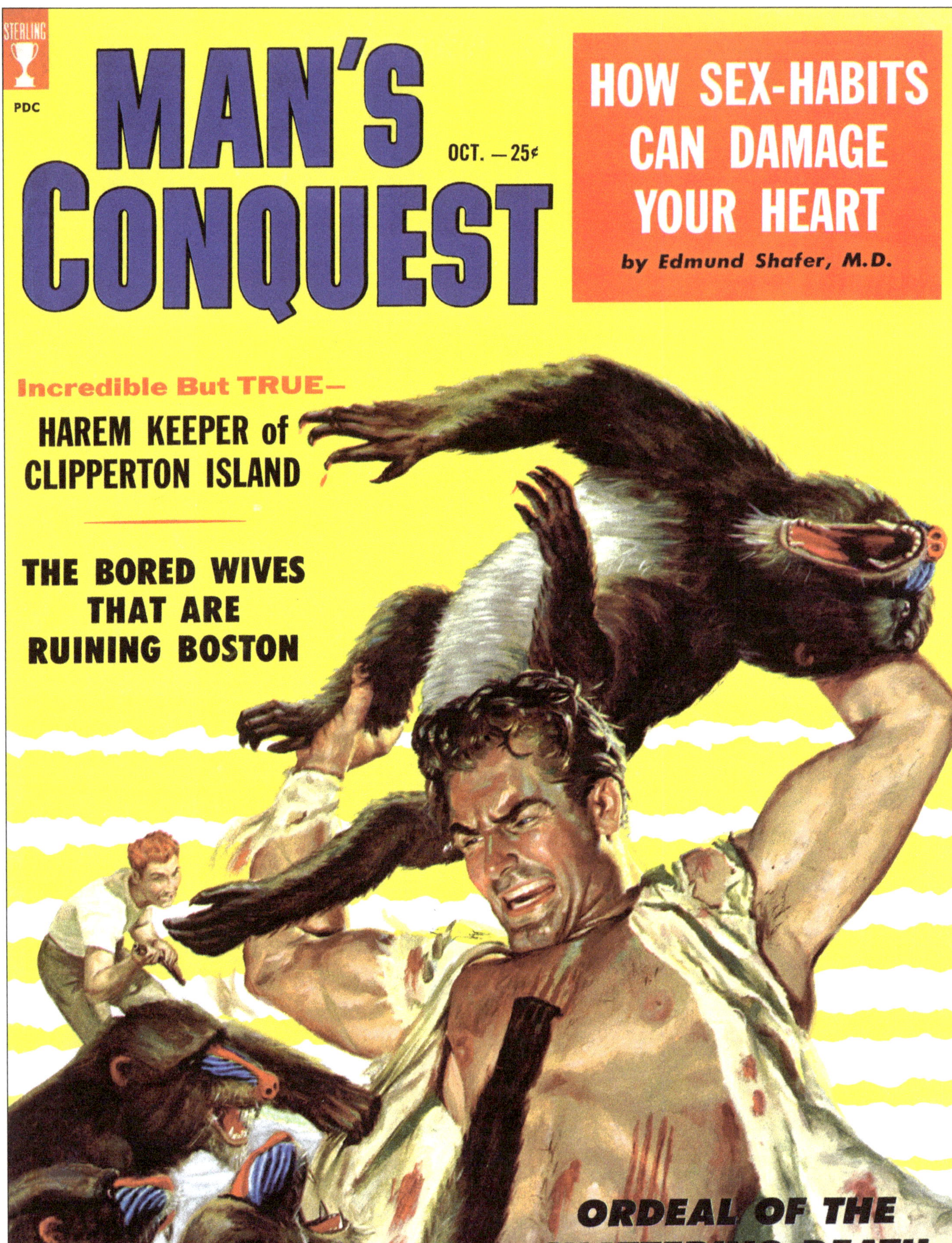

October 1958   *Previously used for* **Man's Illustrated** April 1956

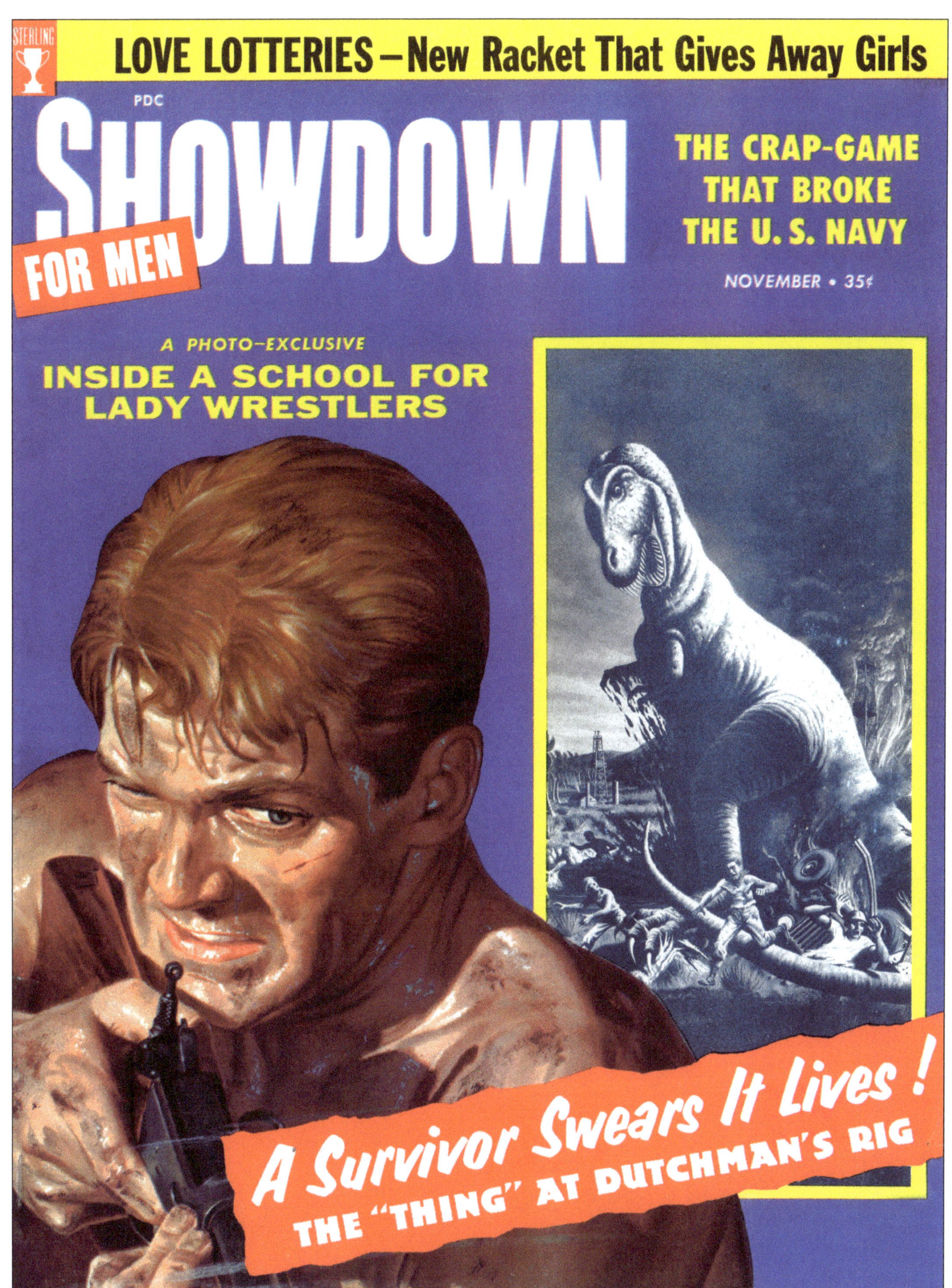

November 1958   *Previously used for* **Man's Illustrated** August 1956

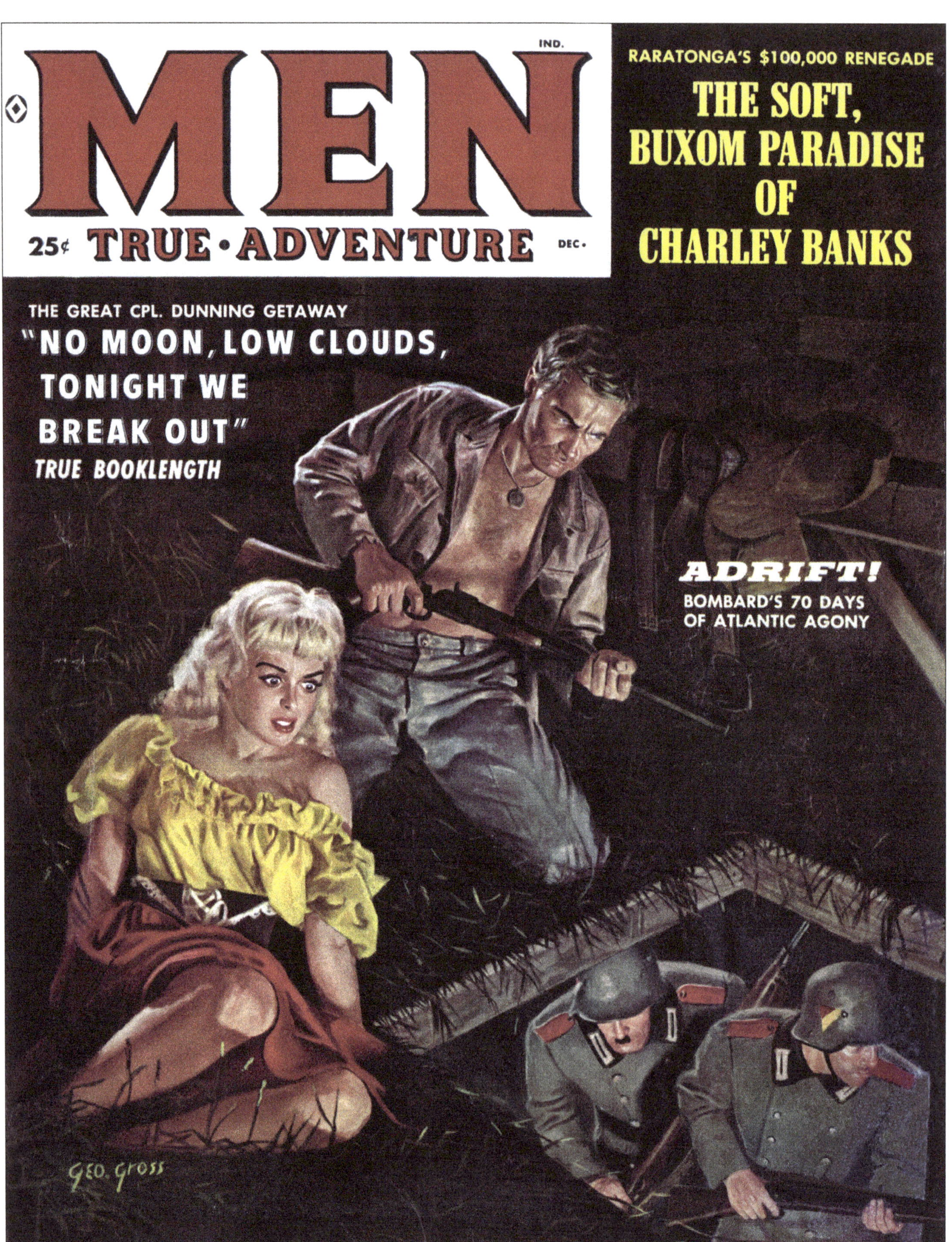

December 1958

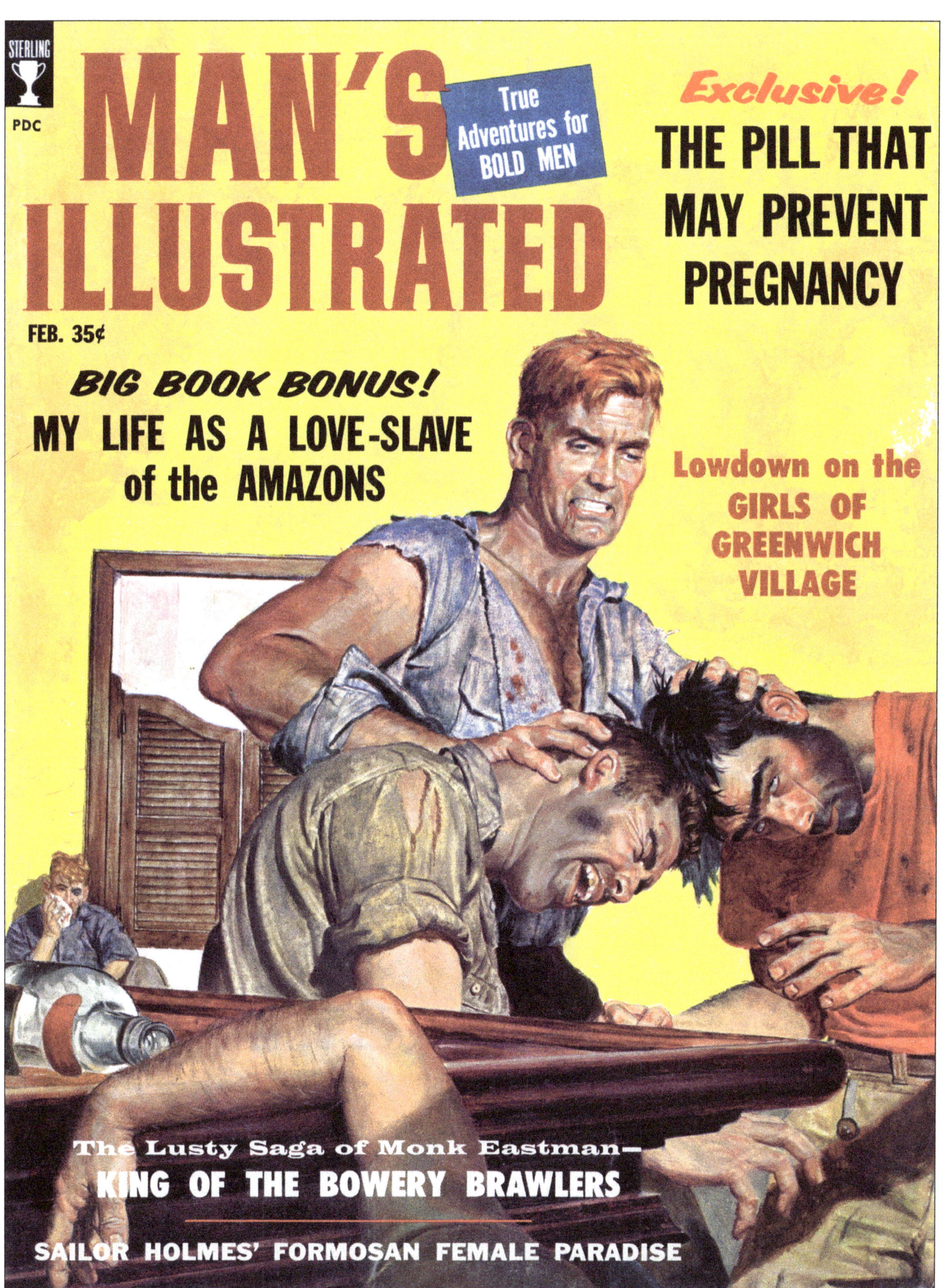

February 1959

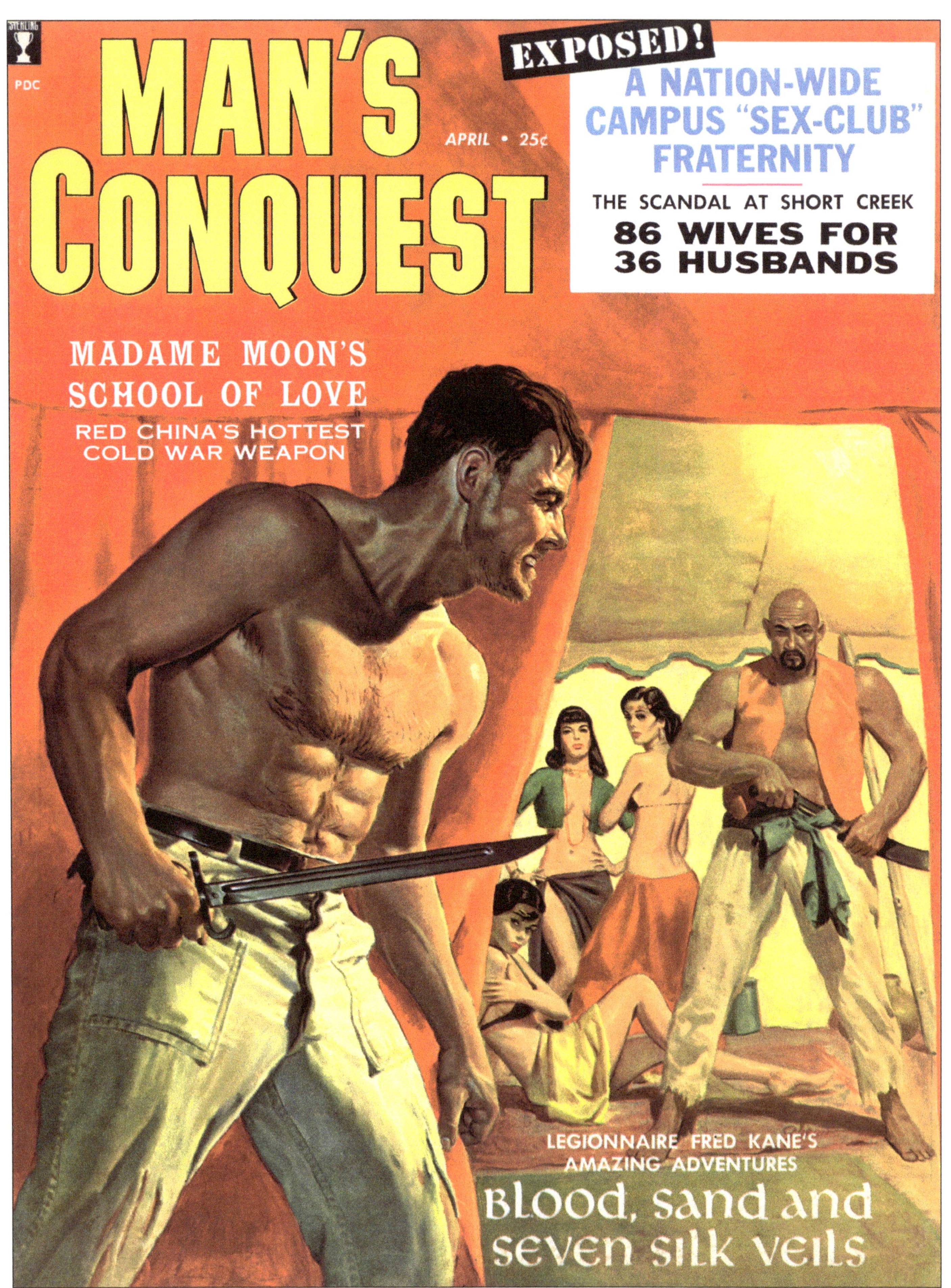

STERLING
PDC
MAN'S CONQUEST
APRIL • 25¢
EXPOSED!
A NATION-WIDE CAMPUS "SEX-CLUB" FRATERNITY
THE SCANDAL AT SHORT CREEK
86 WIVES FOR 36 HUSBANDS
MADAME MOON'S SCHOOL OF LOVE
RED CHINA'S HOTTEST COLD WAR WEAPON
LEGIONNAIRE FRED KANE'S AMAZING ADVENTURES
Blood, sand and seven silk veils

April 1959

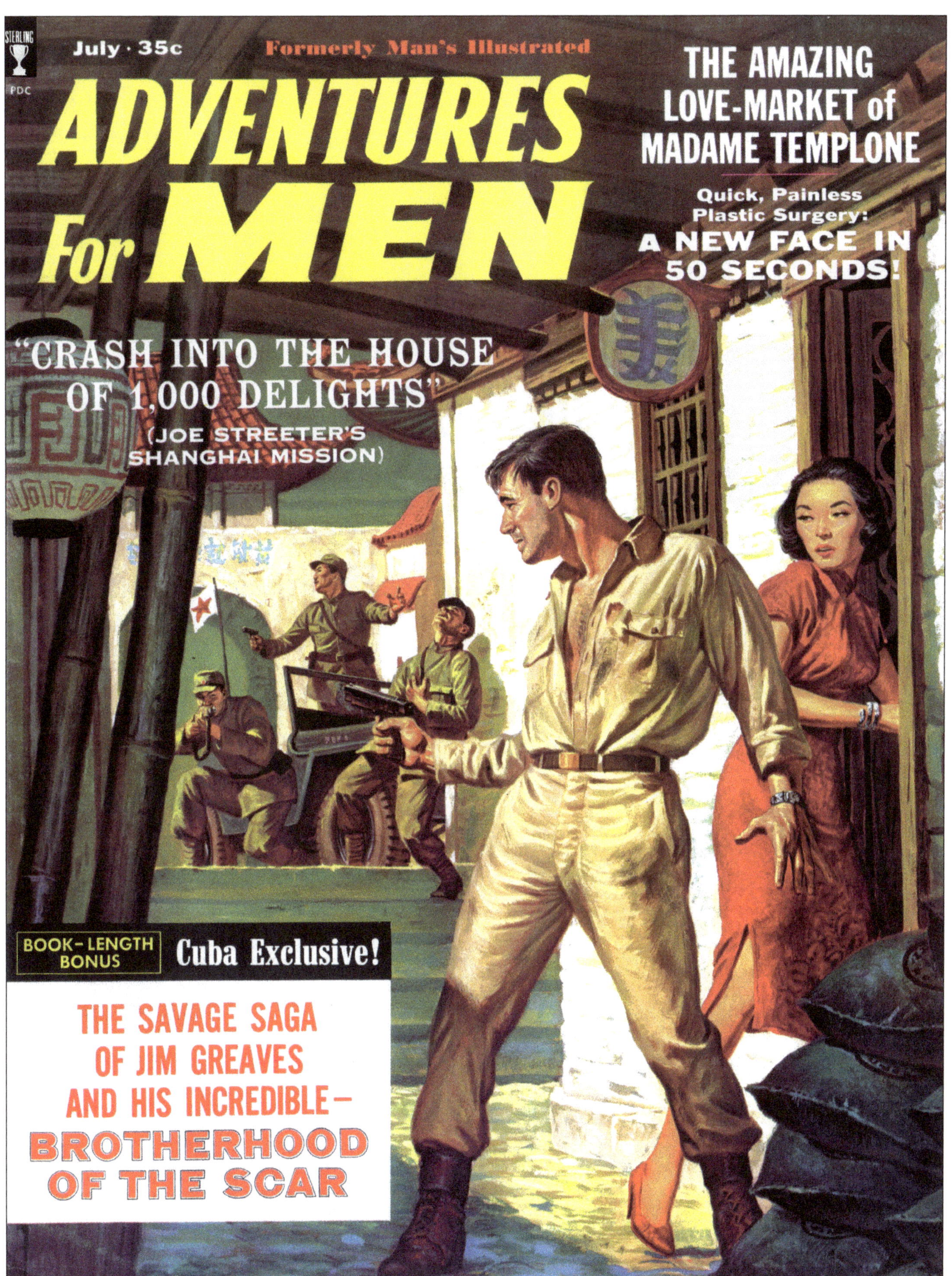

July · 35c
Formerly Man's Illustrated
ADVENTURES For MEN
THE AMAZING LOVE-MARKET of MADAME TEMPLONE
Quick, Painless Plastic Surgery:
A NEW FACE IN 50 SECONDS!
"CRASH INTO THE HOUSE OF 1,000 DELIGHTS"
(JOE STREETER'S SHANGHAI MISSION)
BOOK-LENGTH BONUS
Cuba Exclusive!
THE SAVAGE SAGA OF JIM GREAVES AND HIS INCREDIBLE—
BROTHERHOOD OF THE SCAR
STERLING
PDC

July 1959

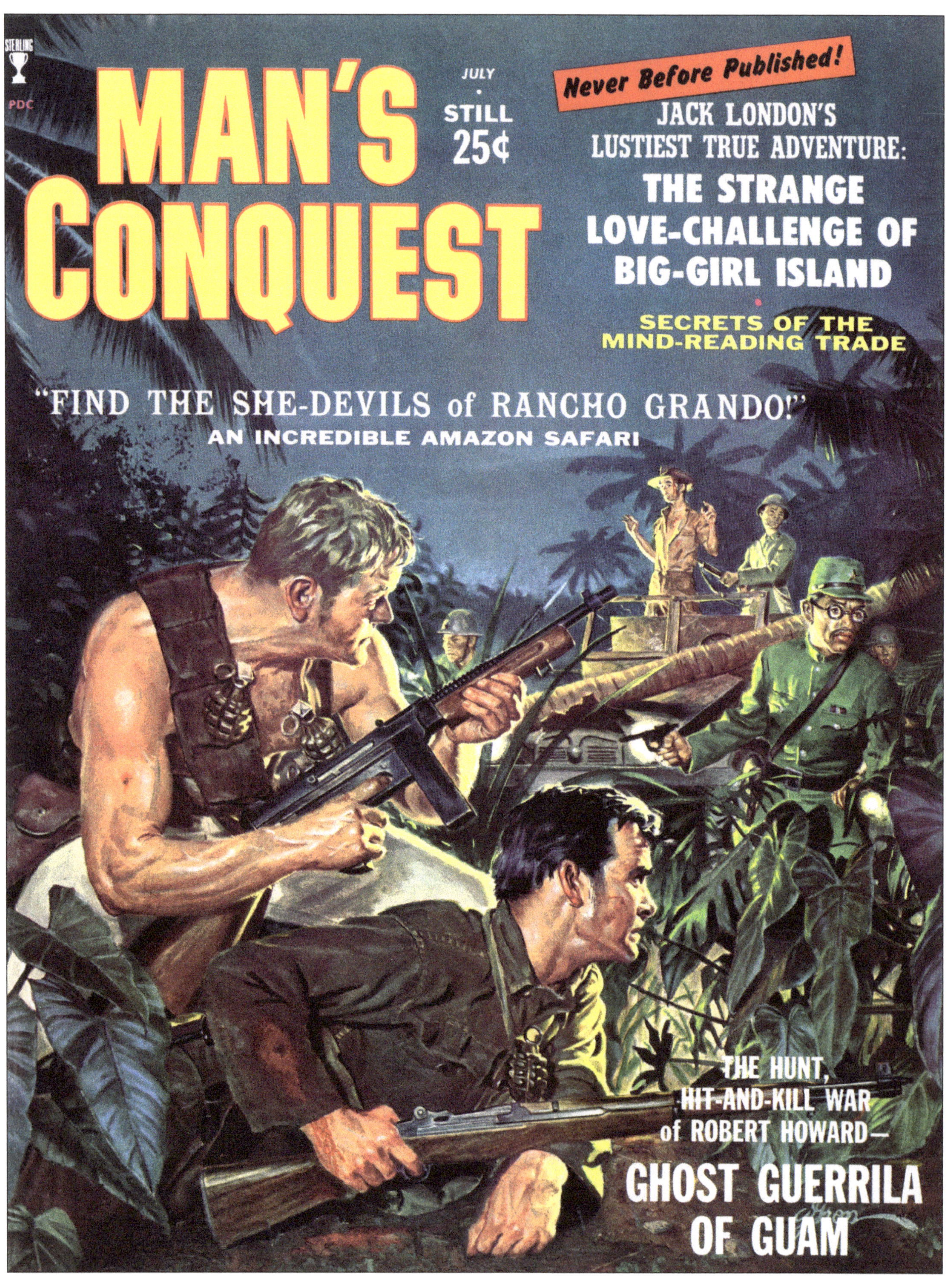

STERLING
PDC
JULY
STILL
25¢
Never Before Published!
JACK LONDON'S
LUSTIEST TRUE ADVENTURE:
THE STRANGE
LOVE-CHALLENGE OF
BIG-GIRL ISLAND
SECRETS OF THE
MIND-READING TRADE
MAN'S
CONQUEST
"FIND THE SHE-DEVILS of RANCHO GRANDO!"
AN INCREDIBLE AMAZON SAFARI
THE HUNT,
HIT-AND-KILL WAR
of ROBERT HOWARD—
GHOST GUERRILA
OF GUAM

July 1959

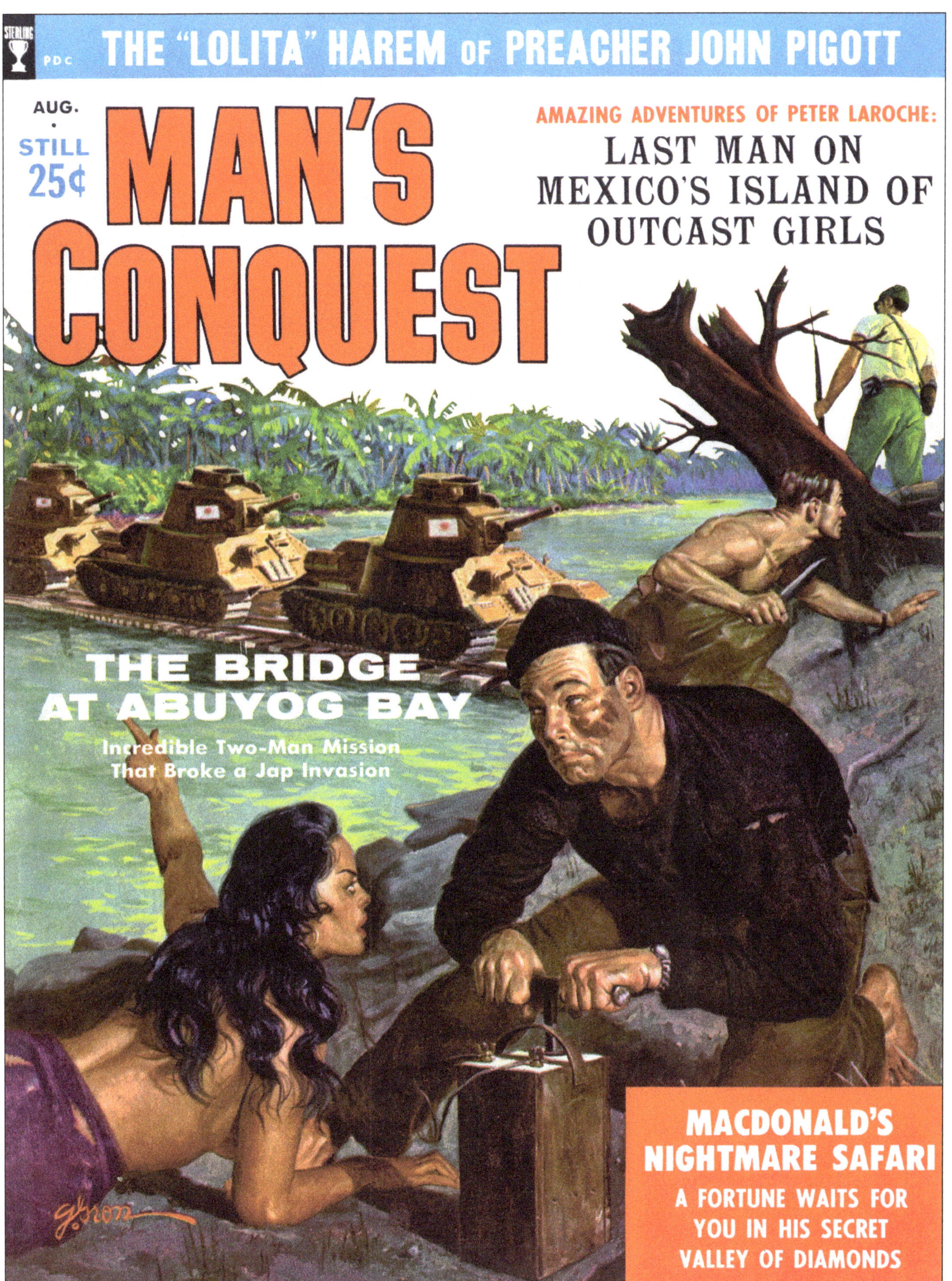

STERLING
PDC
THE "LOLITA" HAREM OF PREACHER JOHN PIGOTT
AUG.
STILL 25¢
MAN'S CONQUEST
AMAZING ADVENTURES OF PETER LAROCHE:
LAST MAN ON MEXICO'S ISLAND OF OUTCAST GIRLS
THE BRIDGE AT ABUYOG BAY
Incredible Two-Man Mission That Broke a Jap Invasion
MACDONALD'S NIGHTMARE SAFARI
A FORTUNE WAITS FOR YOU IN HIS SECRET VALLEY OF DIAMONDS

August 1959

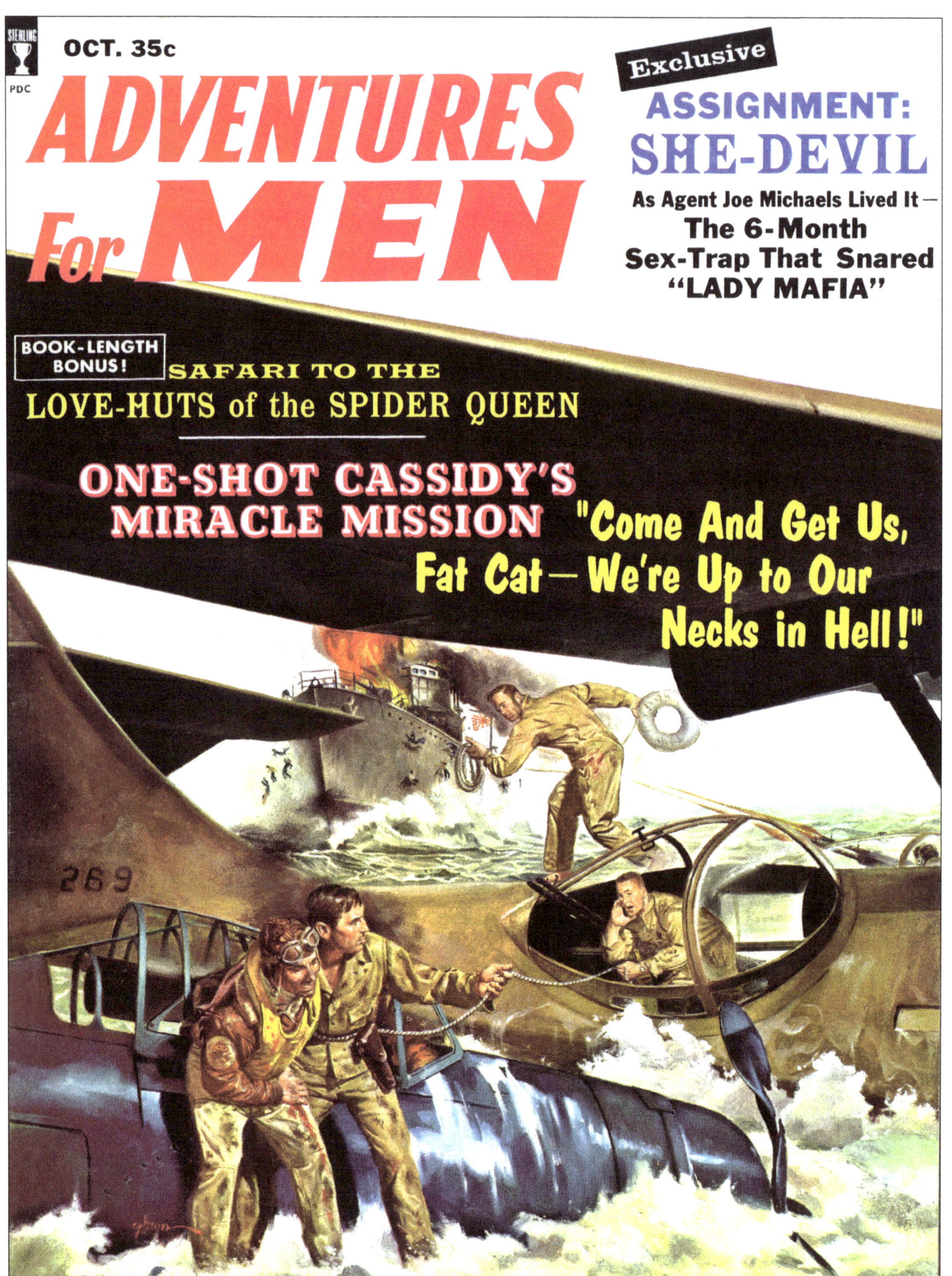

October 1959

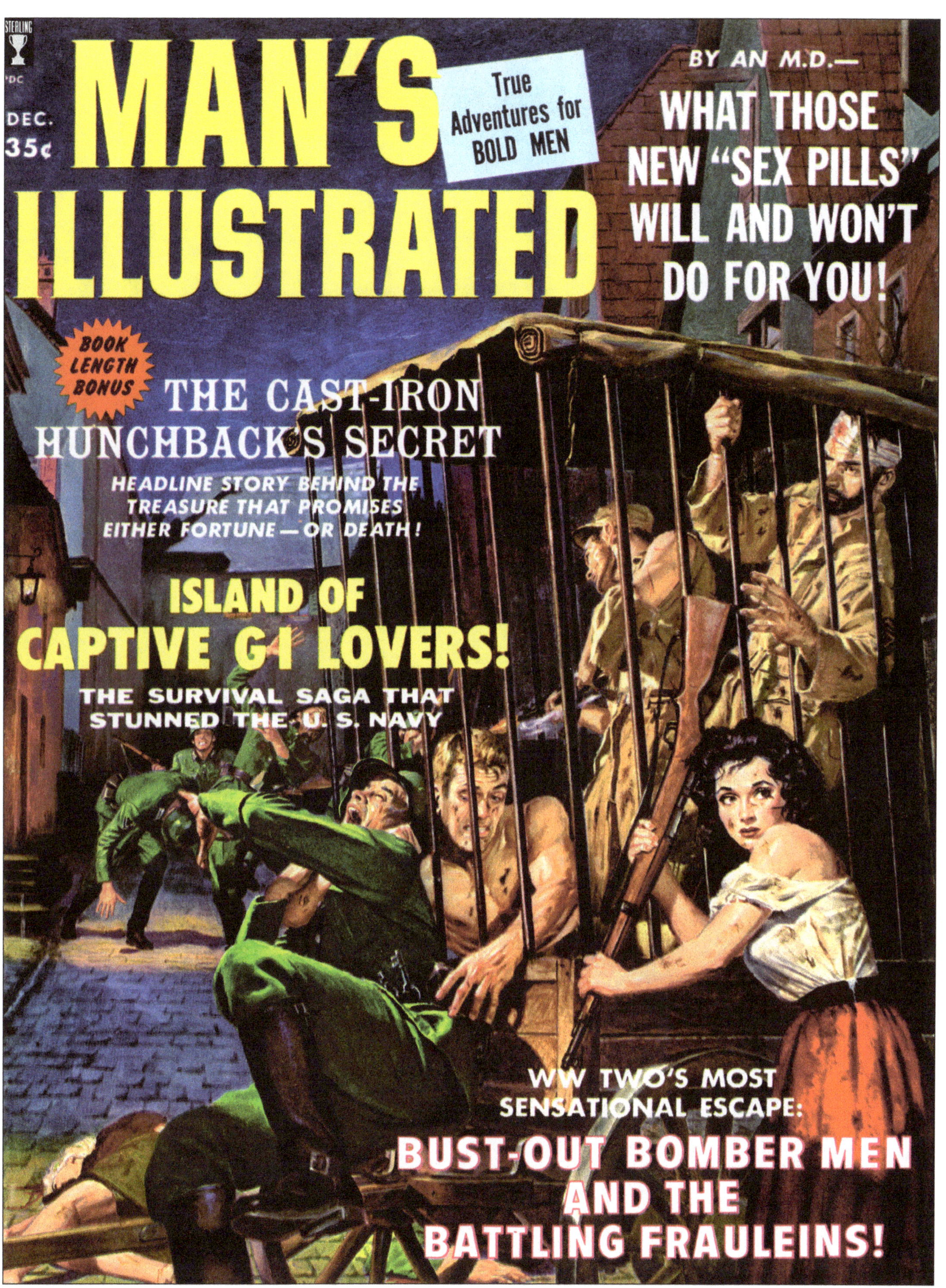

December 1959

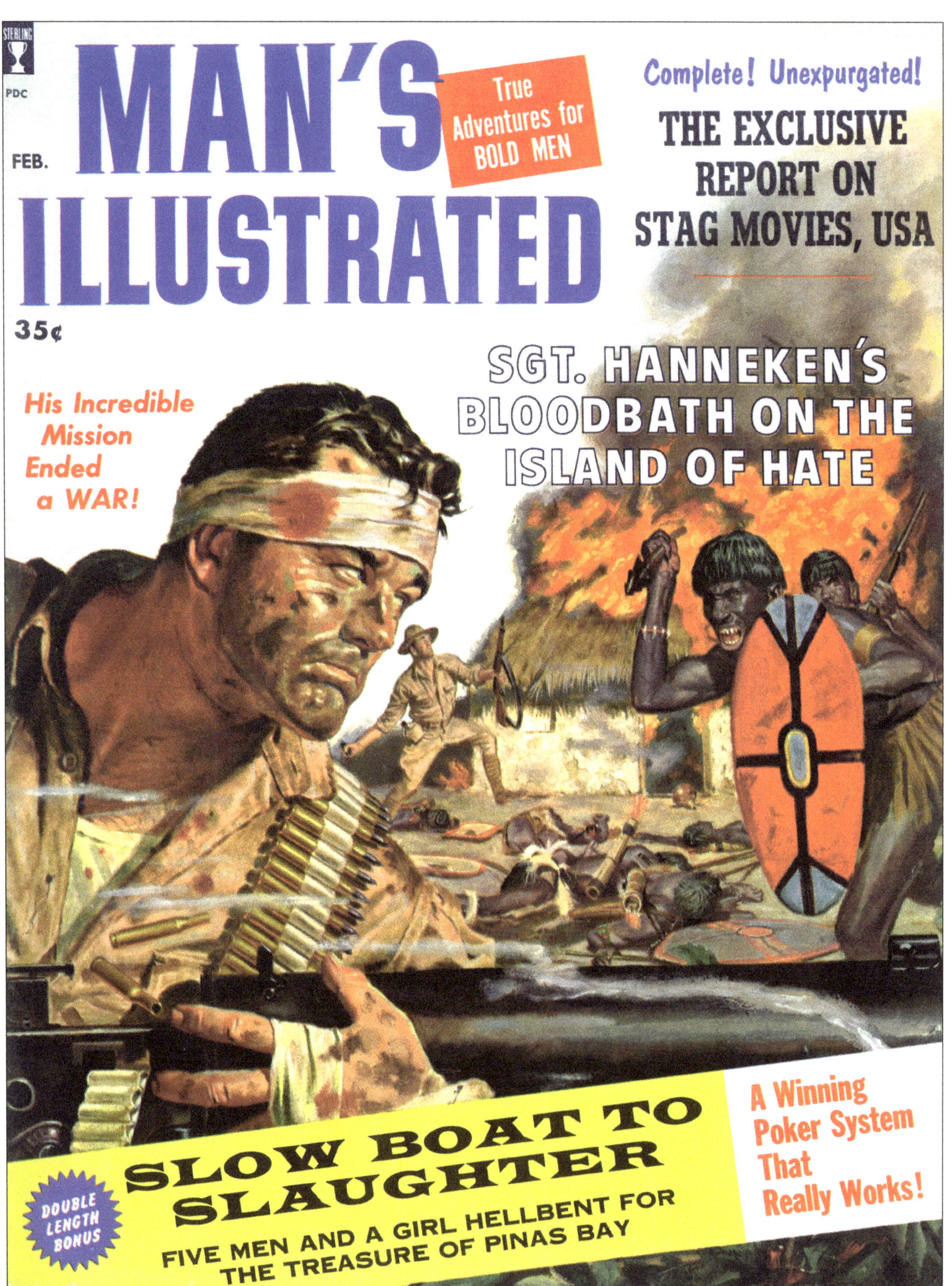

February 1960   *Previously used for* **Impact** October 1957

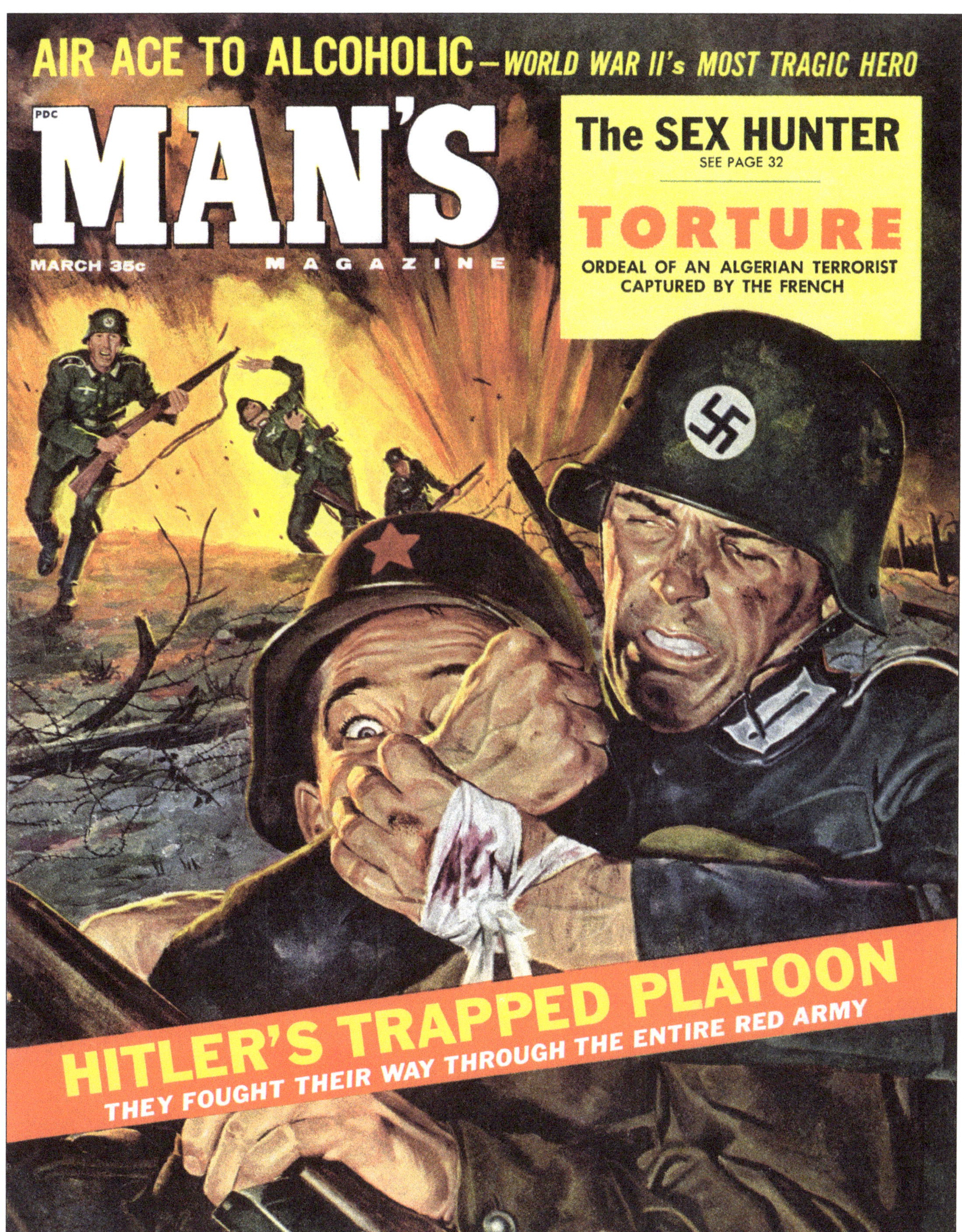
AIR ACE TO ALCOHOLIC—WORLD WAR II's MOST TRAGIC HERO
PDC
MAN'S
MAGAZINE
MARCH 35c
The SEX HUNTER
SEE PAGE 32
TORTURE
ORDEAL OF AN ALGERIAN TERRORIST
CAPTURED BY THE FRENCH
HITLER'S TRAPPED PLATOON
THEY FOUGHT THEIR WAY THROUGH THE ENTIRE RED ARMY

March 1960

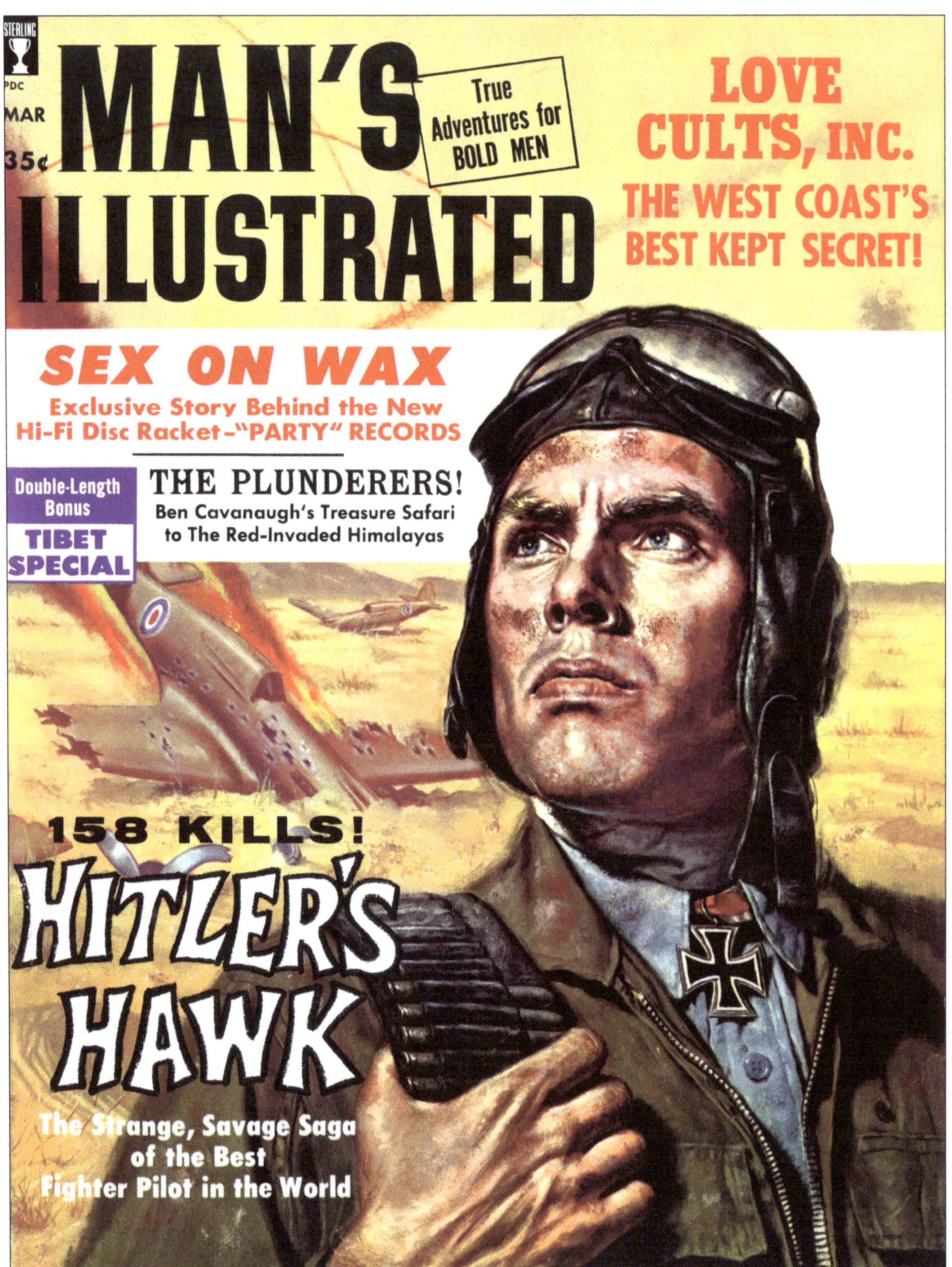

STERLING
PDC
MAR
35¢
MAN'S ILLUSTRATED
True Adventures for BOLD MEN
LOVE CULTS, INC.
THE WEST COAST'S BEST KEPT SECRET!
SEX ON WAX
Exclusive Story Behind the New Hi-Fi Disc Racket—"PARTY" RECORDS
Double-Length Bonus
TIBET SPECIAL
THE PLUNDERERS!
Ben Cavanaugh's Treasure Safari to The Red-Invaded Himalayas
158 KILLS!
HITLER'S HAWK
The Strange, Savage Saga of the Best Fighter Pilot in the World

March 1960

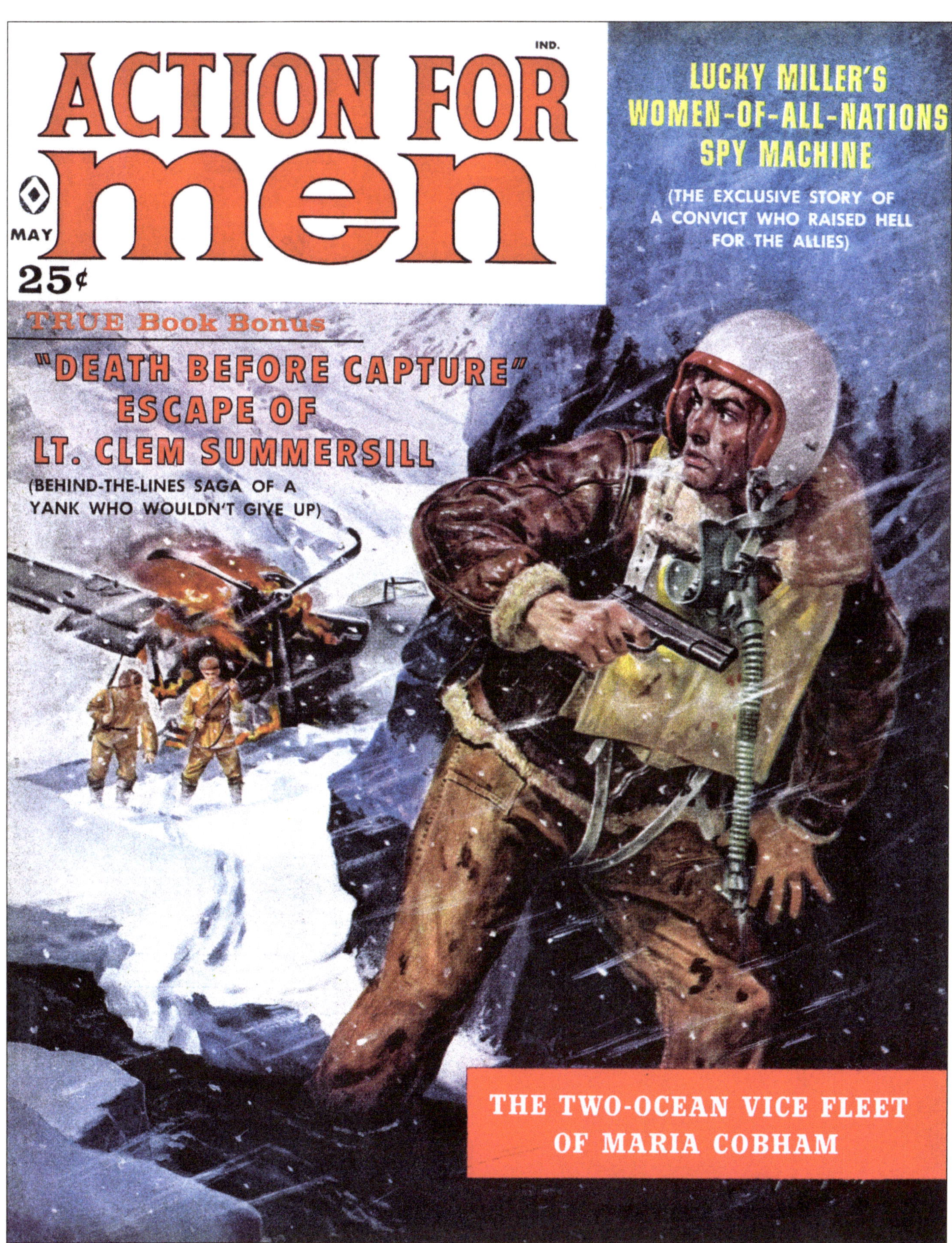

IND.
ACTION FOR men
MAY
25¢
LUCKY MILLER'S
WOMEN-OF-ALL-NATIONS
SPY MACHINE
(THE EXCLUSIVE STORY OF
A CONVICT WHO RAISED HELL
FOR THE ALLIES)
TRUE Book Bonus
"DEATH BEFORE CAPTURE"
ESCAPE OF
LT. CLEM SUMMERSILL
(BEHIND-THE-LINES SAGA OF A
YANK WHO WOULDN'T GIVE UP)
THE TWO-OCEAN VICE FLEET
OF MARIA COBHAM

May 1960

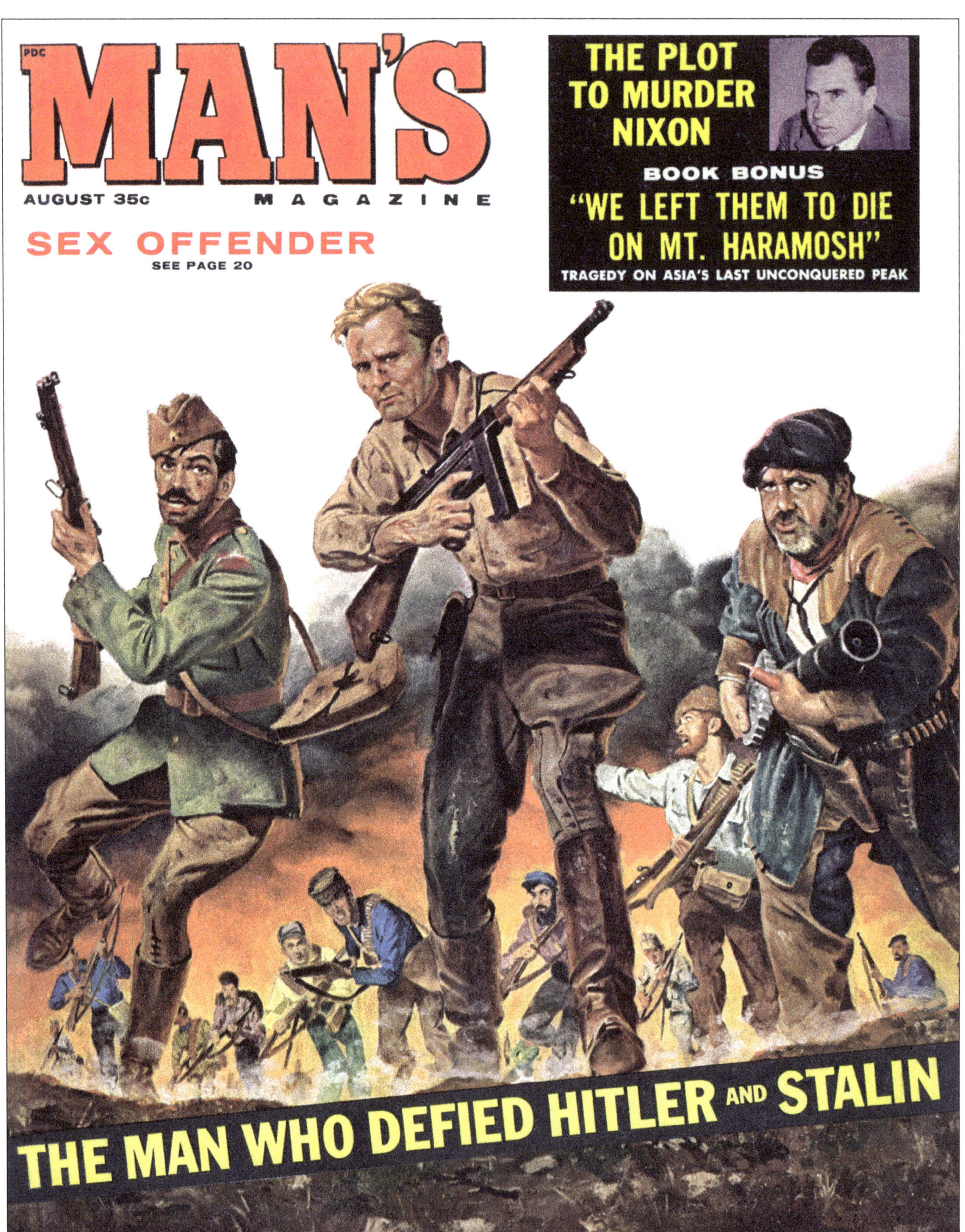
PDC
MAN'S
MAGAZINE
AUGUST 35c
SEX OFFENDER
SEE PAGE 20
THE PLOT TO MURDER NIXON
BOOK BONUS
"WE LEFT THEM TO DIE ON MT. HARAMOSH"
TRAGEDY ON ASIA'S LAST UNCONQUERED PEAK
THE MAN WHO DEFIED HITLER AND STALIN

August 1960

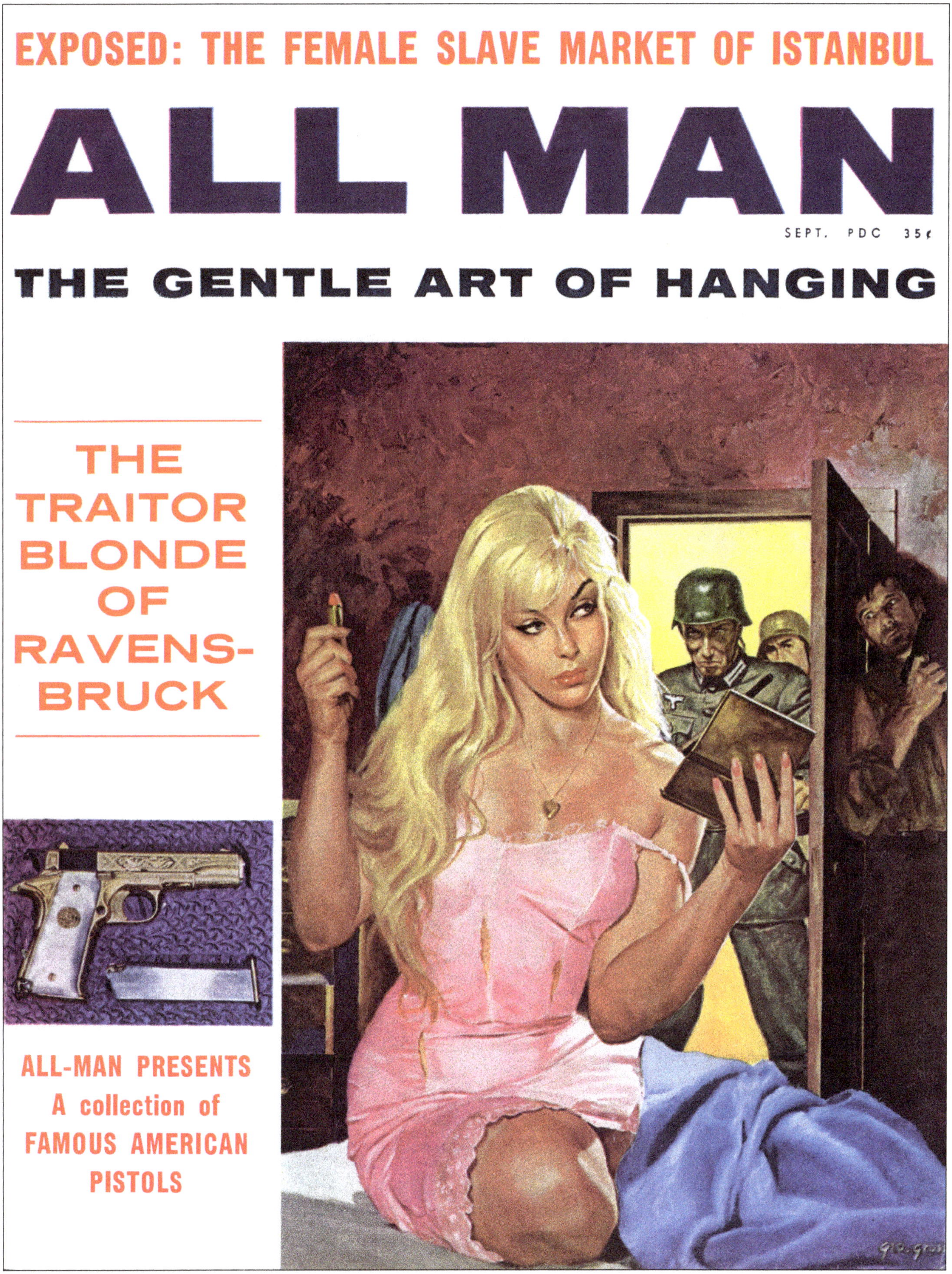

September 1960

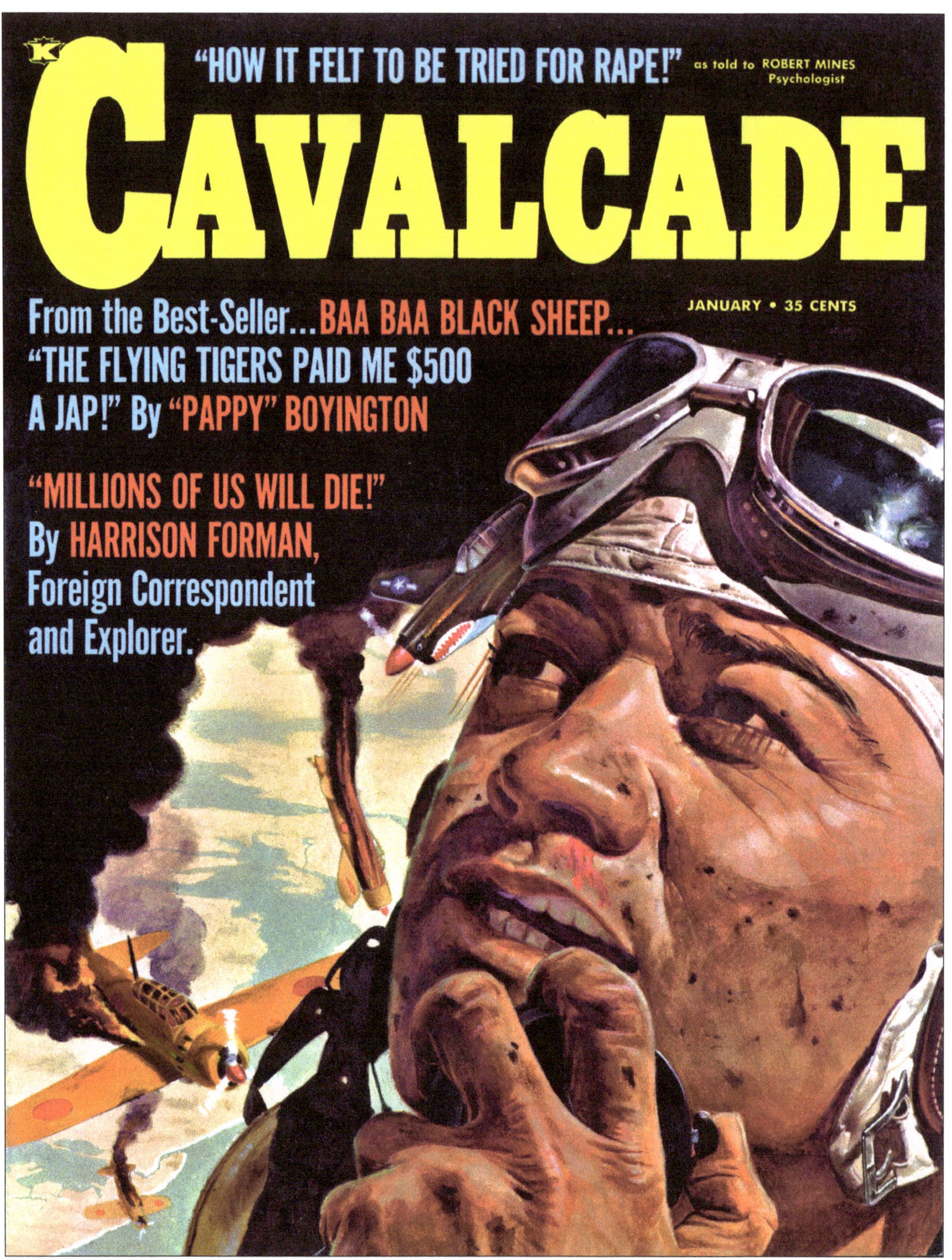

January 1961

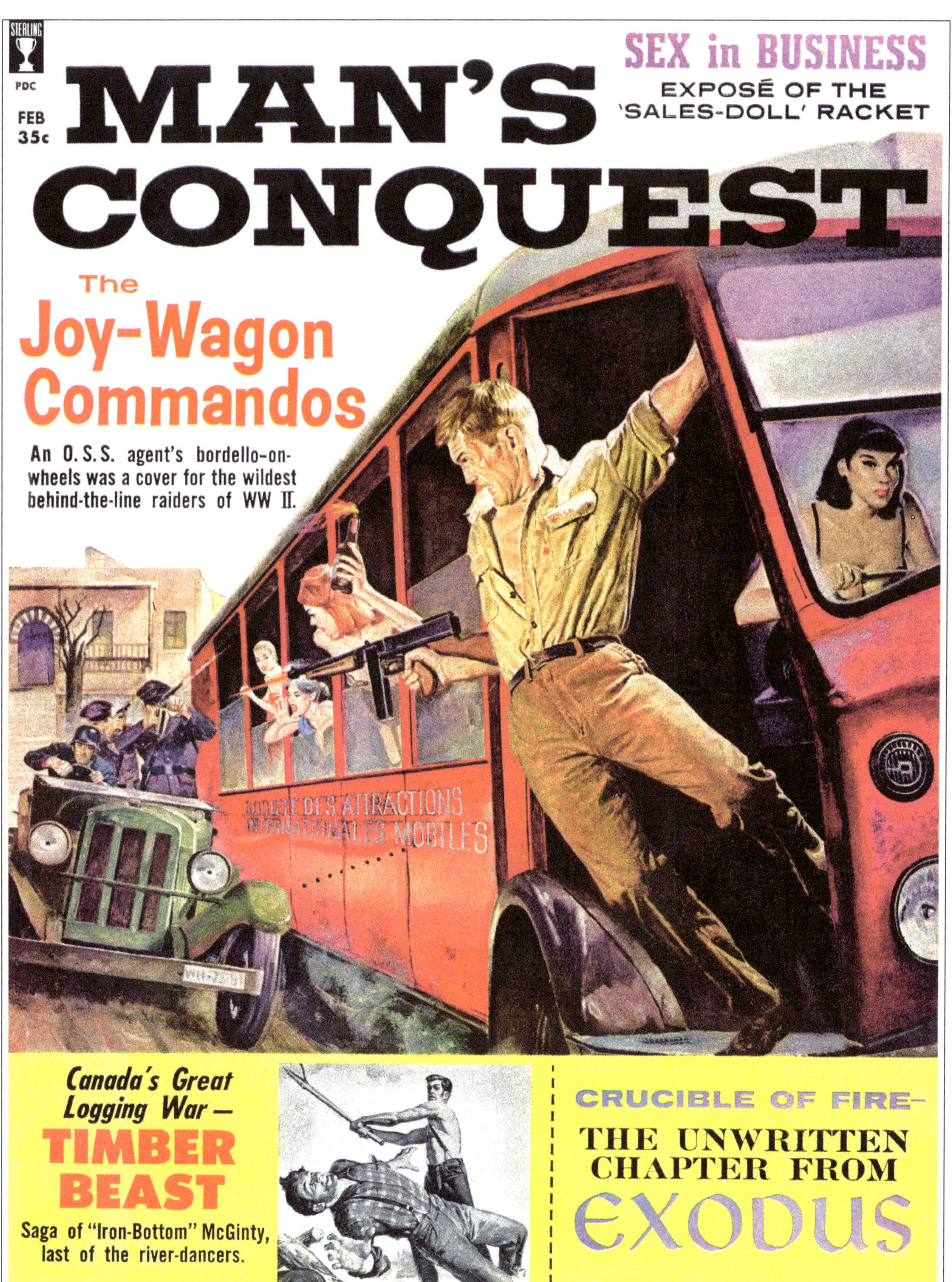

February 1961

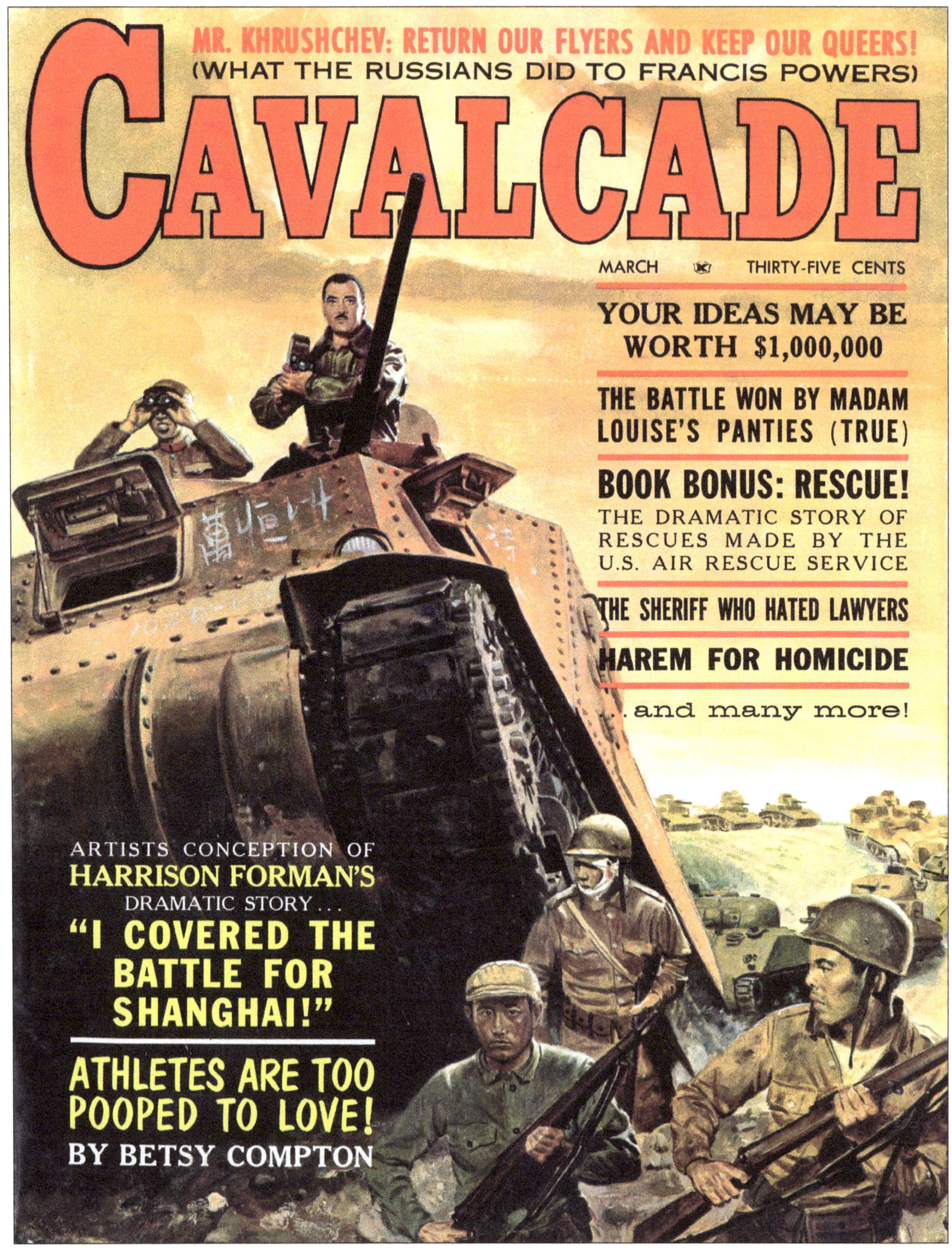

MR. KHRUSHCHEV: RETURN OUR FLYERS AND KEEP OUR QUEERS!
(WHAT THE RUSSIANS DID TO FRANCIS POWERS)
CAVALCADE
MARCH   THIRTY-FIVE CENTS
YOUR IDEAS MAY BE WORTH $1,000,000
THE BATTLE WON BY MADAM LOUISE'S PANTIES (TRUE)
BOOK BONUS: RESCUE!
THE DRAMATIC STORY OF RESCUES MADE BY THE U.S. AIR RESCUE SERVICE
THE SHERIFF WHO HATED LAWYERS
HAREM FOR HOMICIDE
...and many more!
ARTISTS CONCEPTION OF
HARRISON FORMAN'S
DRAMATIC STORY...
"I COVERED THE BATTLE FOR SHANGHAI!"
ATHLETES ARE TOO POOPED TO LOVE!
BY BETSY COMPTON

March 1961

CAVALCADE

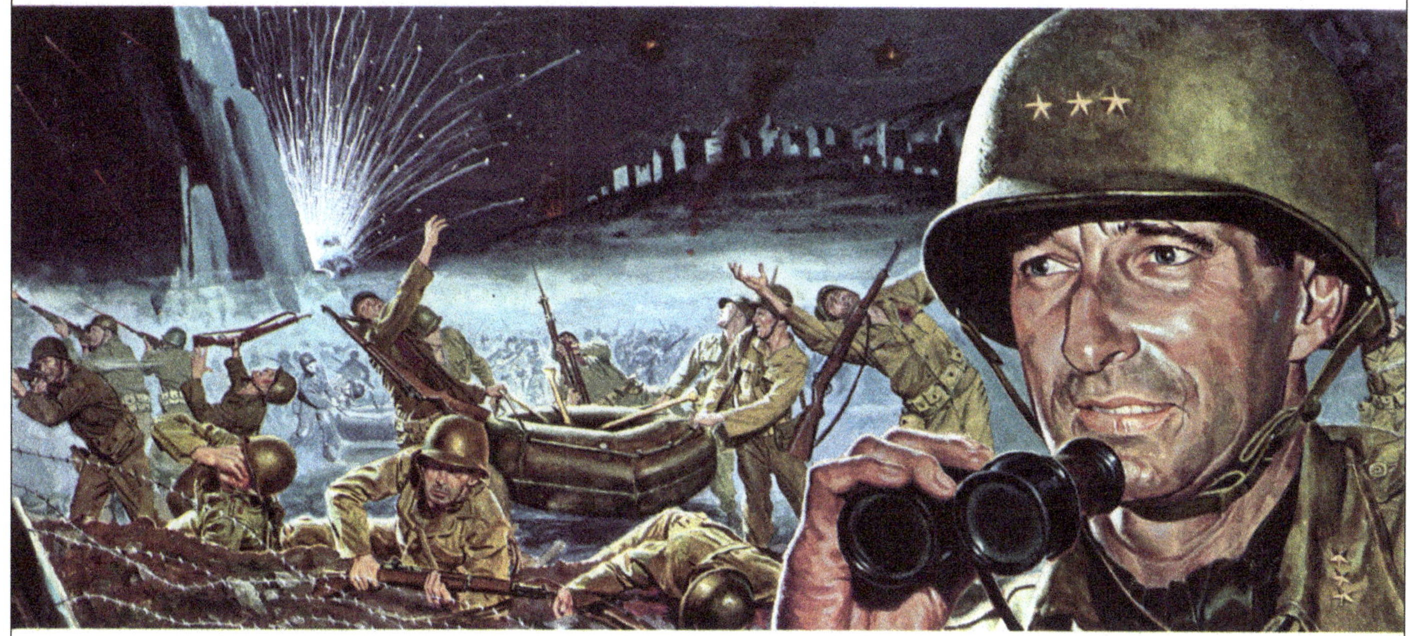

THE GUN MAKERS WHO ASK NO QUESTIONS — HARRISON FORMAN
BETSY COMPTON TELLS . . . 10 WAYS TO MAKE A GIRL SAY YES!
TRUJILLO . . . LADIES' MAN TYRANT OF THE CARIBBEAN
"RED-HOT MAMA . . . CHASTE AS ICE!"
HOW BIG BUSINESS PLANTS SPIES TO GET COMPETITORS' SECRETS
THE DAY THE RAPIDO RAN RED WITH GI BLOOD
JOHN JACOBS' SEARCH FOR HIS LOST $10 MILLION
HARD-HEADED HERMAN . . . HE PROMOTED AMERICA'S FIRST ROAD RACE
A COMBAT PILOT FIGHTS HIS TOUGHEST BATTLE AGAINST HIMSELF
WHAT EVER HAPPENED TO SWEET, VIRTUOUS LITTLE NELL?

May 1961

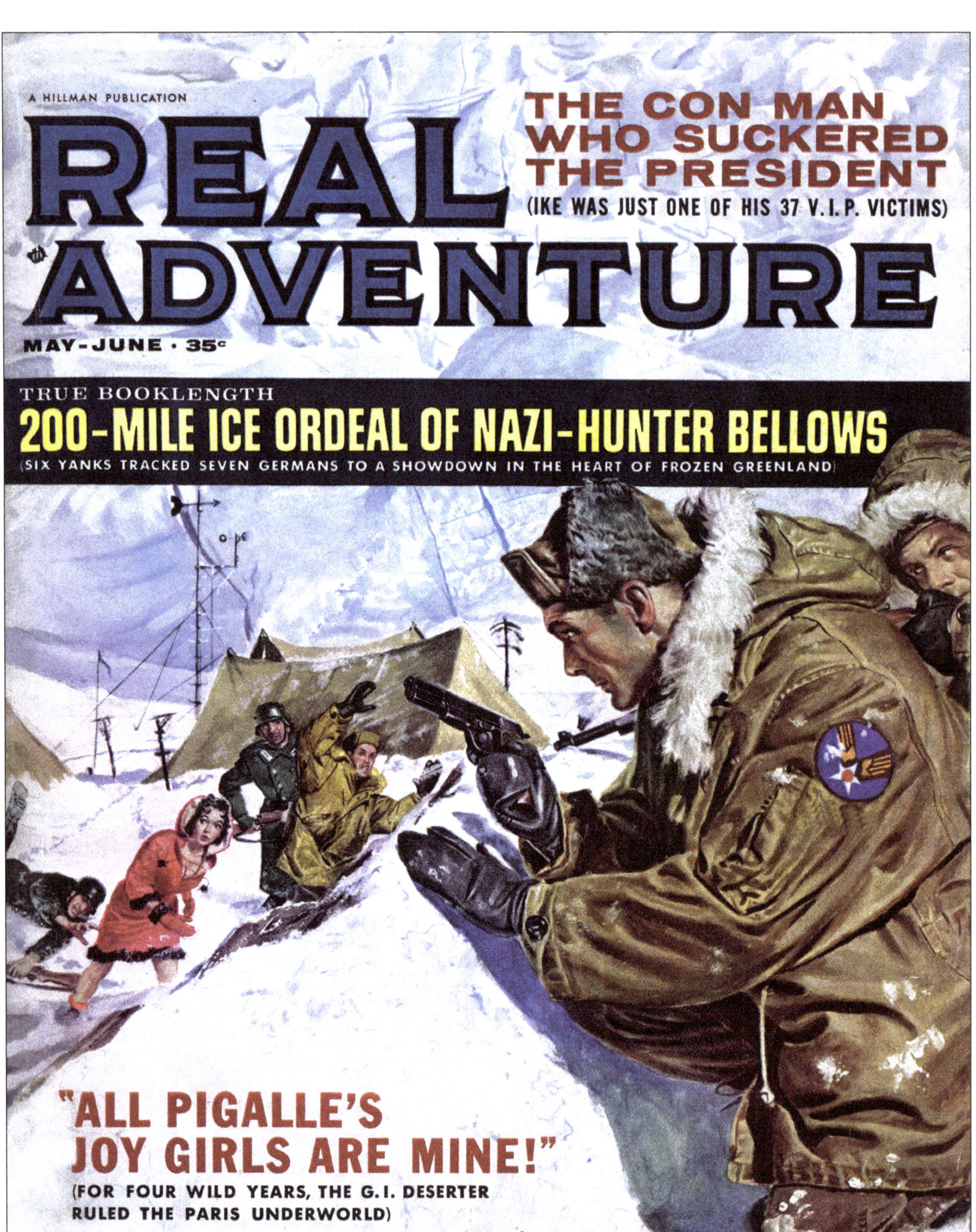

May-June 1961

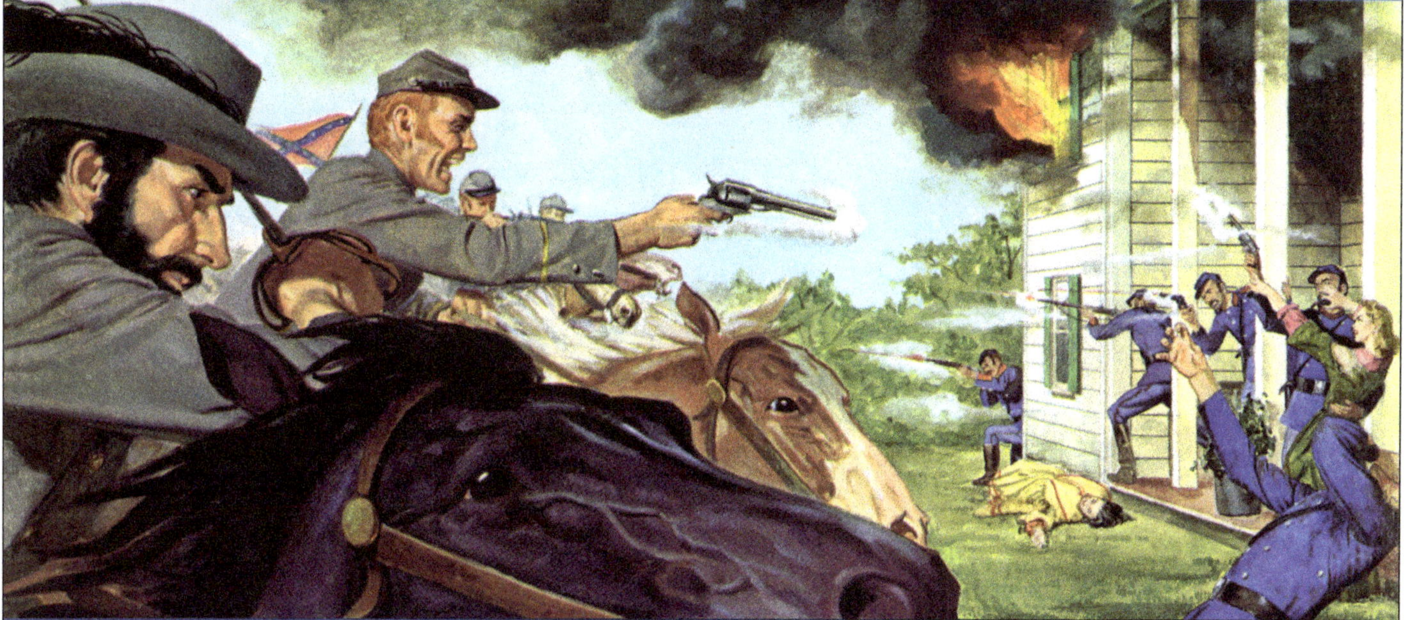

Betsy Compton Tells—"HOW I BED-HOPPED AROUND THE WORLD!"
JULY 1961 ⊠ THIRTY-FIVE CENTS
CAVALCADE
30-year-old General Jeb Stuart—Ladies' Man—Cavalry Genius!
THE MAN WHO BUYS FAMOUS SIGNATURES! (How Men Make Money!)
ADVENTURES OF COL. DAVE STIRLING'S DESERT GHOSTS!
NINE DAYS OF DUNKIRK (Exciting True Book Bonus)
SPECTATOR SEX (Why do men watch Stag Shows and Off-color Movies?)
AFRICAN HAREM BEAUTIES TURNED FREE!
(Trained only in the arts of love, thousands of mistresses of the deposed African leaders are turned loose!)
WHERE THE FISH ARE LARGER THAN FICTION! (Rod & Gun Department)
"HAVE TORTURE KIT, WILL TRAVEL!" (True Crime Thriller!)

July 1961

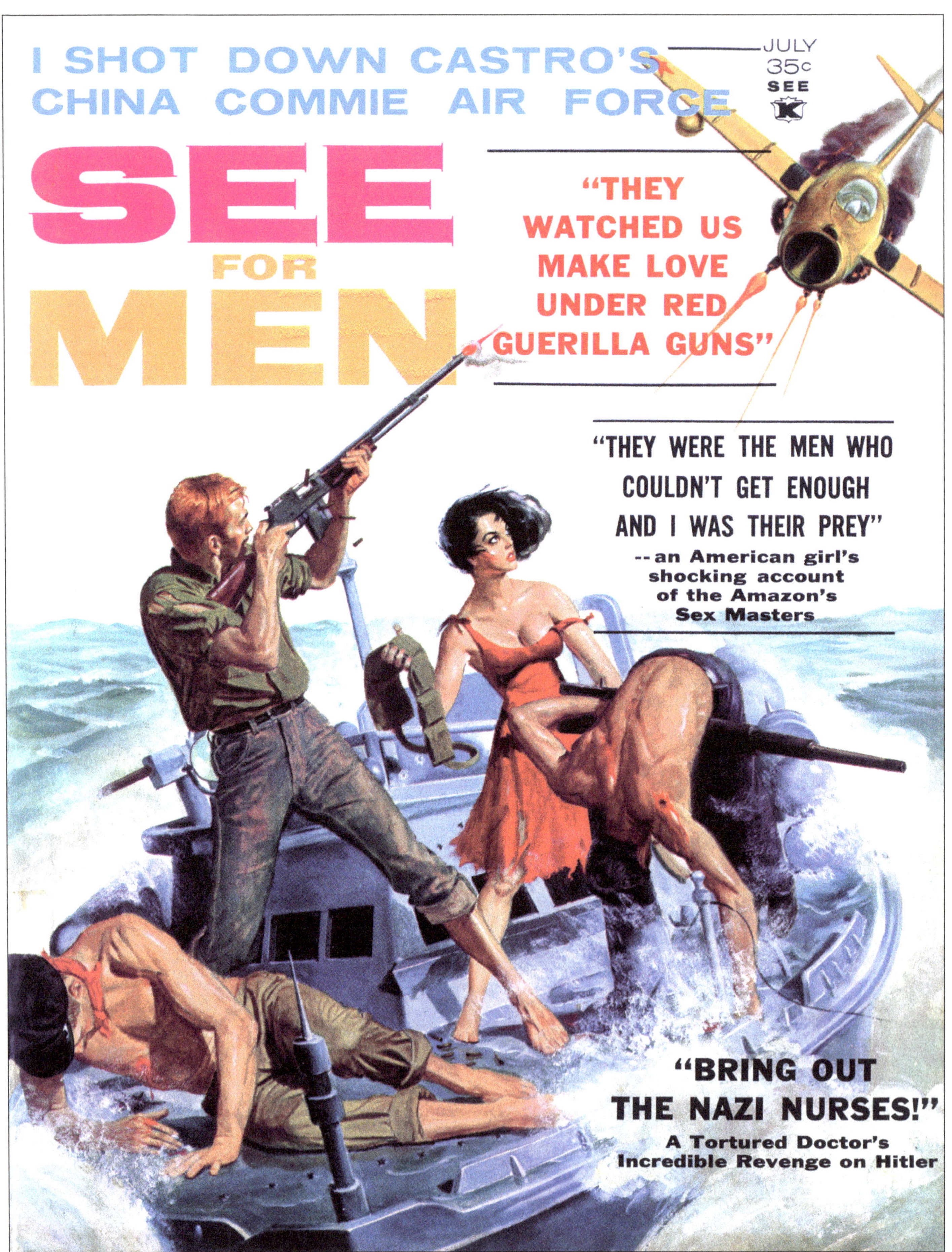

I SHOT DOWN CASTRO'S CHINA COMMIE AIR FORCE
JULY
35c
SEE
SEE
FOR
MEN
"THEY WATCHED US MAKE LOVE UNDER RED GUERILLA GUNS"
"THEY WERE THE MEN WHO COULDN'T GET ENOUGH AND I WAS THEIR PREY"
-- an American girl's shocking account of the Amazon's Sex Masters
"BRING OUT THE NAZI NURSES!"
A Tortured Doctor's Incredible Revenge on Hitler

July 1961

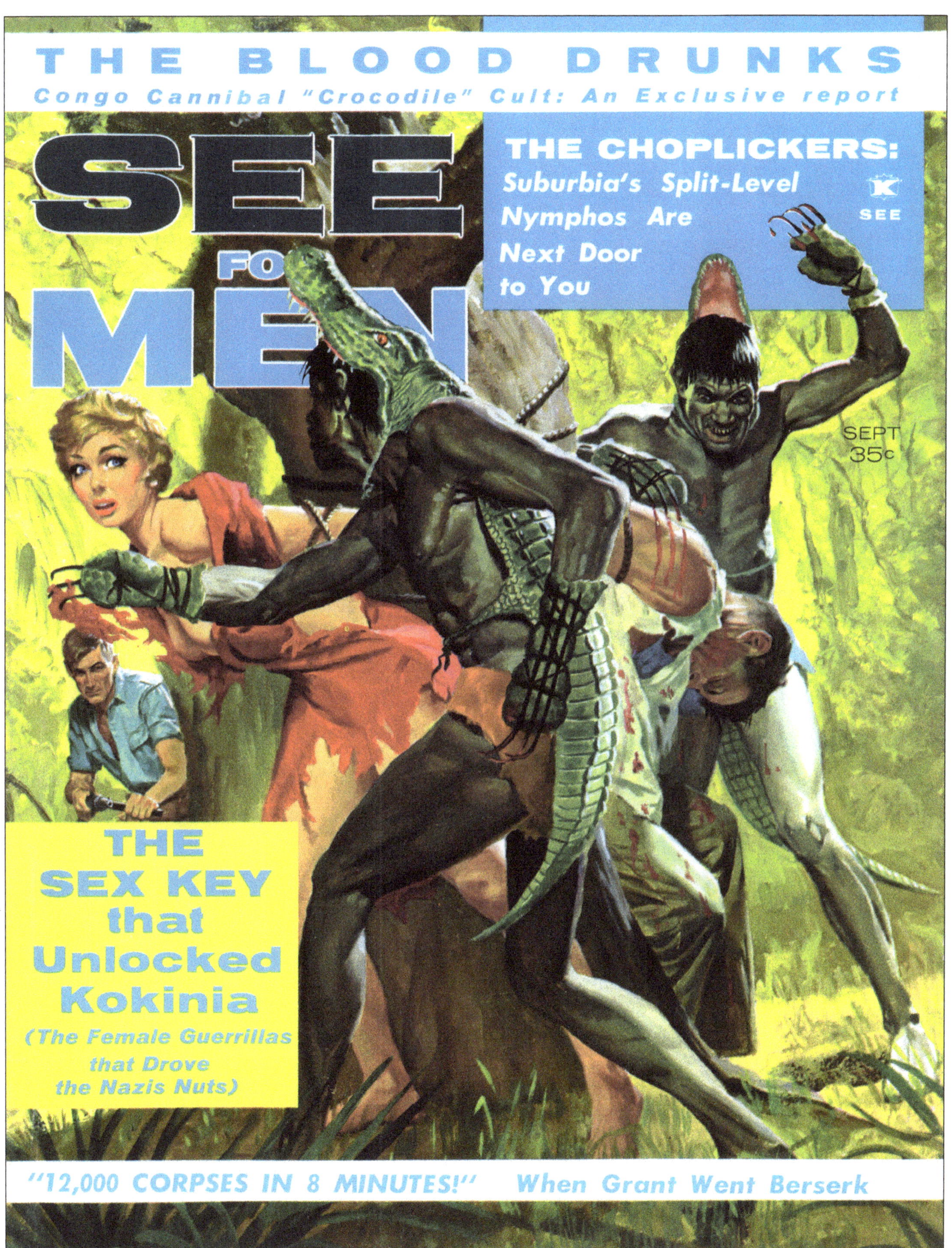

September 1961

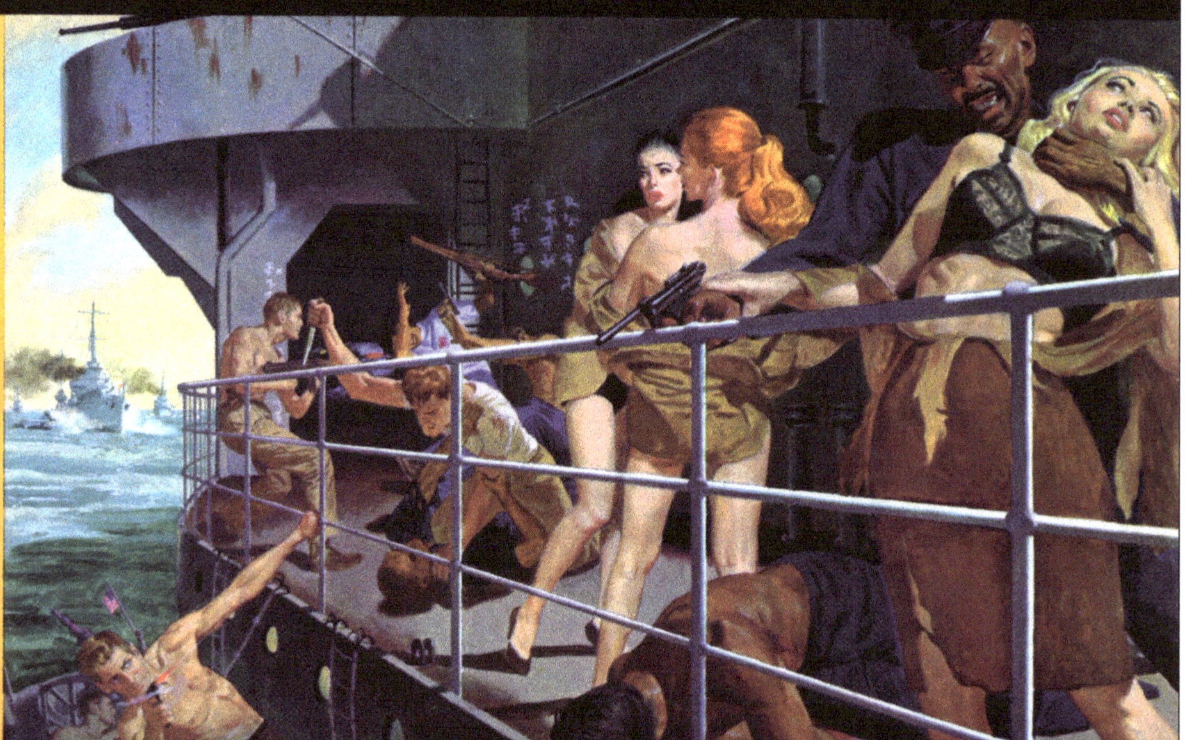

October 1961

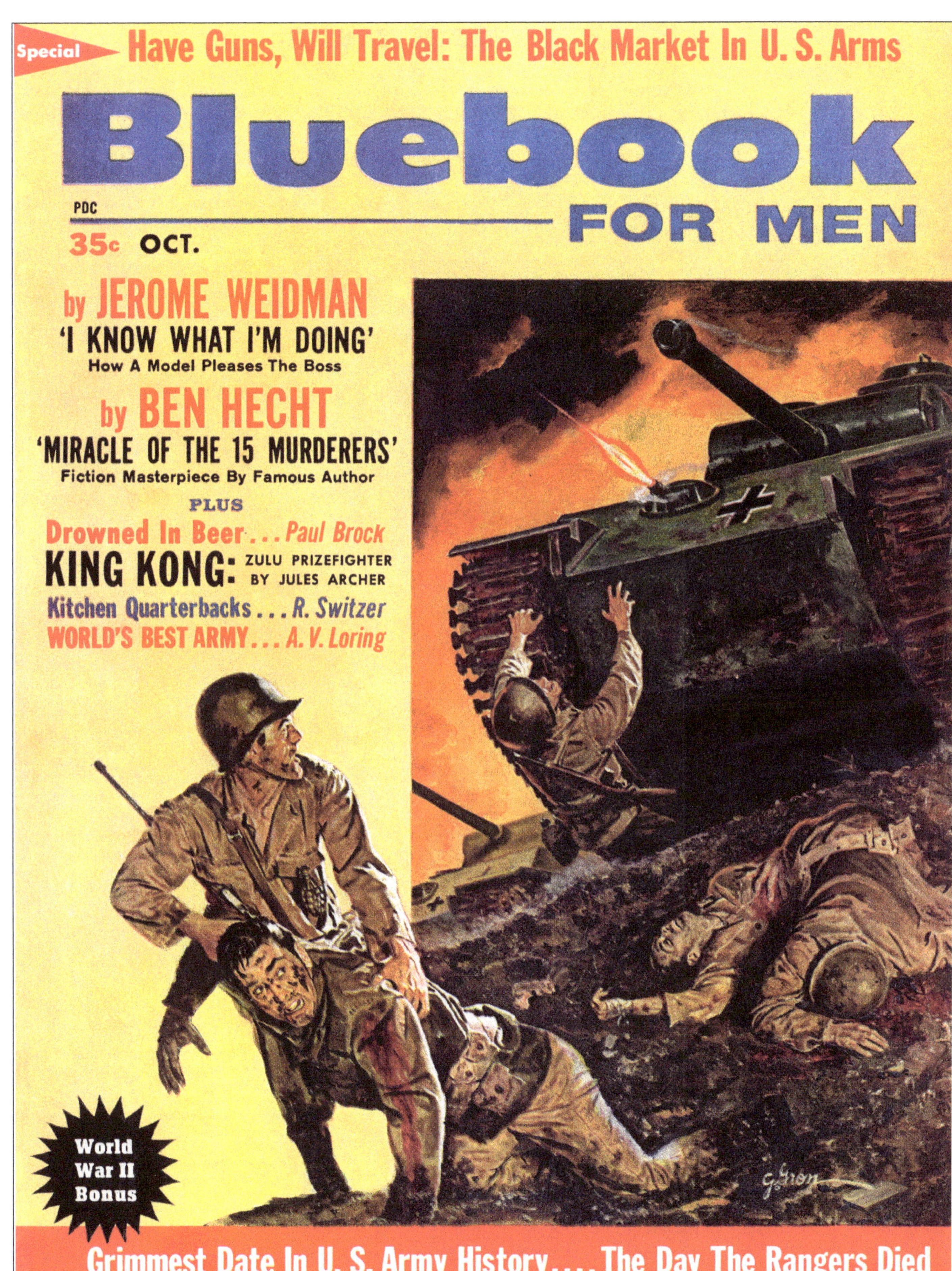

October 1961

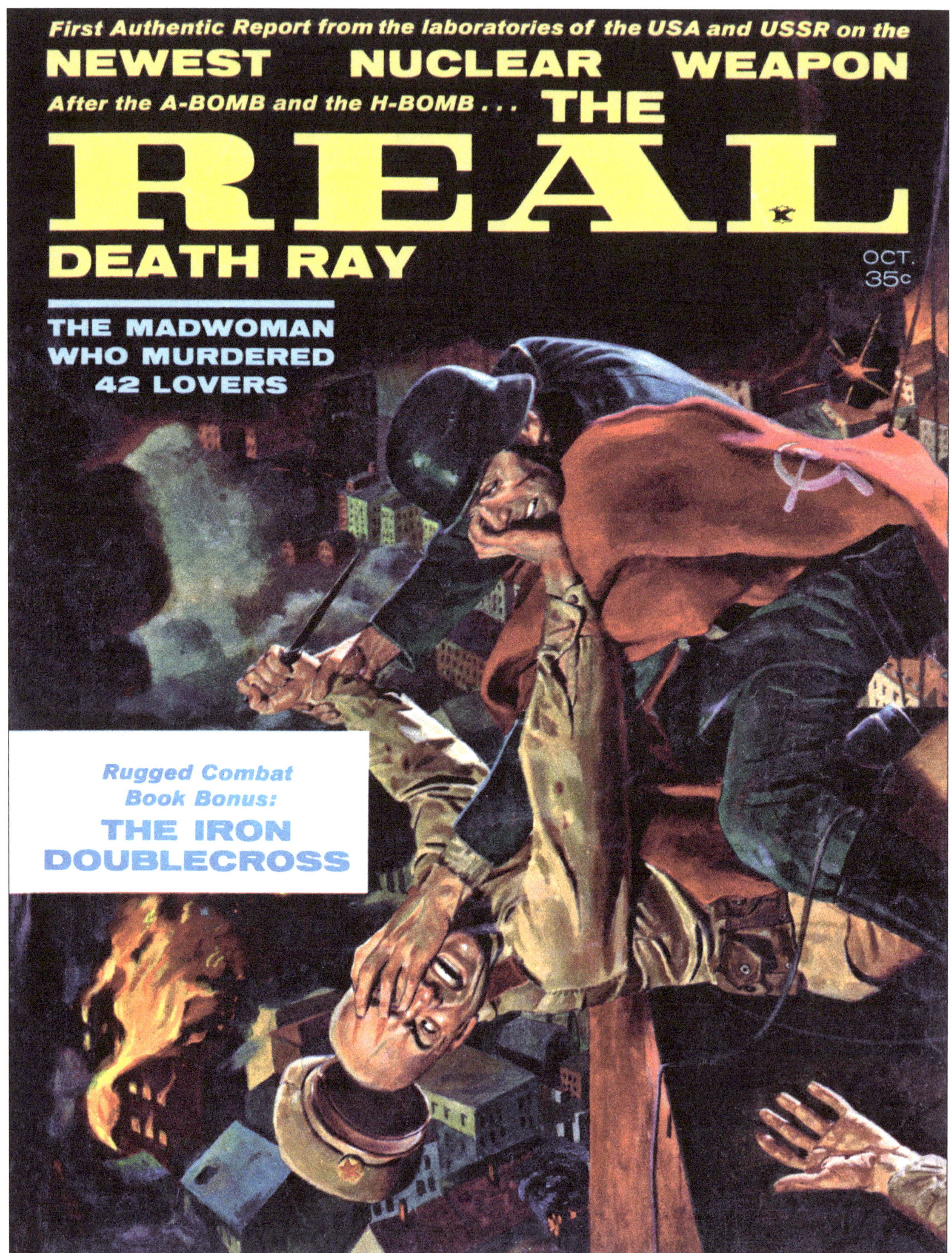
First Authentic Report from the laboratories of the USA and USSR on the
NEWEST NUCLEAR WEAPON
After the A-BOMB and the H-BOMB . . . THE
REAL
DEATH RAY
OCT.
35c
THE MADWOMAN WHO MURDERED 42 LOVERS
Rugged Combat Book Bonus:
THE IRON DOUBLECROSS

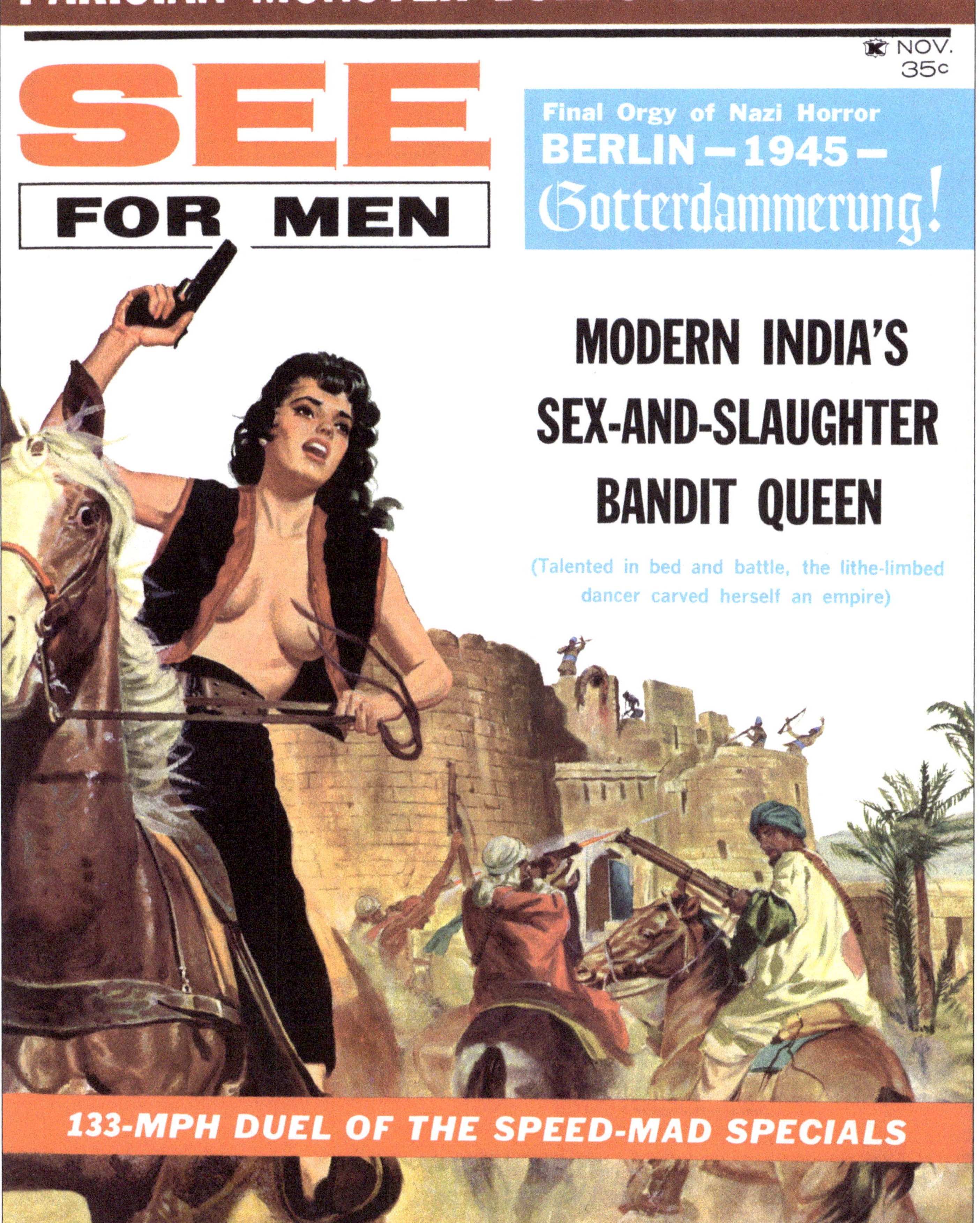

November 1961

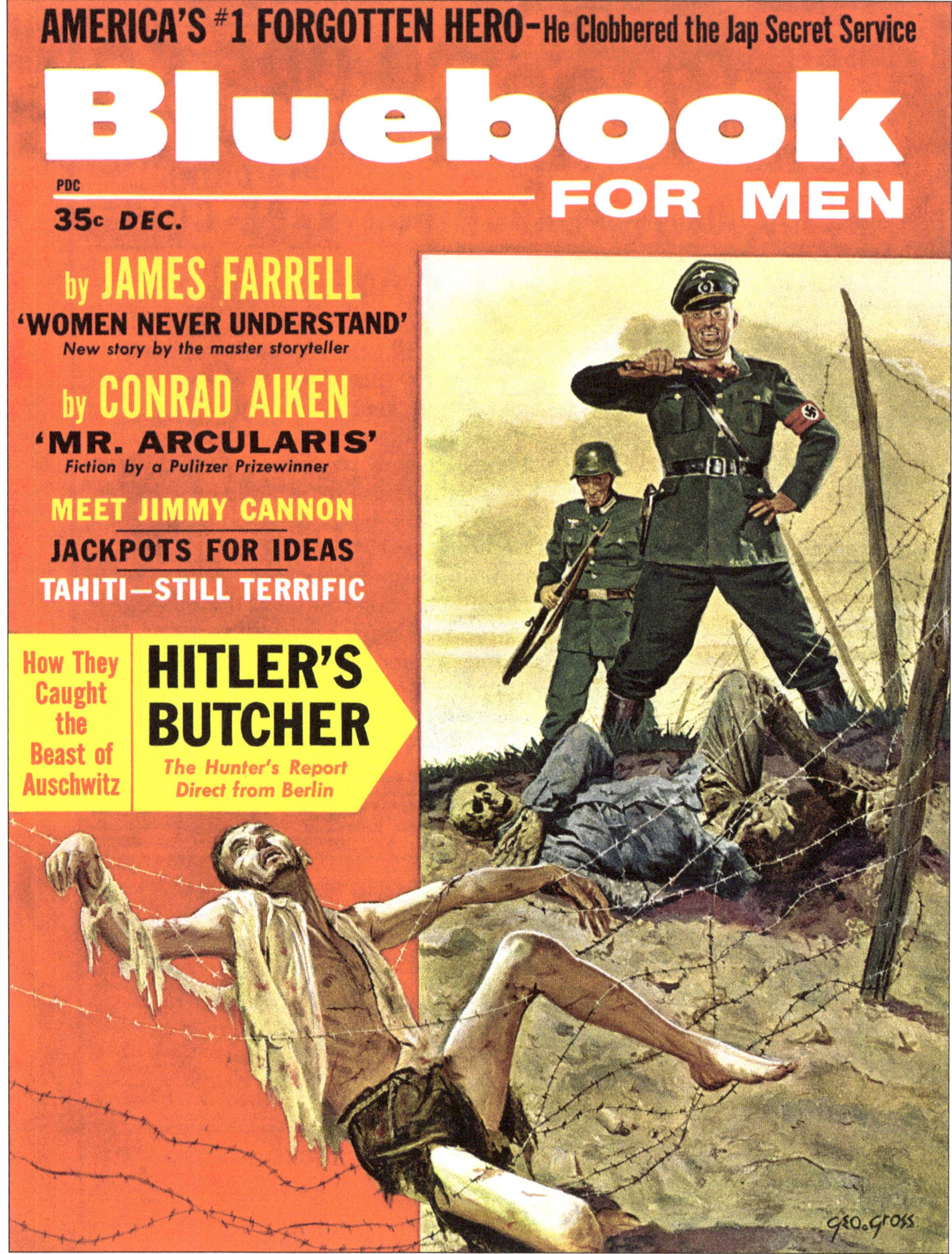
AMERICA'S #1 FORGOTTEN HERO—He Clobbered the Jap Secret Service

Bluebook
FOR MEN

PDC
35¢ DEC.

by JAMES FARRELL
'WOMEN NEVER UNDERSTAND'
New story by the master storyteller

by CONRAD AIKEN
'MR. ARCULARIS'
Fiction by a Pulitzer Prizewinner

MEET JIMMY CANNON
JACKPOTS FOR IDEAS
TAHITI—STILL TERRIFIC

How They Caught the Beast of Auschwitz

HITLER'S BUTCHER
The Hunter's Report Direct from Berlin

geo.Gross

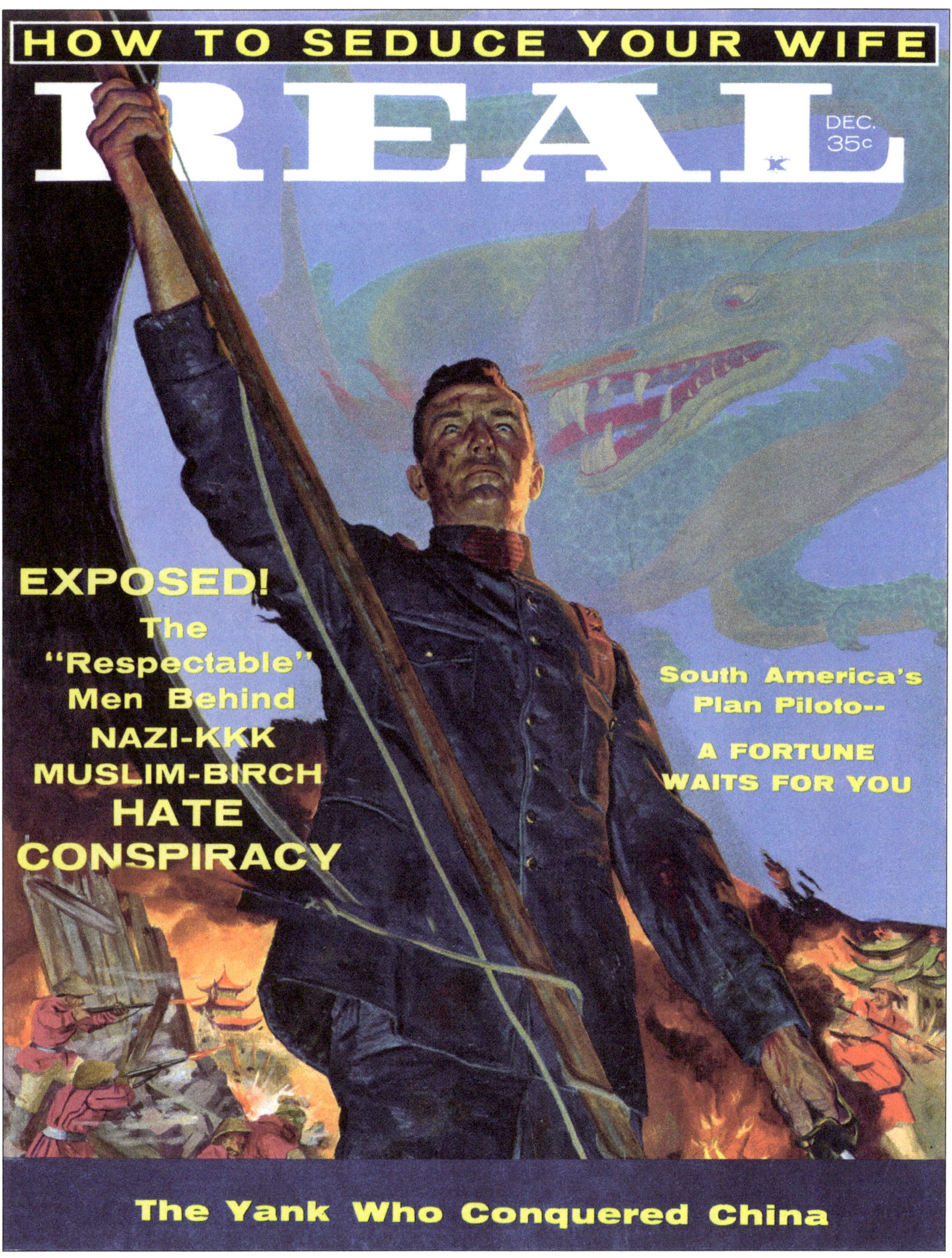

December 1961

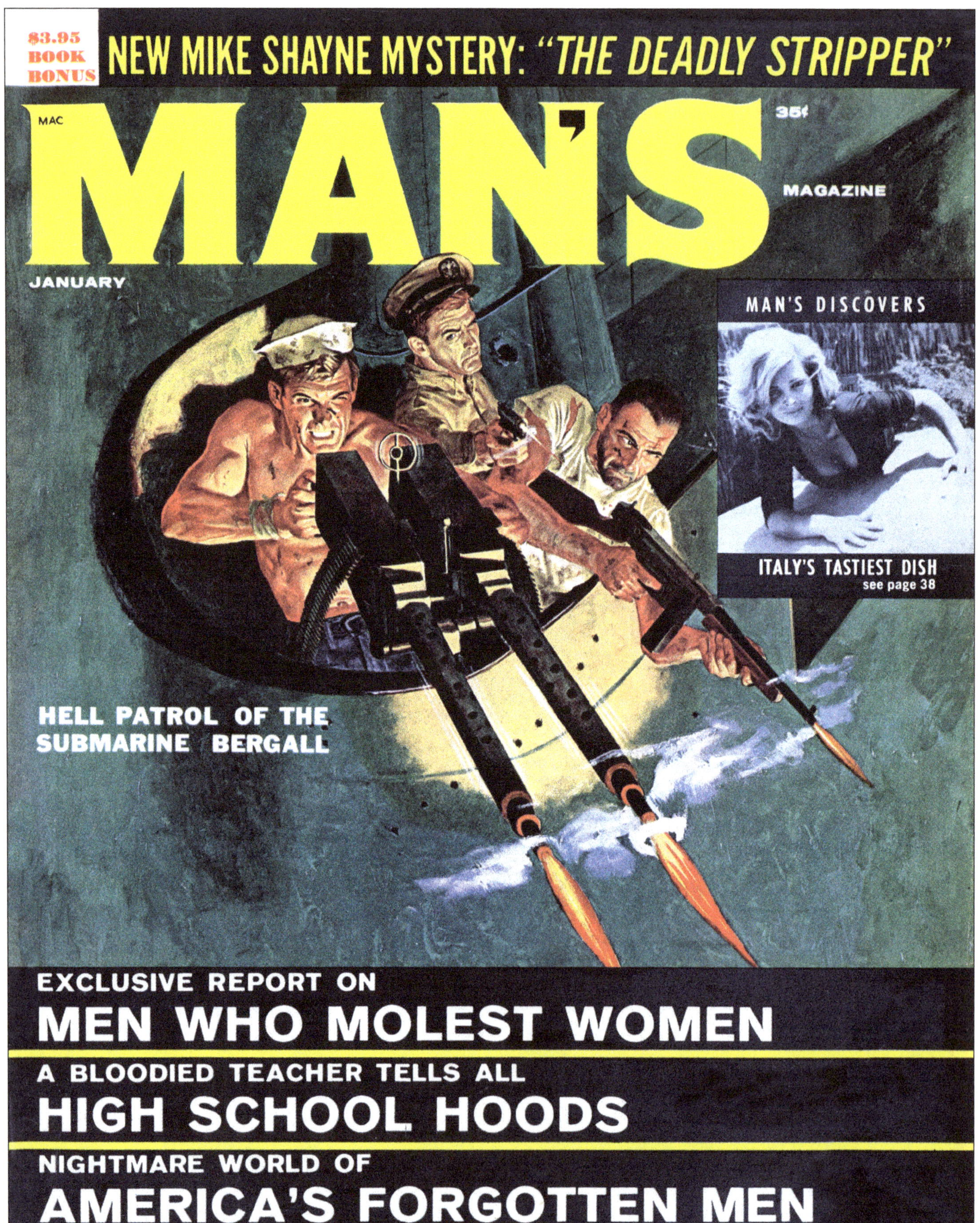

January 1962

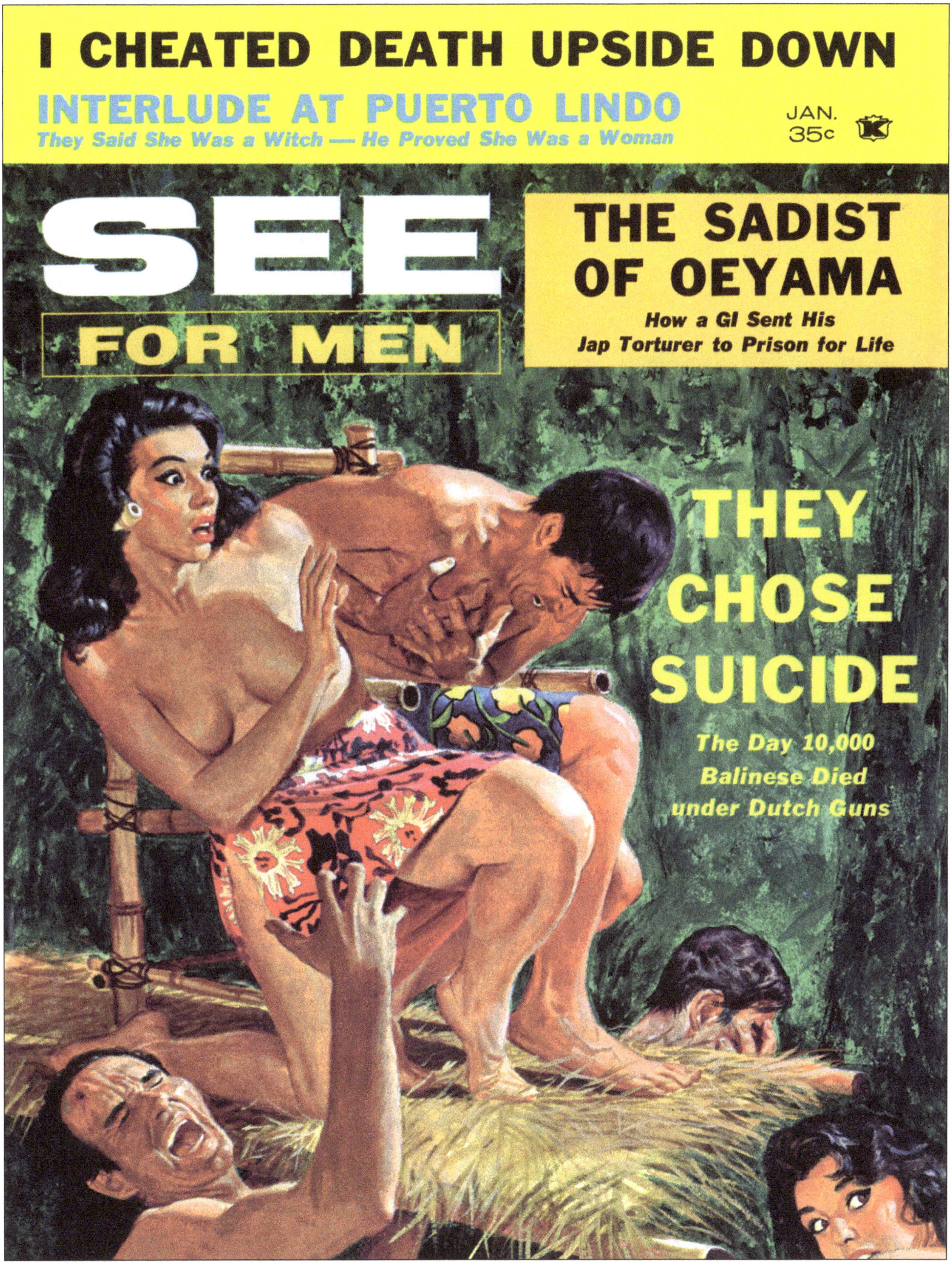

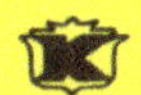

I CHEATED DEATH UPSIDE DOWN
INTERLUDE AT PUERTO LINDO
They Said She Was a Witch — He Proved She Was a Woman
JAN.
35c
SEE
FOR MEN
THE SADIST OF OEYAMA
How a GI Sent His
Jap Torturer to Prison for Life
THEY CHOSE SUICIDE
The Day 10,000 Balinese Died under Dutch Guns

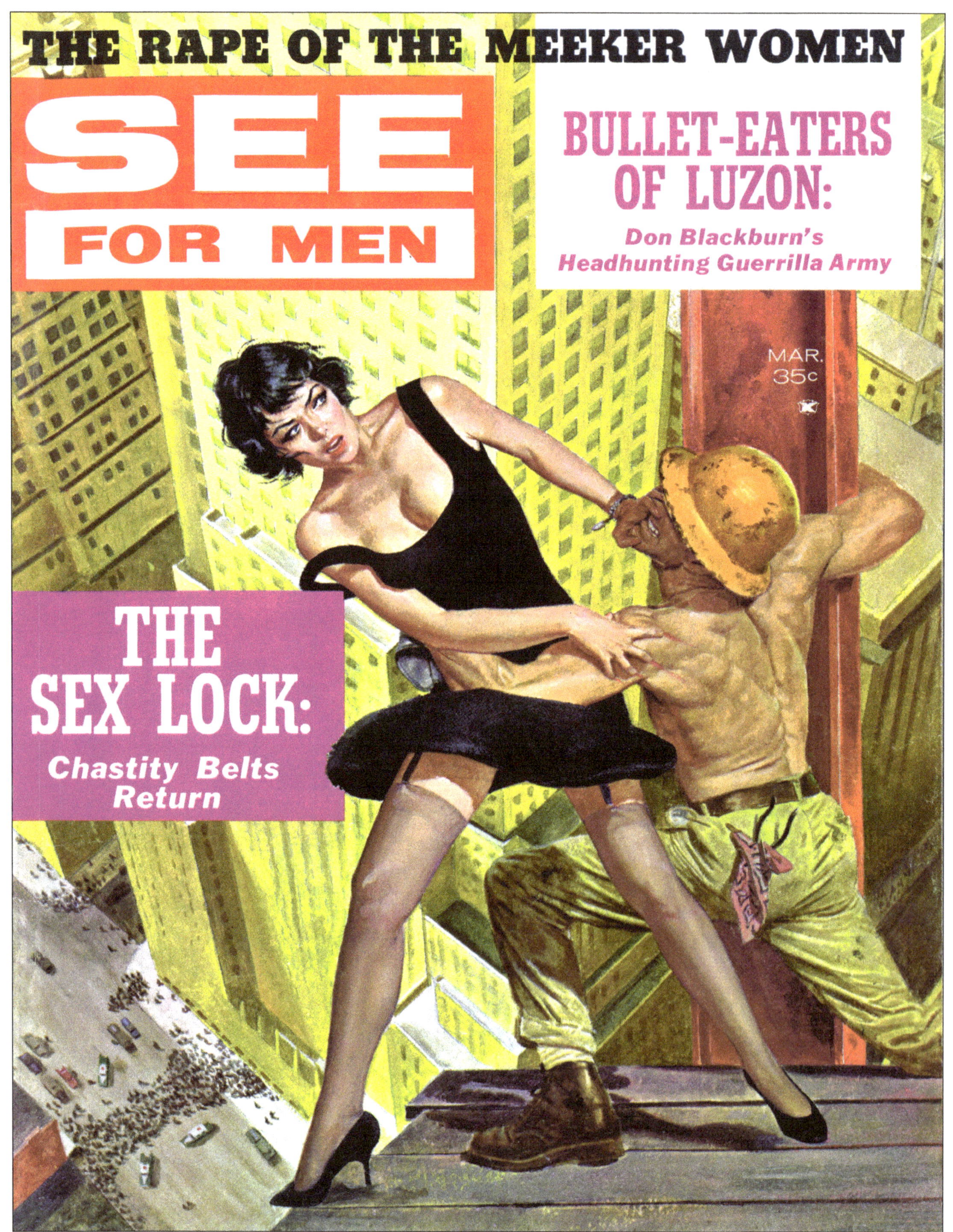

THE RAPE OF THE MEEKER WOMEN
SEE
FOR MEN
BULLET-EATERS OF LUZON:
Don Blackburn's Headhunting Guerrilla Army
MAR. 35c
THE SEX LOCK: Chastity Belts Return

March 1962

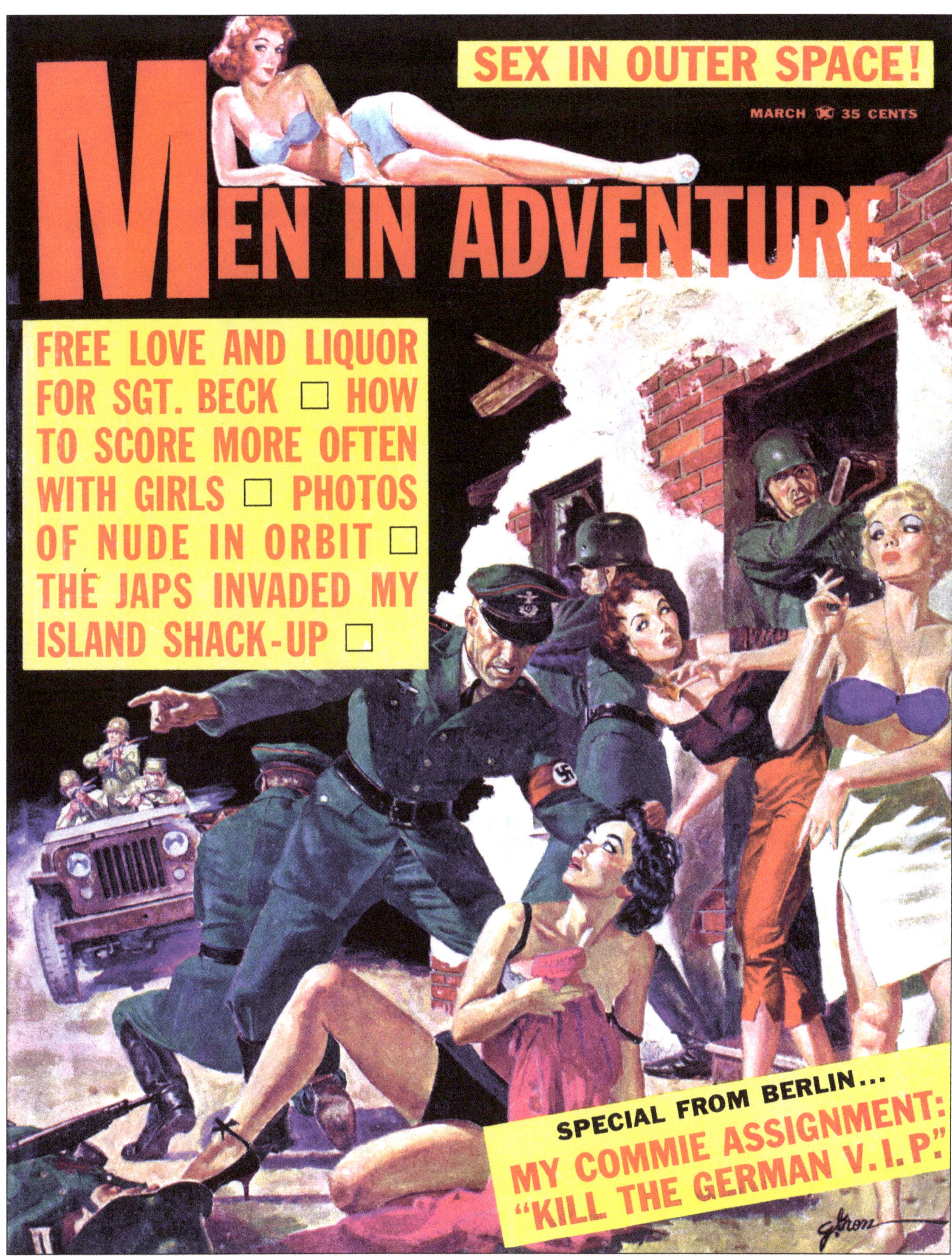

SEX IN OUTER SPACE!
MARCH 35 CENTS
MEN IN ADVENTURE
FREE LOVE AND LIQUOR FOR SGT. BECK □ HOW TO SCORE MORE OFTEN WITH GIRLS □ PHOTOS OF NUDE IN ORBIT □ THE JAPS INVADED MY ISLAND SHACK-UP □
SPECIAL FROM BERLIN...
MY COMMIE ASSIGNMENT: "KILL THE GERMAN V.I.P."

March 1962

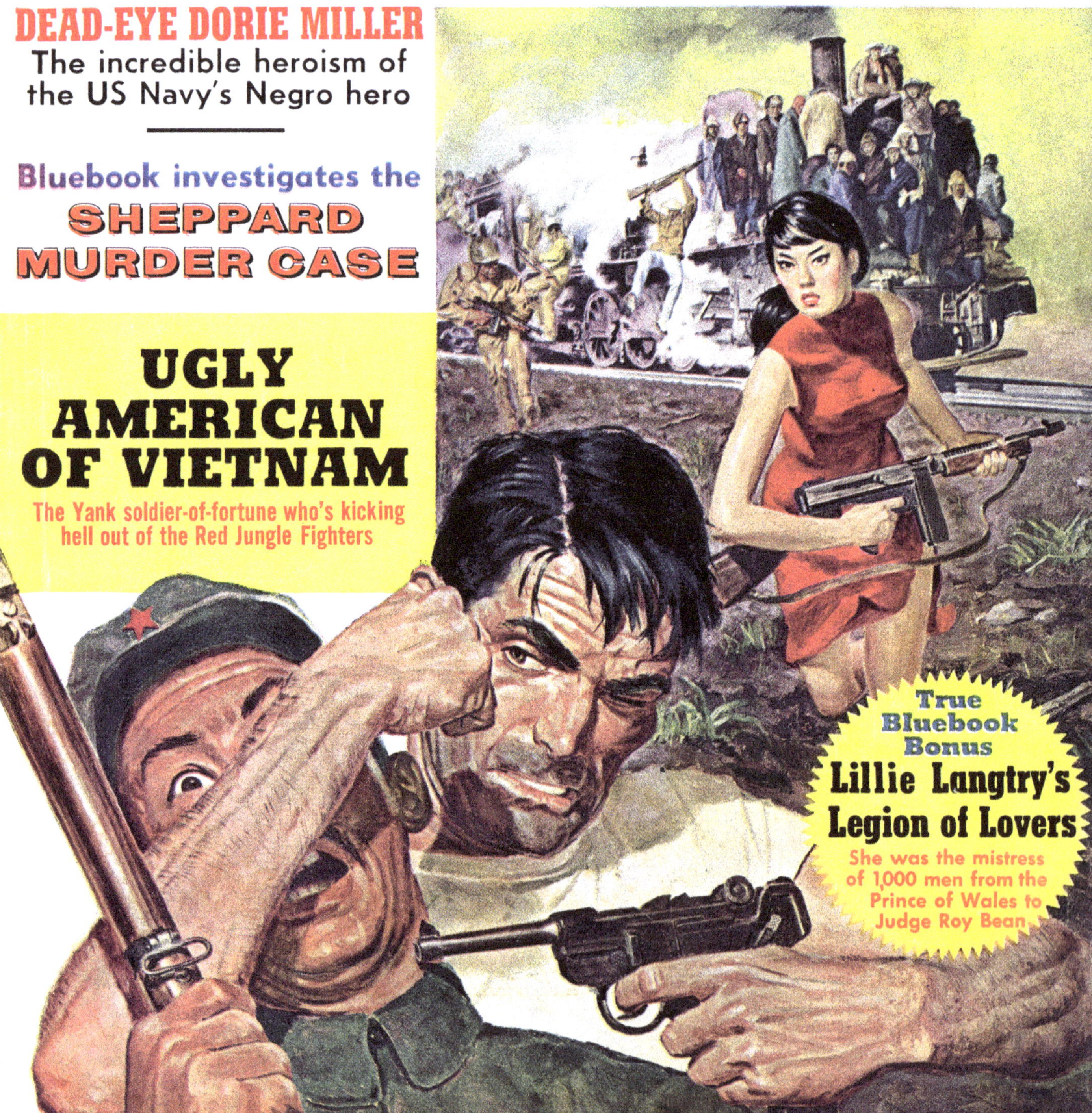

now monthly
Did Big Business Kill The Bordello? by Lee Mortimer
Bluebook
FOR MEN
PDC
35¢ MARCH
DEAD-EYE DORIE MILLER
The incredible heroism of the US Navy's Negro hero
Bluebook investigates the
SHEPPARD MURDER CASE
UGLY AMERICAN OF VIETNAM
The Yank soldier-of-fortune who's kicking hell out of the Red Jungle Fighters
True Bluebook Bonus
Lillie Langtry's Legion of Lovers
She was the mistress of 1,000 men from the Prince of Wales to Judge Roy Bean

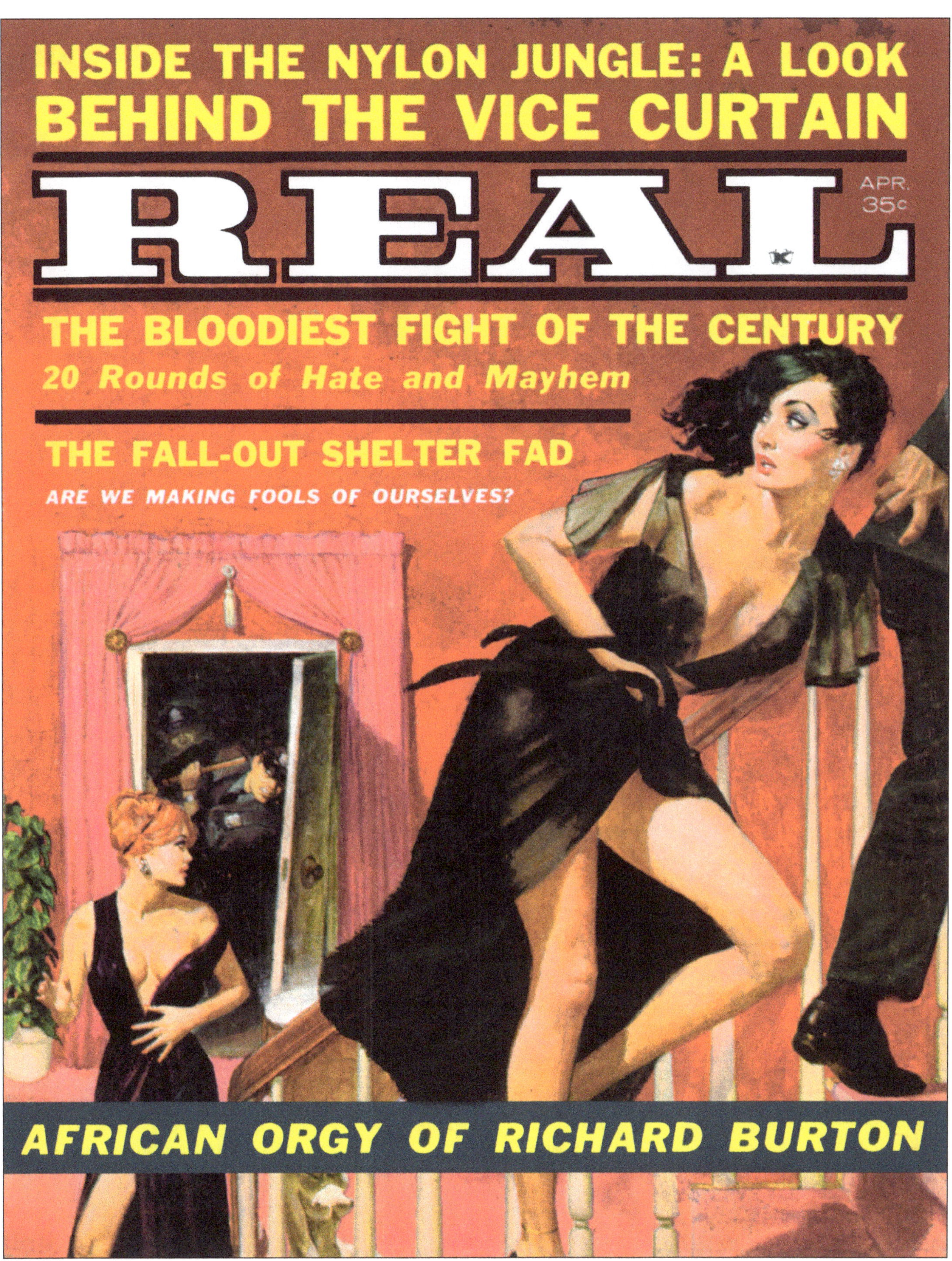
INSIDE THE NYLON JUNGLE: A LOOK
BEHIND THE VICE CURTAIN
REAL
APR.
35c
THE BLOODIEST FIGHT OF THE CENTURY
20 Rounds of Hate and Mayhem
THE FALL-OUT SHELTER FAD
ARE WE MAKING FOOLS OF OURSELVES?
AFRICAN ORGY OF RICHARD BURTON

April 1962

now monthly

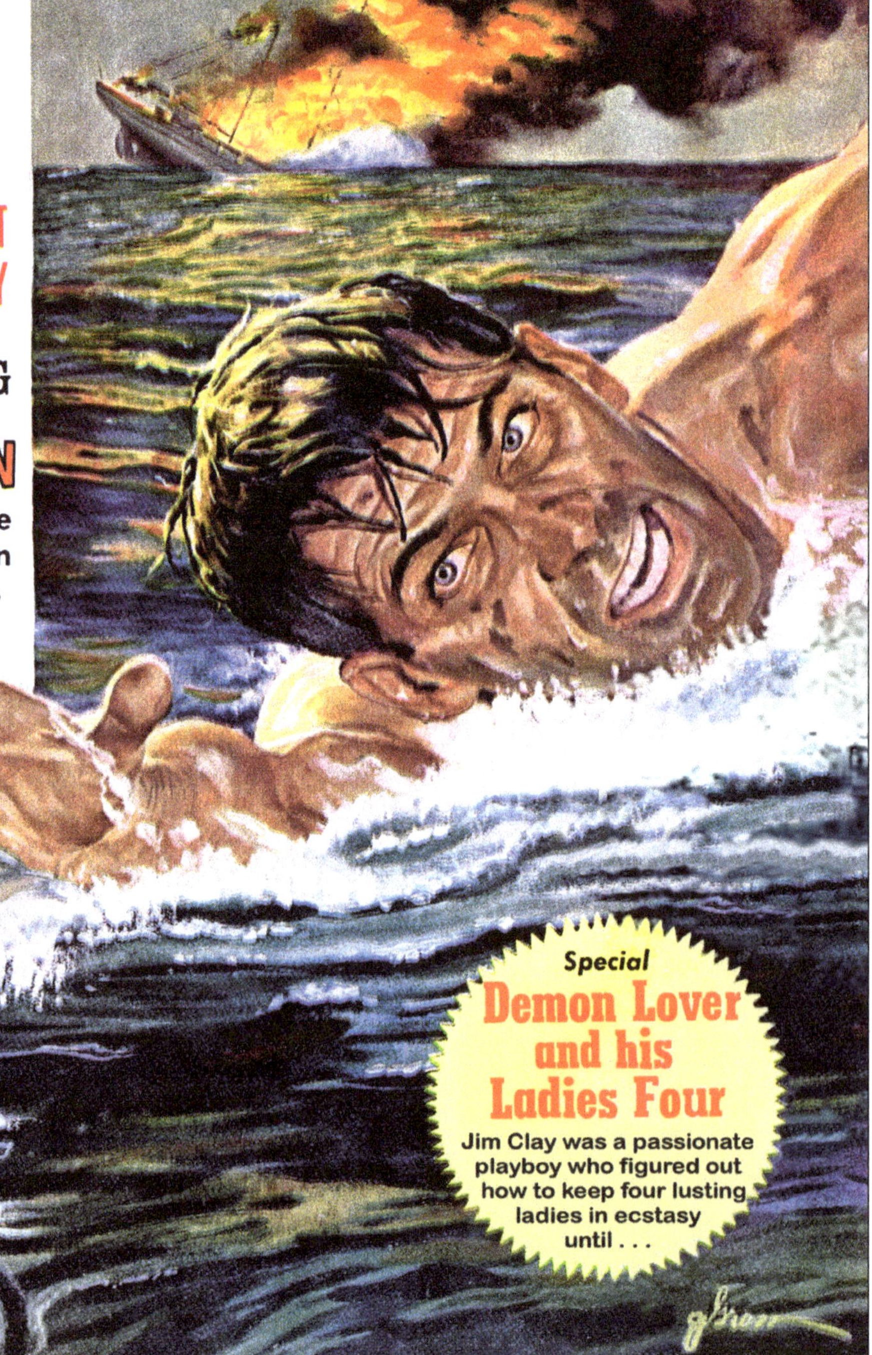
'I'll Be The Next Heavyweight Champ'—Sonny Liston

Bluebook
FOR MEN

PDC
35¢   APRIL

Book Bonus

LAST VOYAGE OF THE KETCH BLUEBILL
From out of today's headlines comes this tense tale of terror on the high seas

AVOID THESE 15 STOCK MARKET MISTAKES — AND MAKE MONEY

SERGEANTS ARE FOR DYING

TORPEDO JUNCTION
Eye-witness story of Midway, the death of a U.S. Torpedo squadron and the sinking of 4 Jap carriers

Special
Demon Lover and his Ladies Four
Jim Clay was a passionate playboy who figured out how to keep four lusting ladies in ecstasy until . . .

April 1962

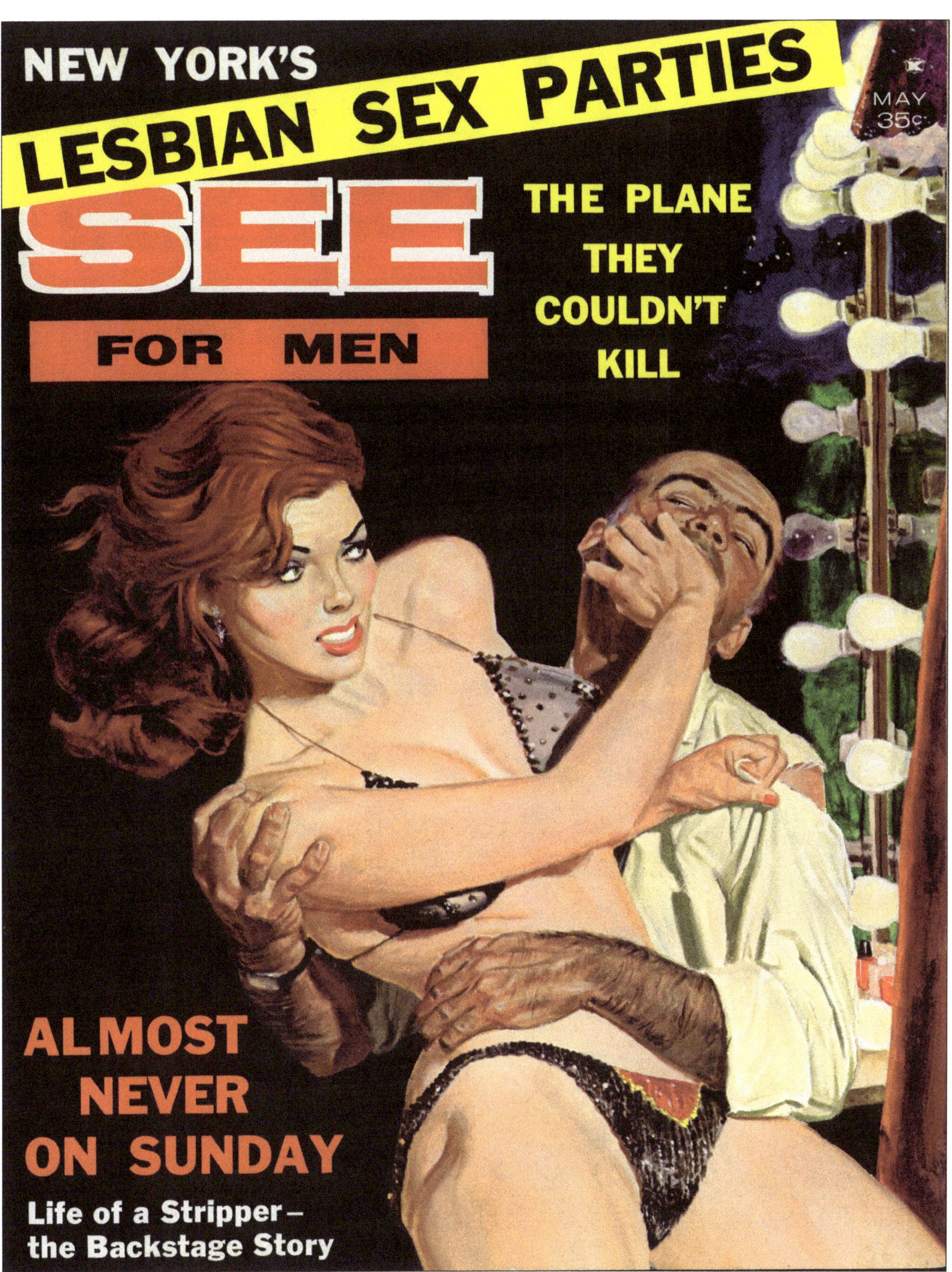

NEW YORK'S
LESBIAN SEX PARTIES
MAY 35¢
SEE
FOR MEN
THE PLANE THEY COULDN'T KILL
ALMOST NEVER ON SUNDAY
Life of a Stripper—
the Backstage Story

May 1962

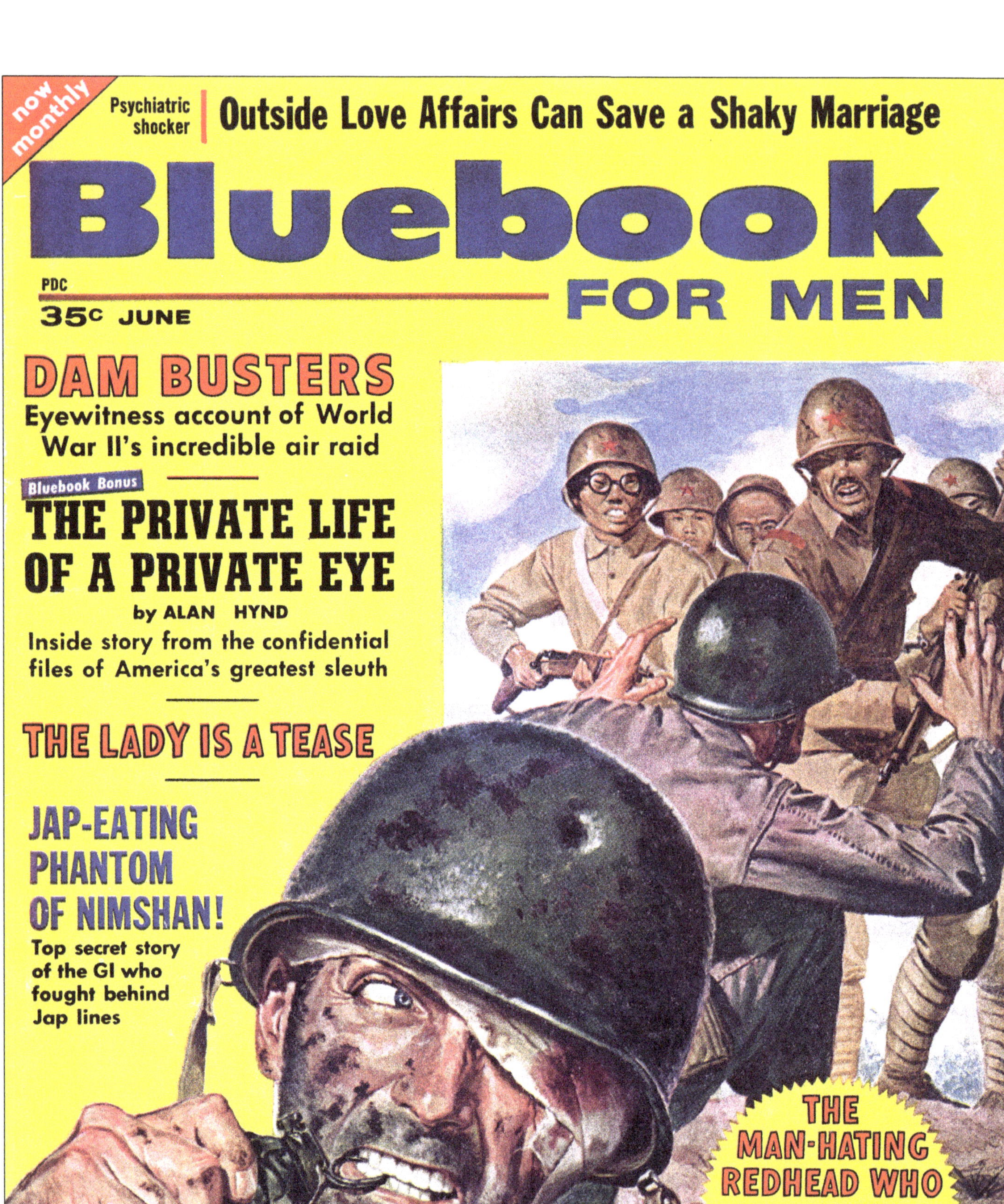

now monthly
Psychiatric shocker
Outside Love Affairs Can Save a Shaky Marriage
Bluebook
FOR MEN
PDC
35¢ JUNE
DAM BUSTERS
Eyewitness account of World War II's incredible air raid
Bluebook Bonus
THE PRIVATE LIFE OF A PRIVATE EYE
by ALAN HYND
Inside story from the confidential files of America's greatest sleuth
THE LADY IS A TEASE
JAP-EATING PHANTOM OF NIMSHAN!
Top secret story of the GI who fought behind Jap lines
THE MAN-HATING REDHEAD WHO RULED THE SPANISH MAIN

June 1962

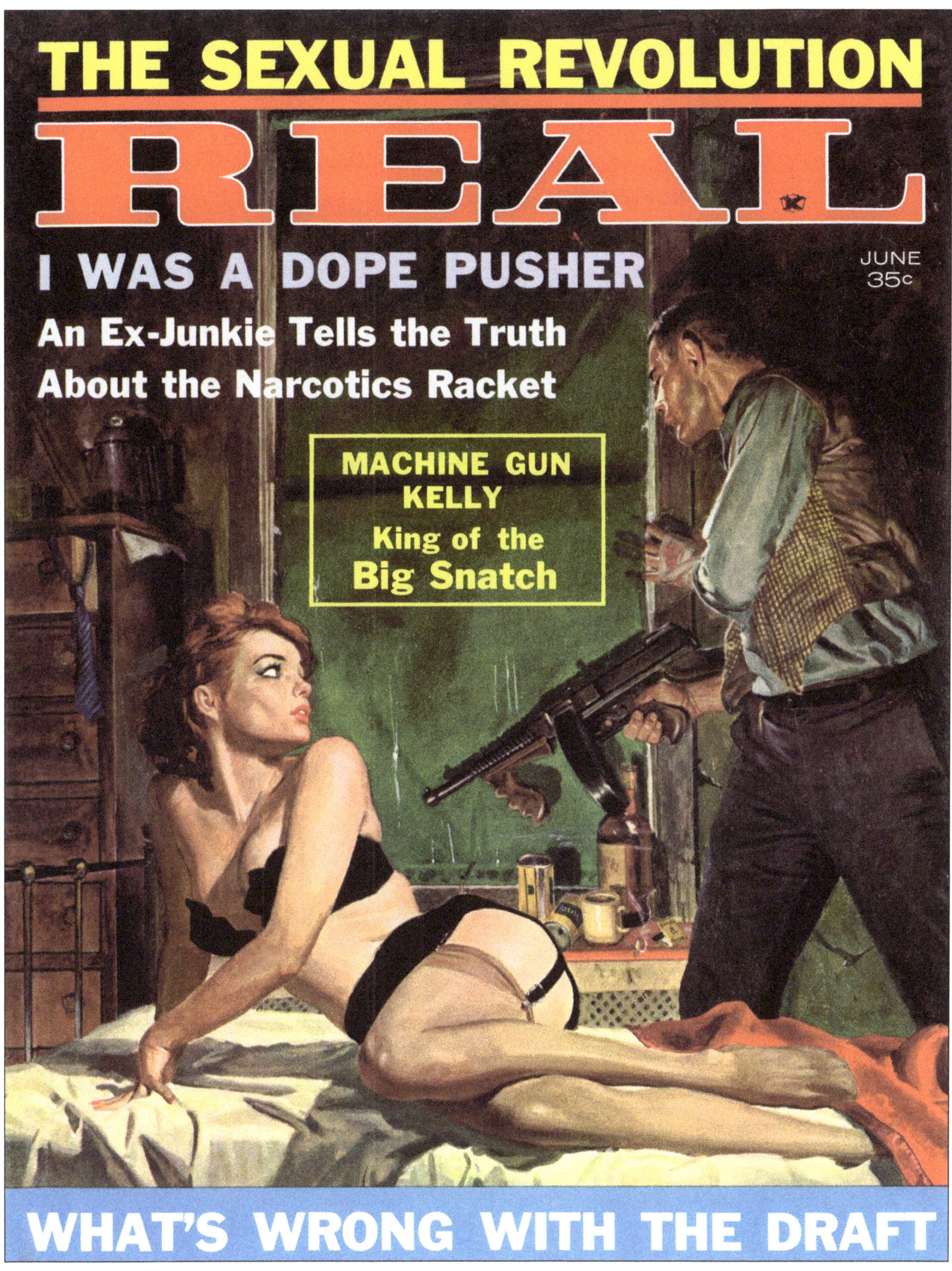
THE SEXUAL REVOLUTION
REAL
I WAS A DOPE PUSHER
An Ex-Junkie Tells the Truth
About the Narcotics Racket
JUNE
35c
MACHINE GUN
KELLY
King of the
Big Snatch
WHAT'S WRONG WITH THE DRAFT

June 1962

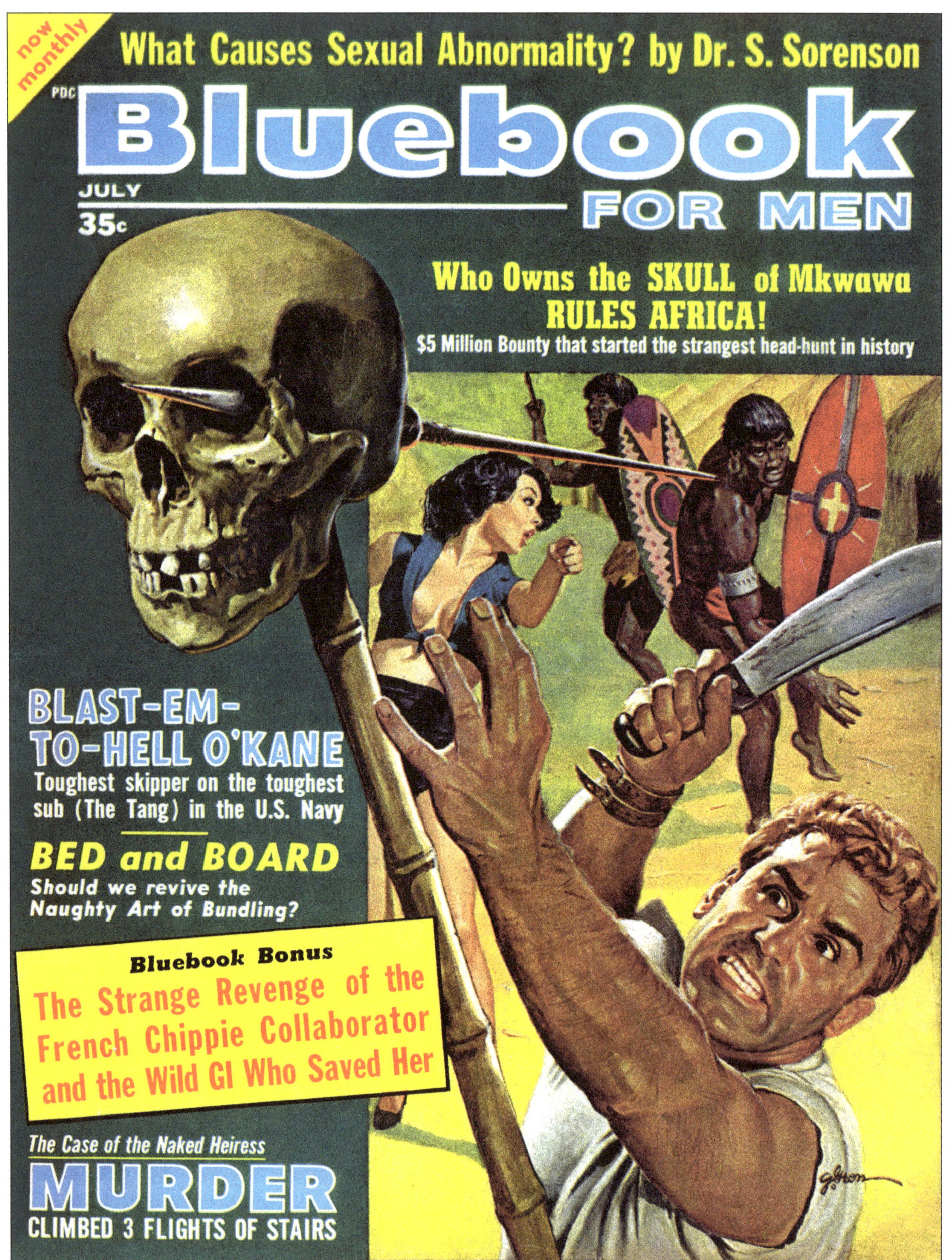

now monthly
PDC
What Causes Sexual Abnormality? by Dr. S. Sorenson
Bluebook
FOR MEN
JULY
35c
Who Owns the SKULL of Mkwawa RULES AFRICA!
$5 Million Bounty that started the strangest head-hunt in history
BLAST-EM-TO-HELL O'KANE
Toughest skipper on the toughest sub (The Tang) in the U.S. Navy
BED and BOARD
Should we revive the Naughty Art of Bundling?
Bluebook Bonus
The Strange Revenge of the French Chippie Collaborator and the Wild GI Who Saved Her
The Case of the Naked Heiress
MURDER
CLIMBED 3 FLIGHTS OF STAIRS

July 1962

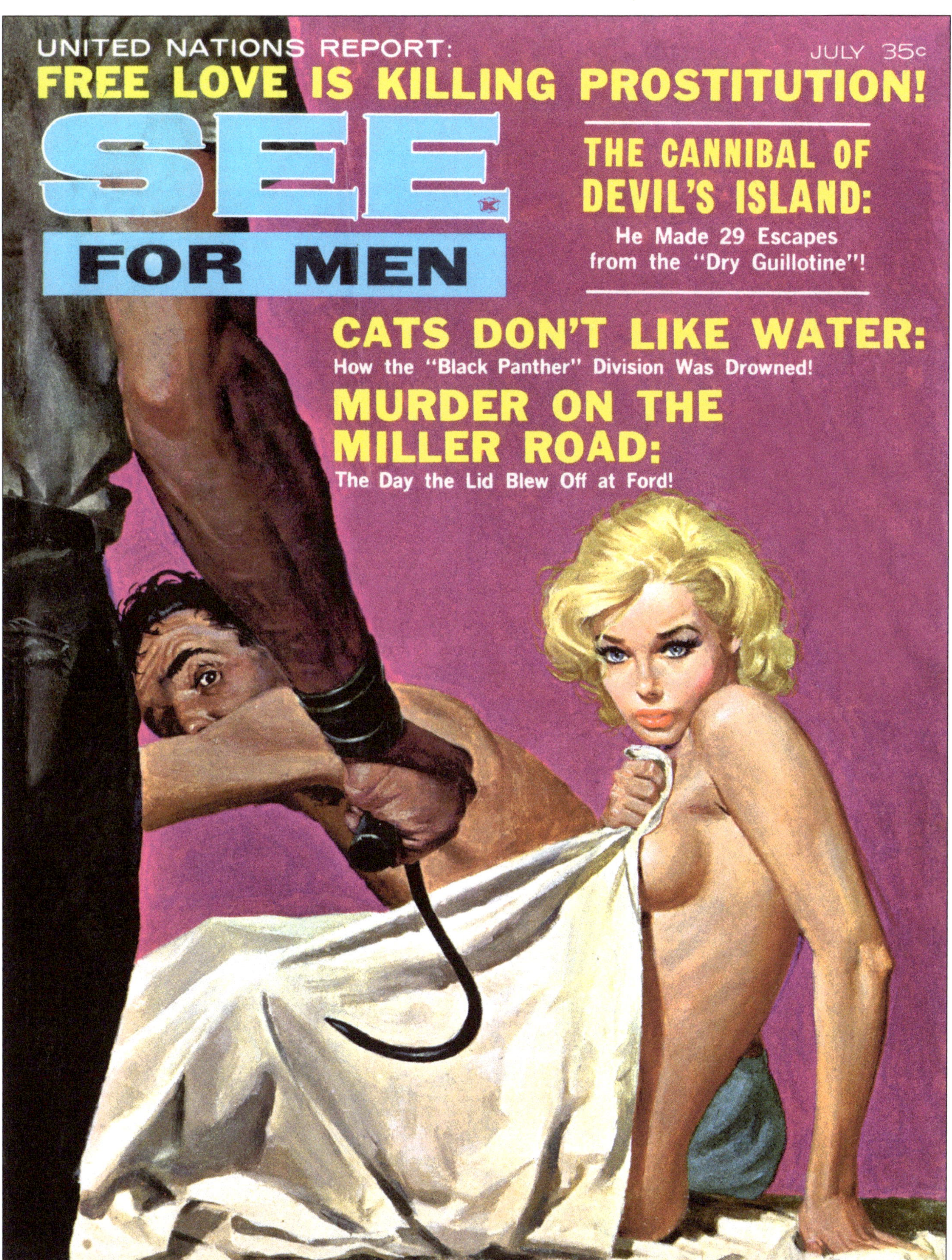

UNITED NATIONS REPORT:
FREE LOVE IS KILLING PROSTITUTION!
SEE
FOR MEN
JULY 35¢
THE CANNIBAL OF DEVIL'S ISLAND:
He Made 29 Escapes from the "Dry Guillotine"!
CATS DON'T LIKE WATER:
How the "Black Panther" Division Was Drowned!
MURDER ON THE MILLER ROAD:
The Day the Lid Blew Off at Ford!

July 1962

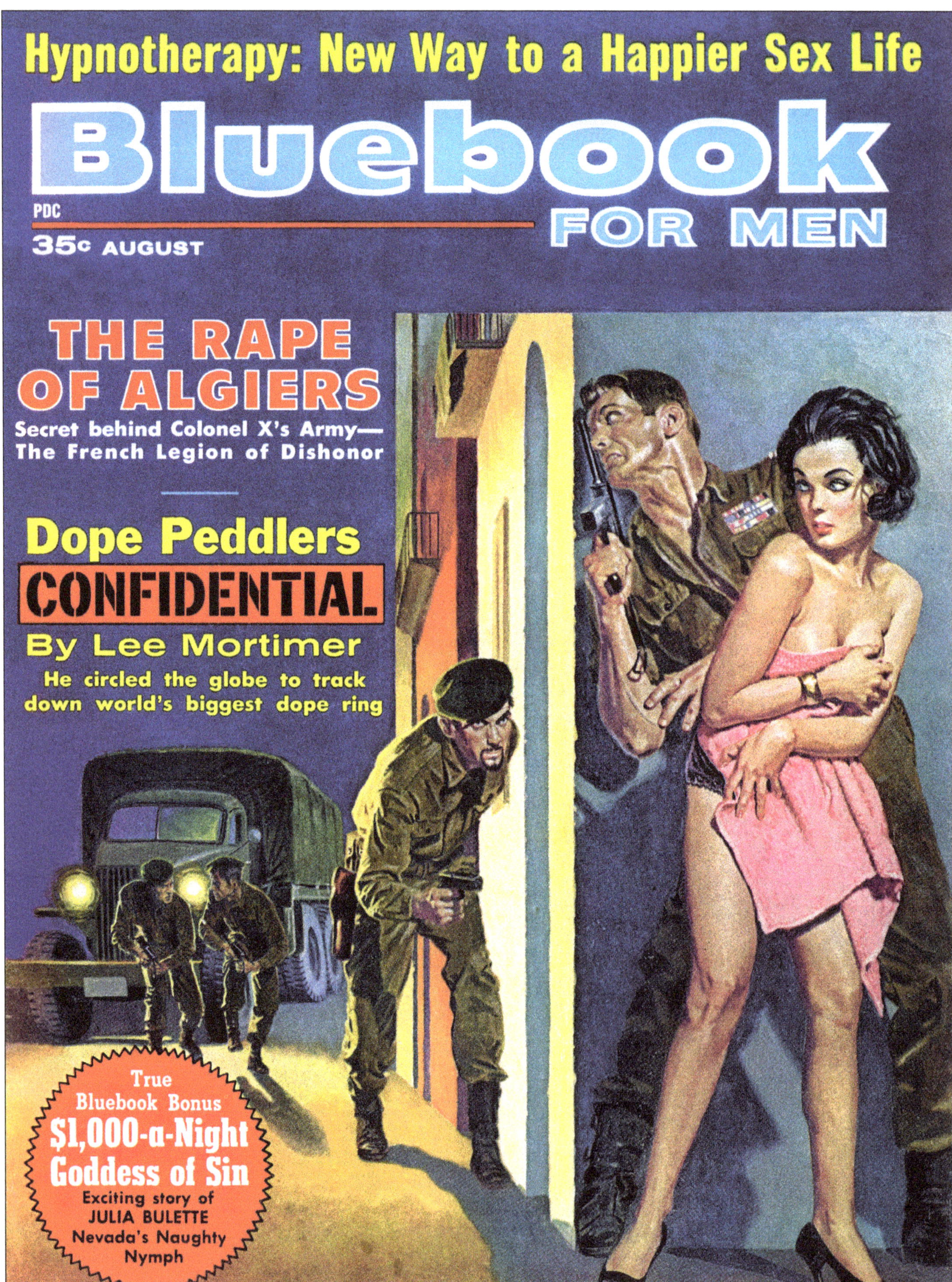
Hypnotherapy: New Way to a Happier Sex Life
Bluebook
FOR MEN
PDC
35¢ AUGUST
THE RAPE OF ALGIERS
Secret behind Colonel X's Army—
The French Legion of Dishonor
Dope Peddlers
CONFIDENTIAL
By Lee Mortimer
He circled the globe to track
down world's biggest dope ring
True
Bluebook Bonus
$1,000-a-Night
Goddess of Sin
Exciting story of
JULIA BULETTE
Nevada's Naughty
Nymph

August 1962

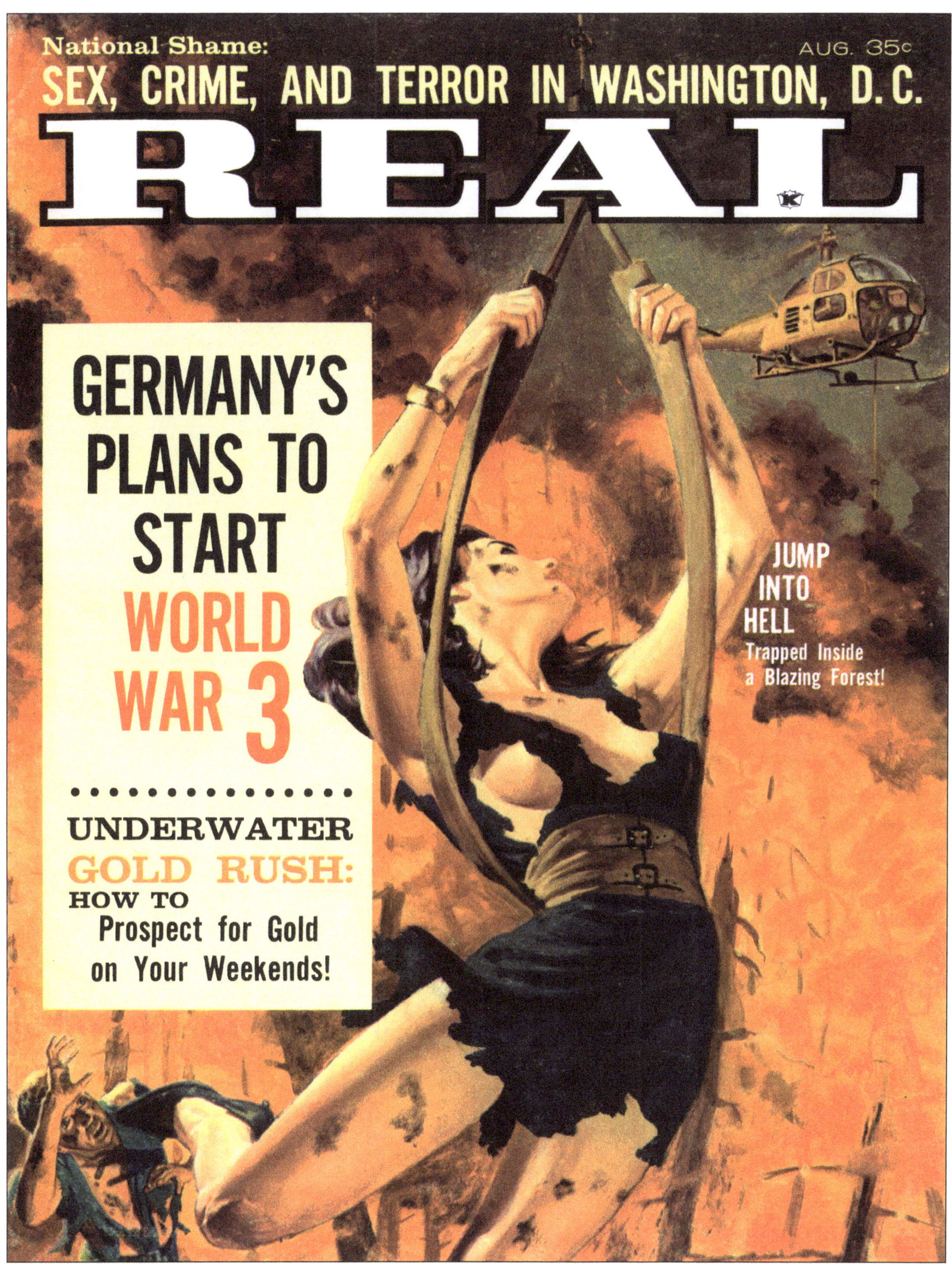

National Shame:
SEX, CRIME, AND TERROR IN WASHINGTON, D.C.
AUG. 35c
REAL
GERMANY'S PLANS TO START WORLD WAR 3
UNDERWATER GOLD RUSH: HOW TO Prospect for Gold on Your Weekends!
JUMP INTO HELL
Trapped Inside a Blazing Forest!

August 1962

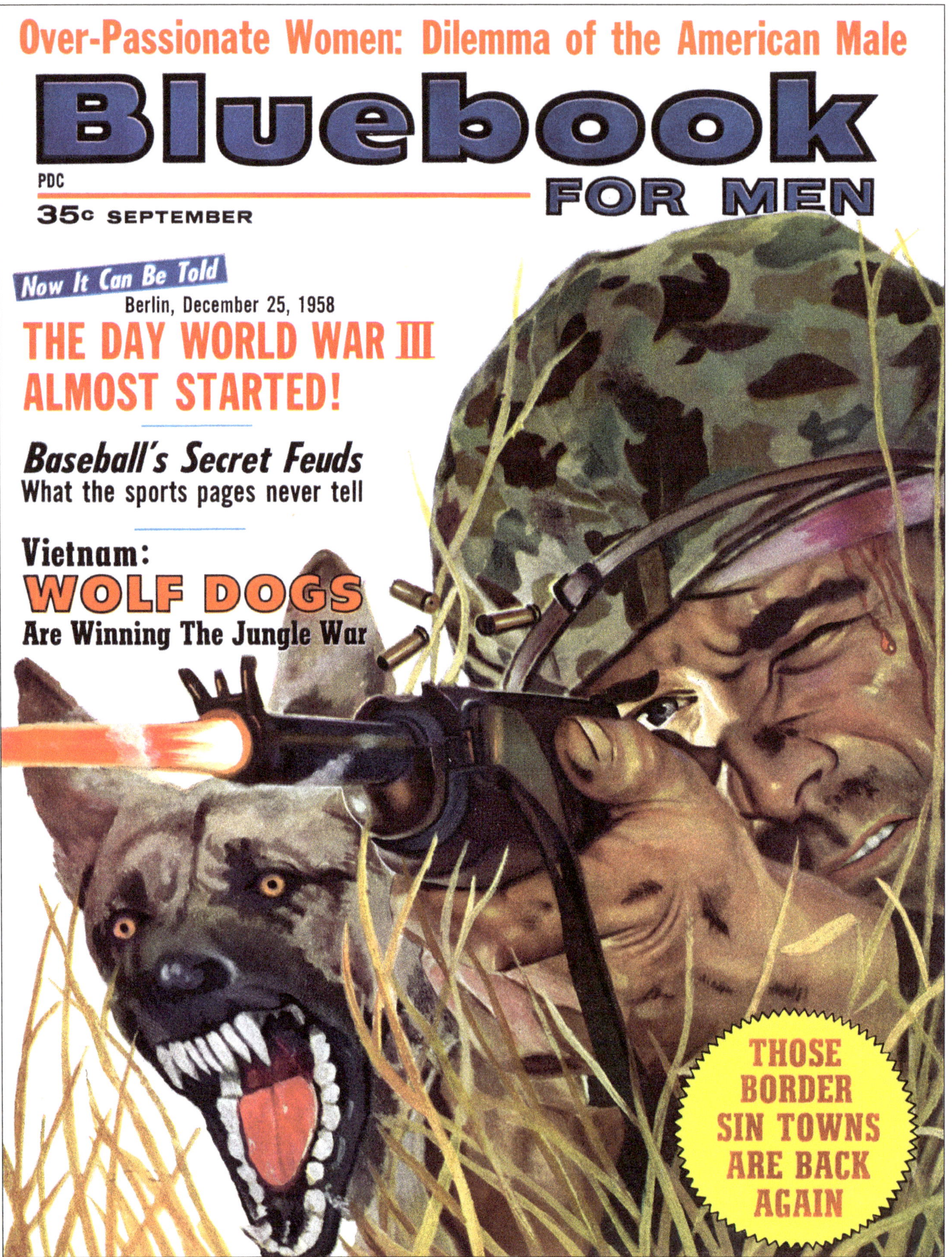

September 1962

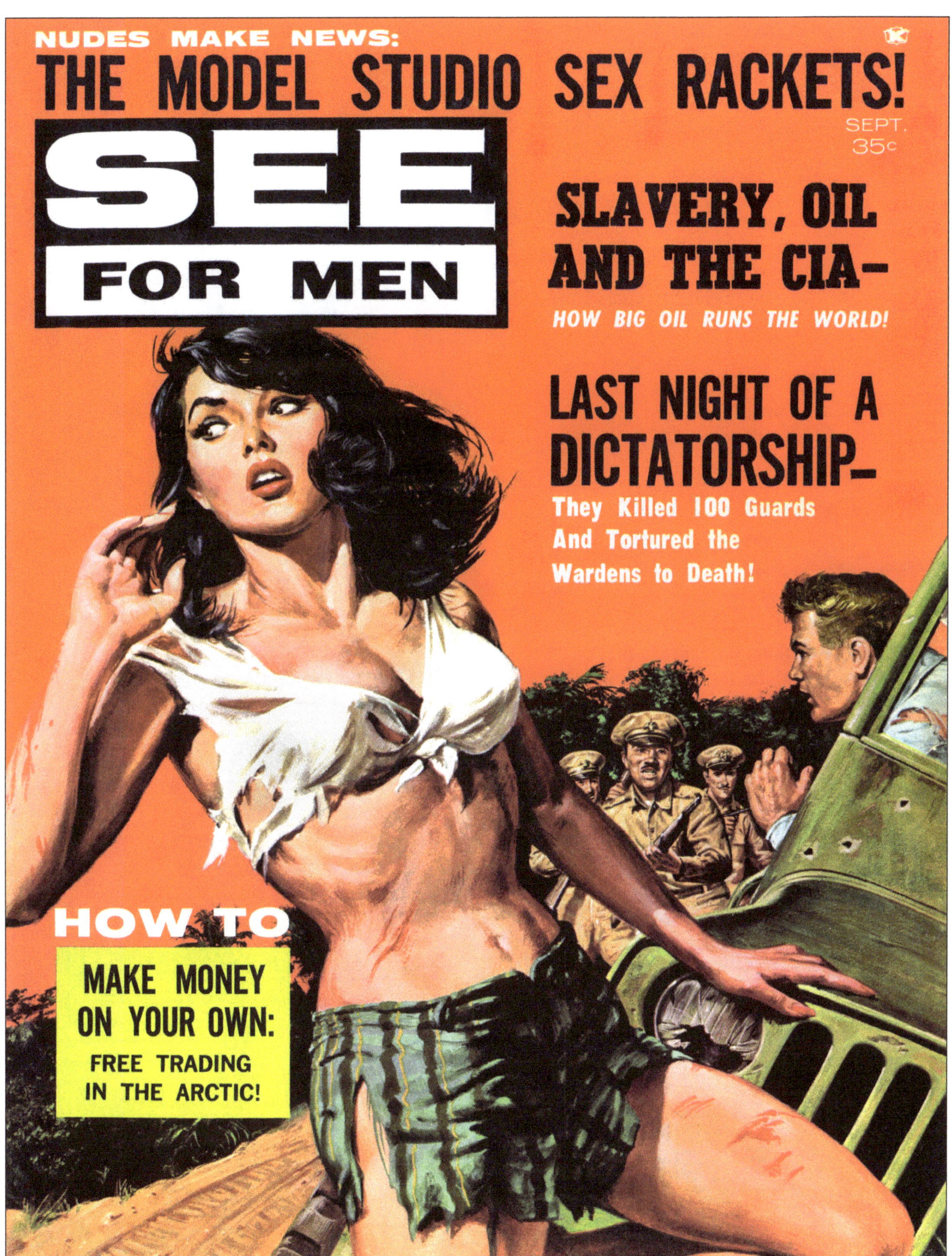

September 1962

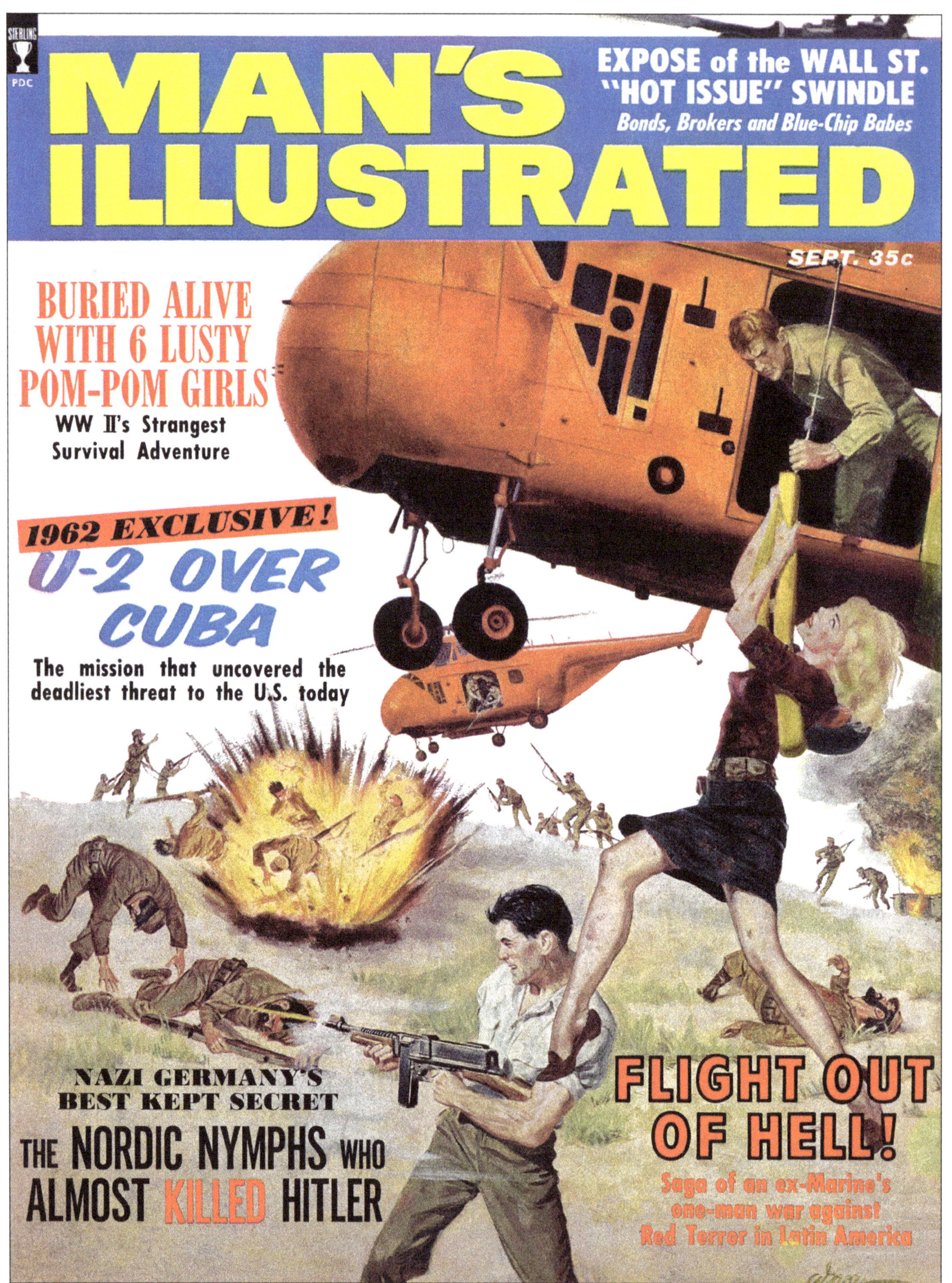

September 1962

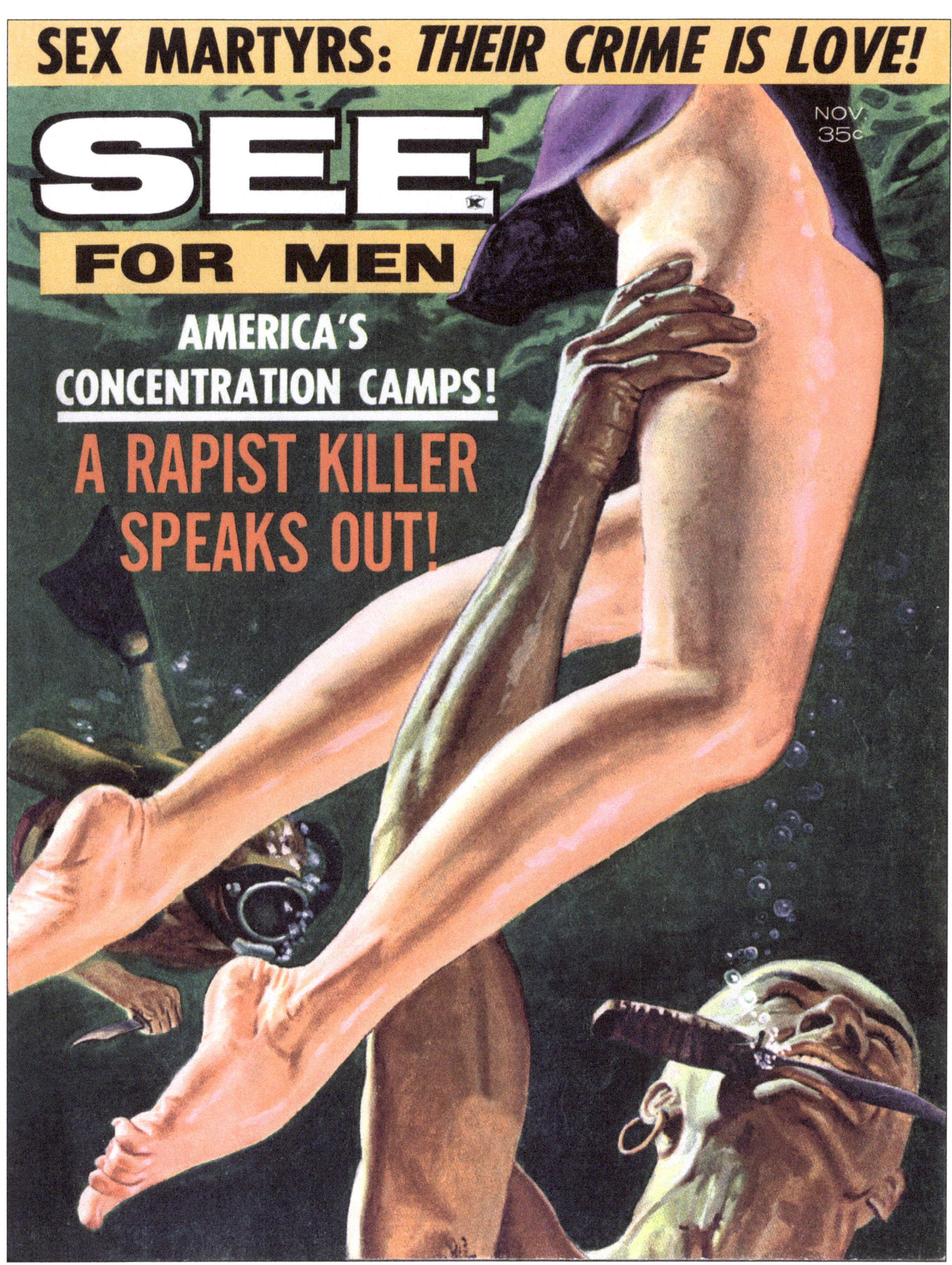

November 1962

TRUE ACTION

TRUE BOOKLENGTH ADVENTURE

FRÄULEIN SEDUCTRESS WHO LURED YANKS INTO A P.O.W. PENAL HOLE

35¢

THE BLONDE WHO LED A RENEGADE LEGIONNAIRE 2000 MILES TO FT. BECHAR

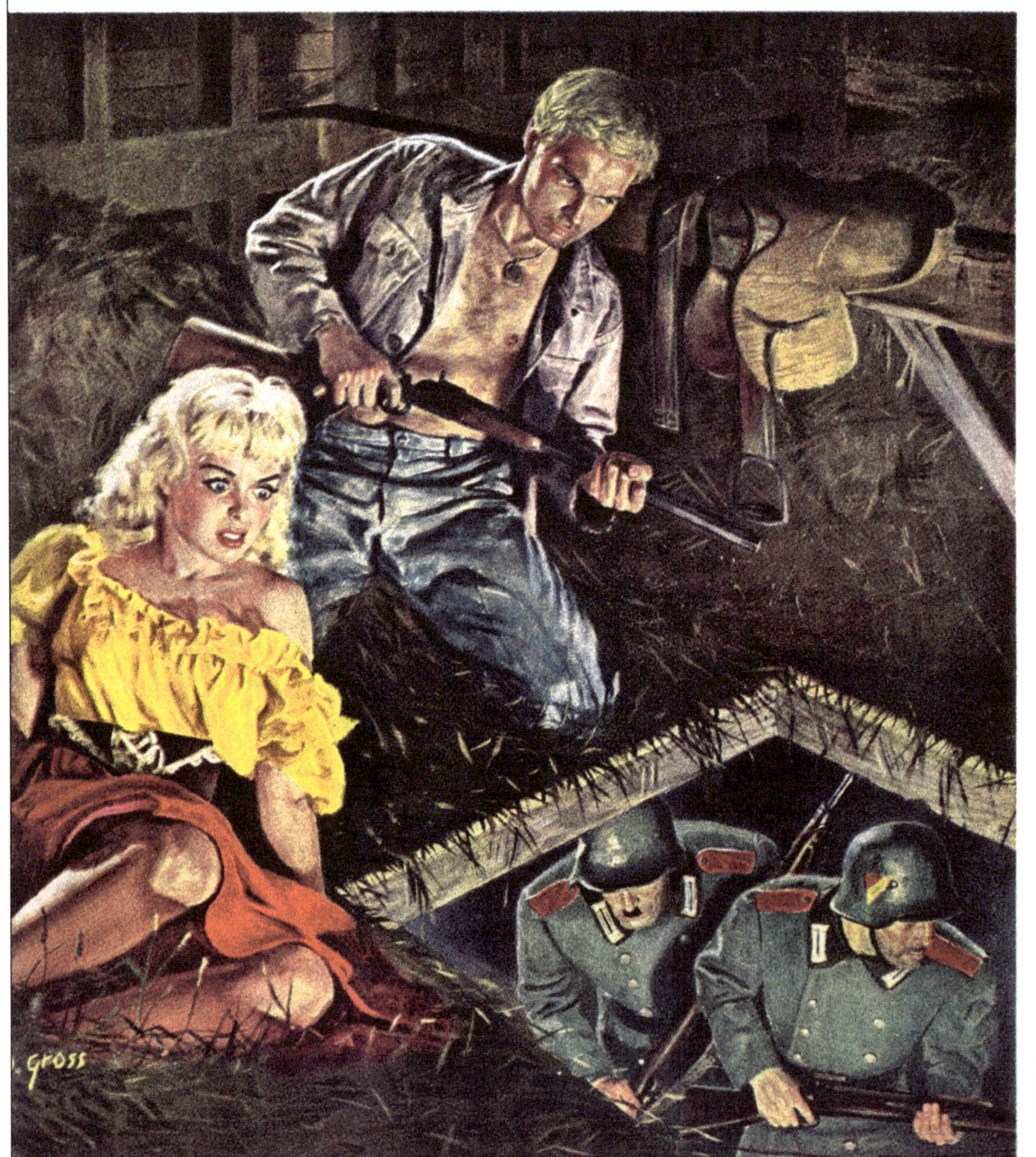

ALLIED AIR ACE AND HIS AMAZING FLYING CANNON

King Rawlings' Strange Harem Of Far North Love Brides

November 1962   *Previously used for* **Men** December 1958

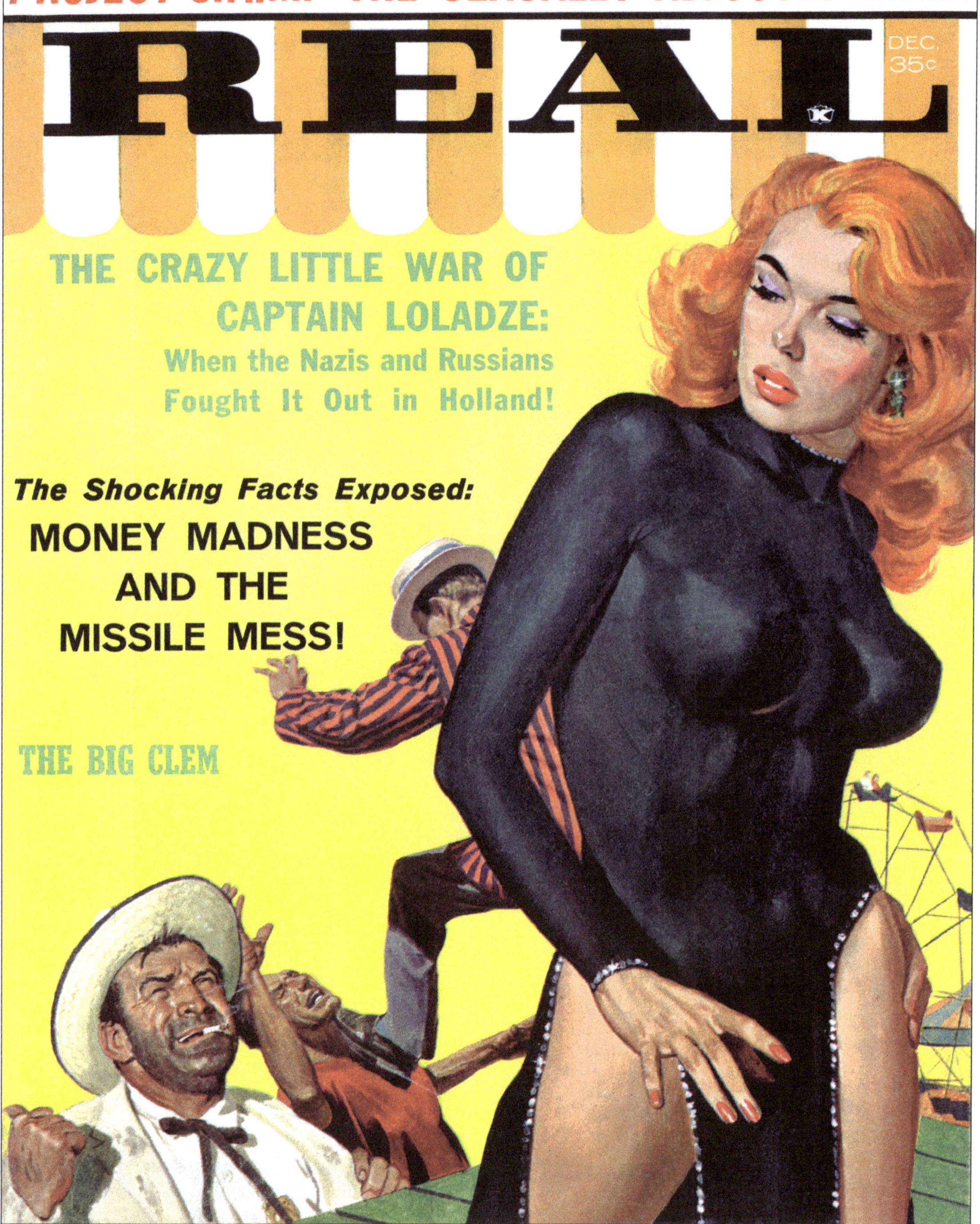

December 1962

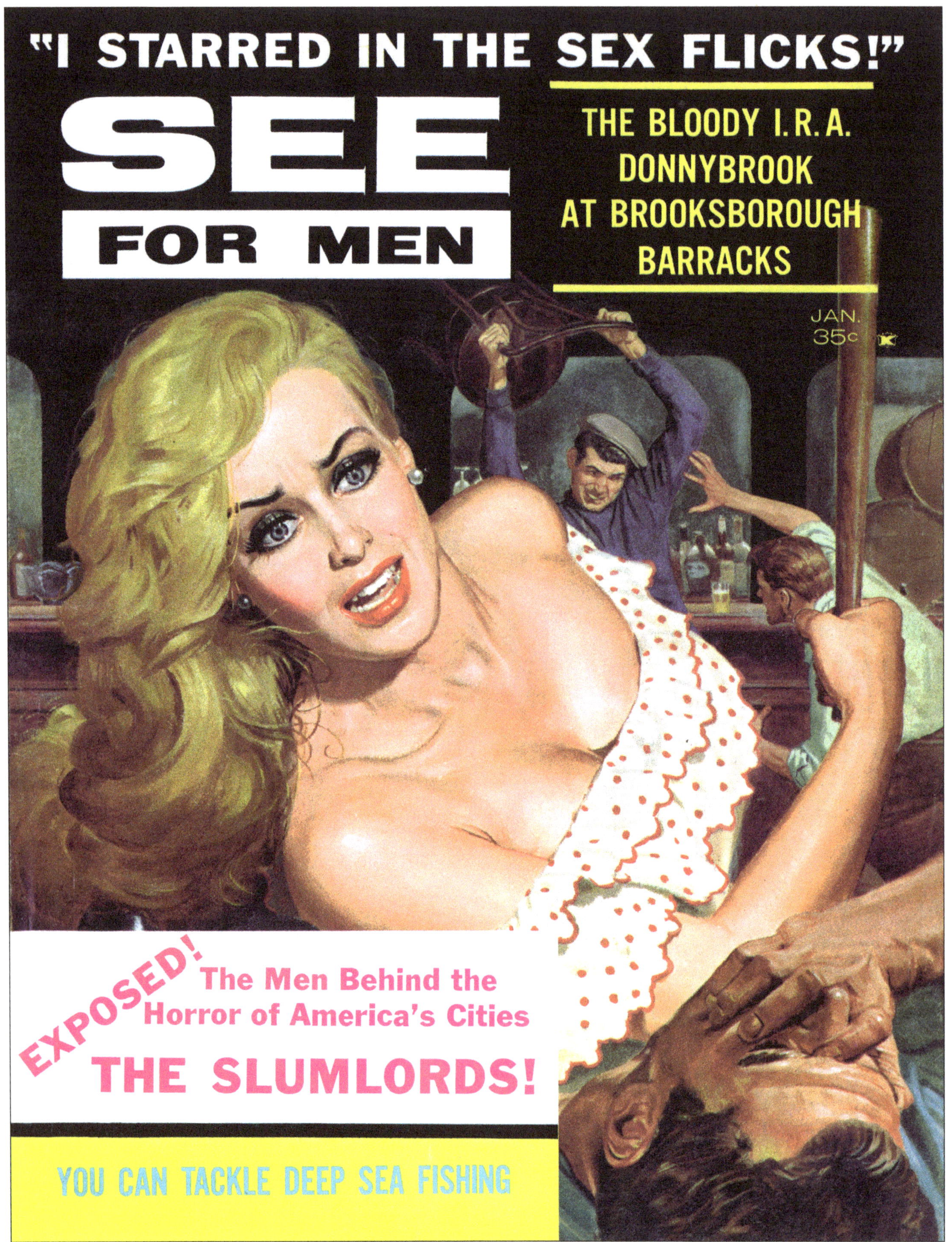

January 1963

New Facts About:
YOUR SEX DRIVE AND YOUR SANITY

Special Report:
BUG-KILLING CHEMICALS ARE POISONING YOU

REAL

FEB.
35¢

"I HID ON GUAM FOR 16 YEARS!"

THE ALASKAN MASSACRE THAT STOPPED A RUSSIAN INVASION OF AMERICA

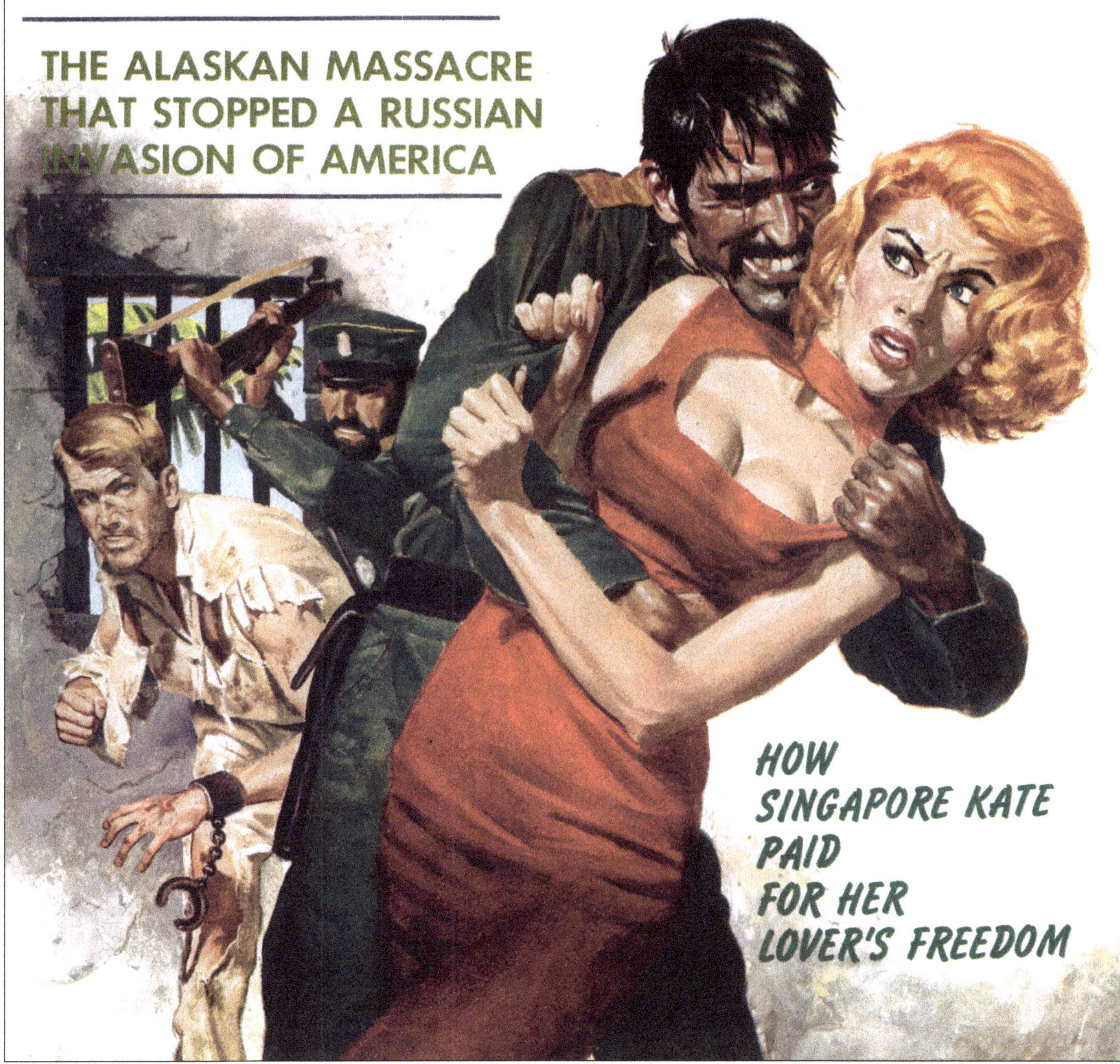

HOW SINGAPORE KATE PAID FOR HER LOVER'S FREEDOM

February 1963

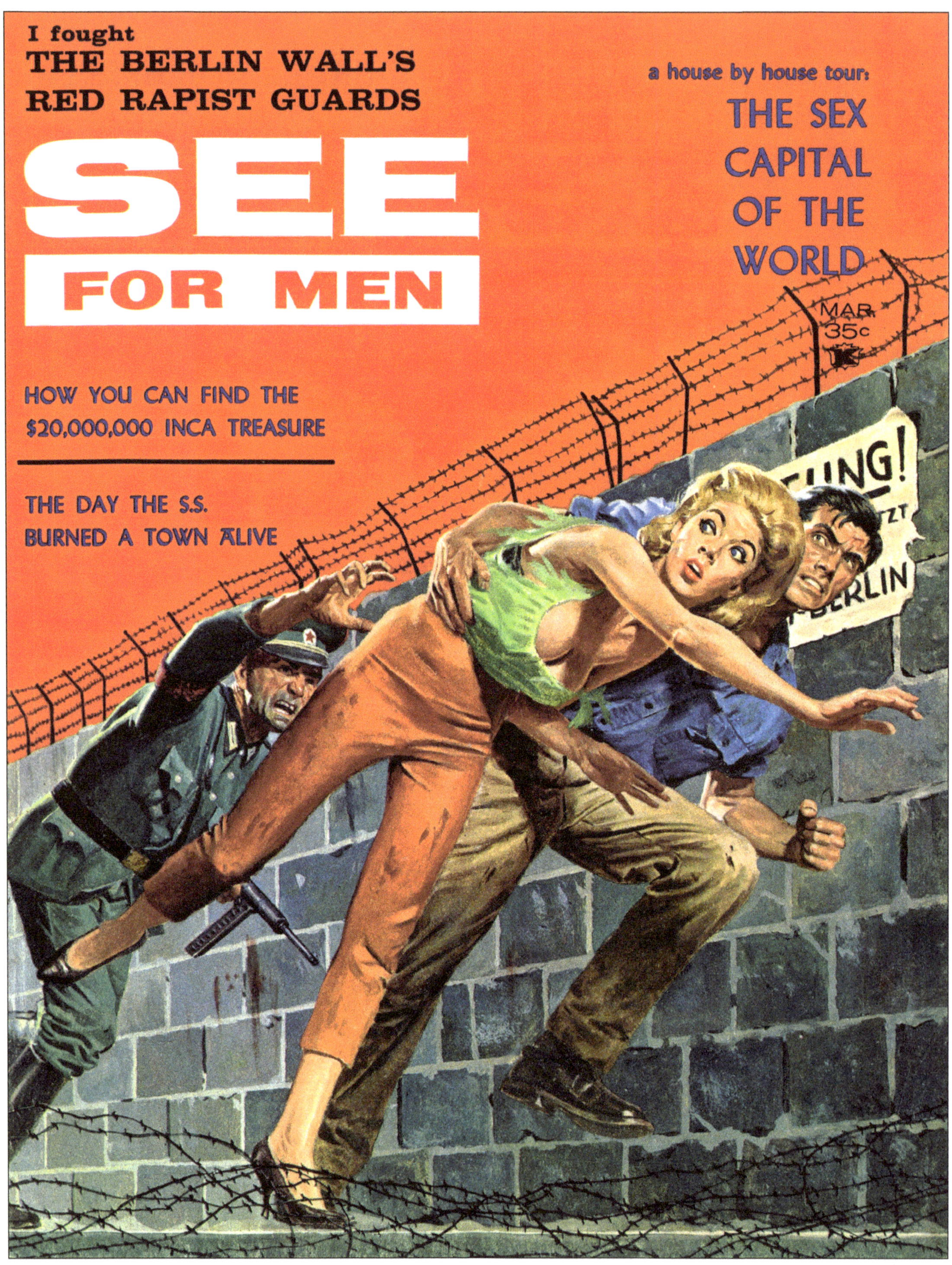

I fought
THE BERLIN WALL'S
RED RAPIST GUARDS
SEE
FOR MEN
a house by house tour:
THE SEX CAPITAL OF THE WORLD
MAR. 35c
HOW YOU CAN FIND THE $20,000,000 INCA TREASURE
THE DAY THE S.S. BURNED A TOWN ALIVE
TUNG!
BERLIN

March 1963

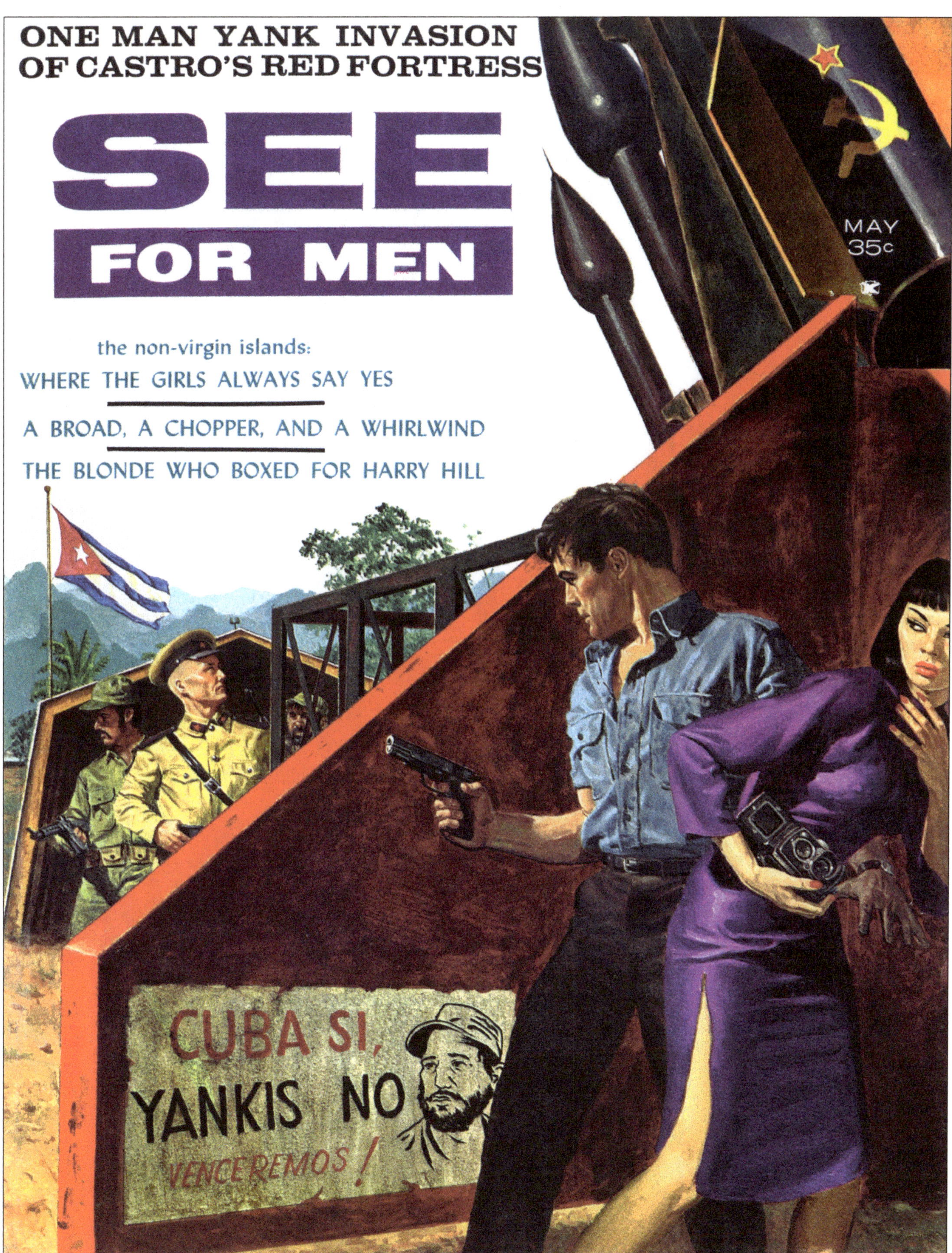

ONE MAN YANK INVASION
OF CASTRO'S RED FORTRESS

SEE
FOR MEN

MAY
35c

the non-virgin islands:
WHERE THE GIRLS ALWAYS SAY YES

A BROAD, A CHOPPER, AND A WHIRLWIND

THE BLONDE WHO BOXED FOR HARRY HILL

CUBA SI,
YANKIS NO
VENCEREMOS!

May 1963

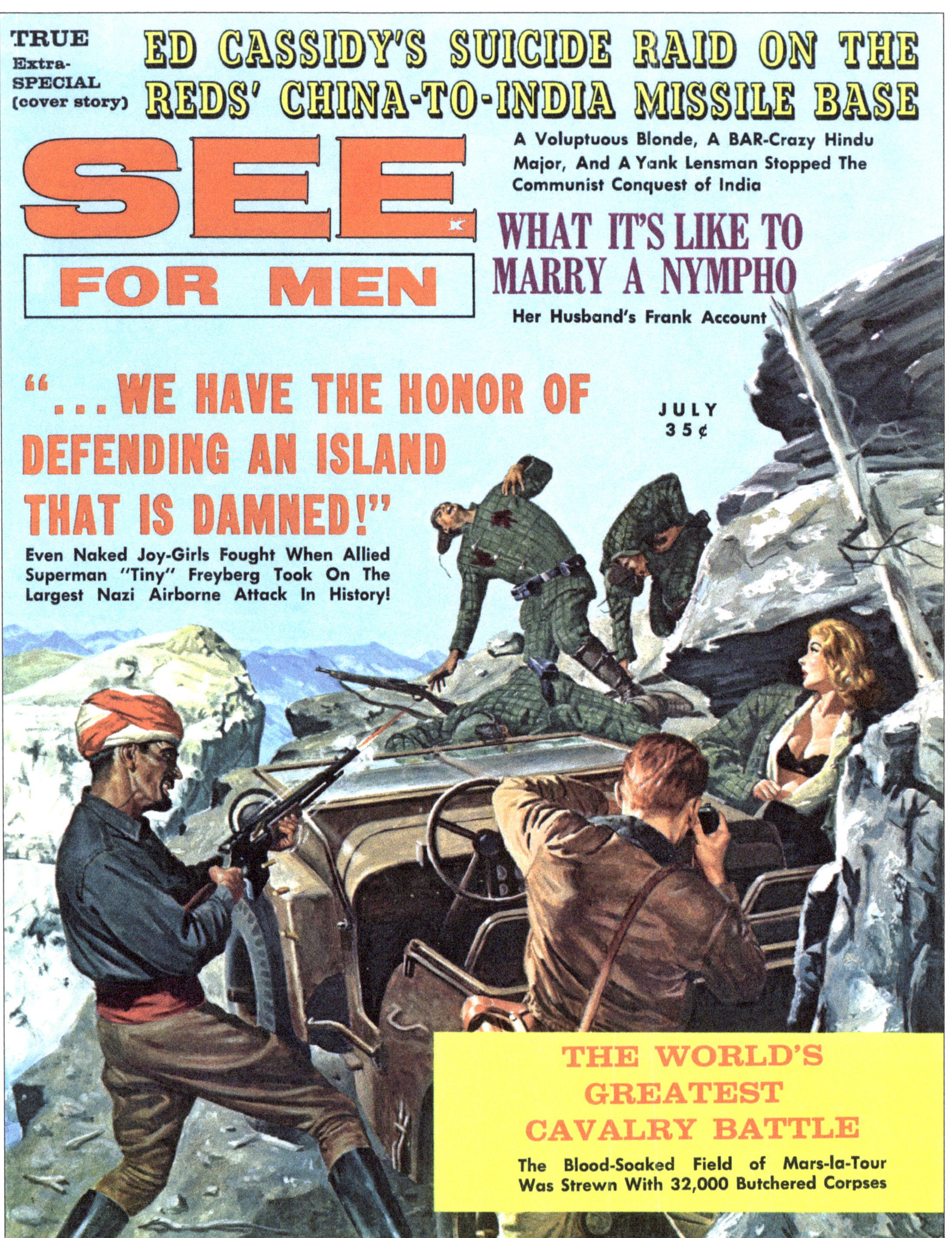
TRUE
Extra-
SPECIAL
(cover story)

ED CASSIDY'S SUICIDE RAID ON THE REDS' CHINA-TO-INDIA MISSILE BASE

SEE
FOR MEN

A Voluptuous Blonde, A BAR-Crazy Hindu Major, And A Yank Lensman Stopped The Communist Conquest of India

WHAT IT'S LIKE TO MARRY A NYMPHO
Her Husband's Frank Account

"...WE HAVE THE HONOR OF DEFENDING AN ISLAND THAT IS DAMNED!"
Even Naked Joy-Girls Fought When Allied Superman "Tiny" Freyberg Took On The Largest Nazi Airborne Attack In History!

JULY
35¢

THE WORLD'S GREATEST CAVALRY BATTLE
The Blood-Soaked Field of Mars-la-Tour Was Strewn With 32,000 Butchered Corpses

July 1963

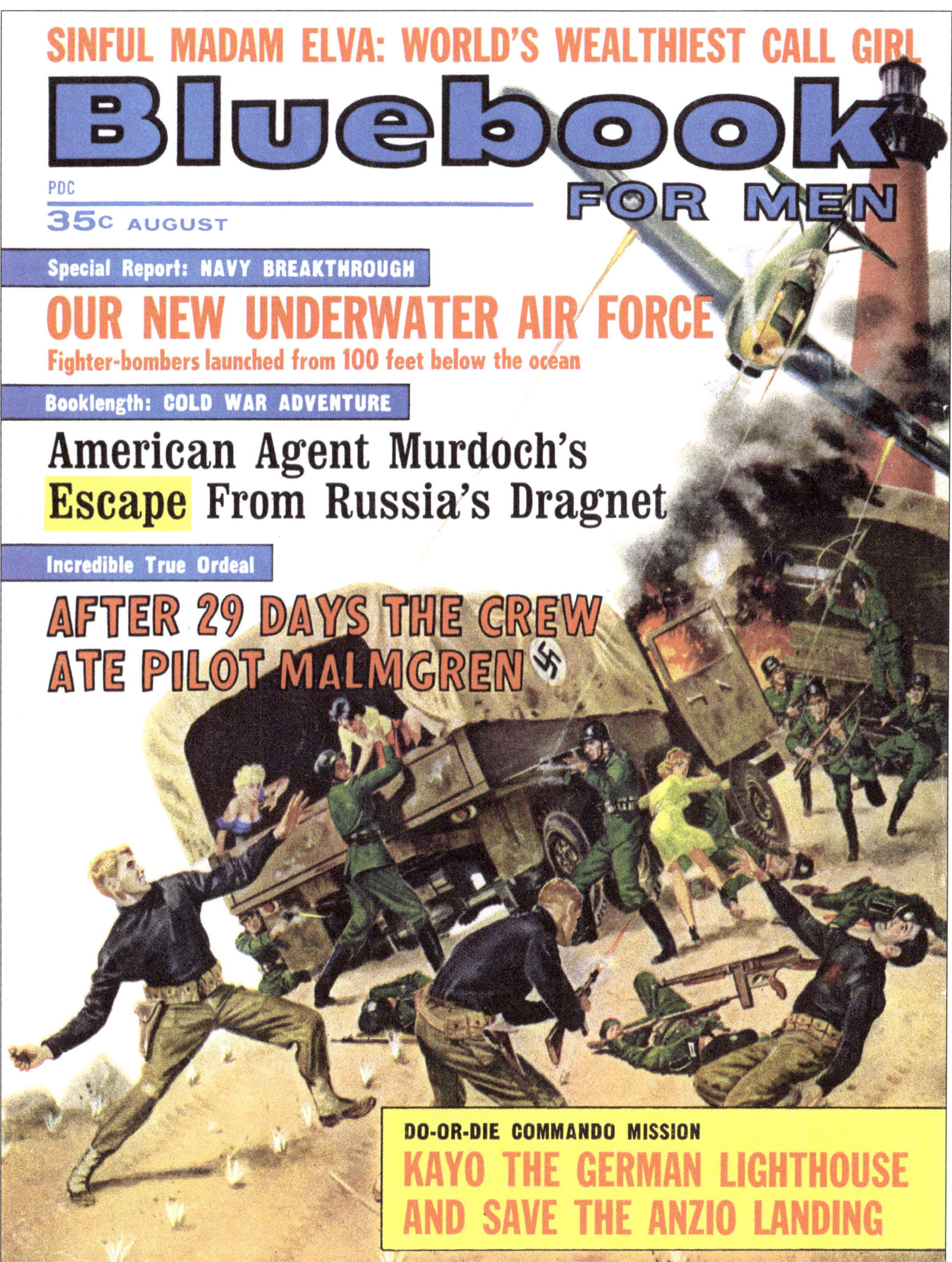

SINFUL MADAM ELVA: WORLD'S WEALTHIEST CALL GIRL
Bluebook
FOR MEN
PDC
35c AUGUST
Special Report: NAVY BREAKTHROUGH
OUR NEW UNDERWATER AIR FORCE
Fighter-bombers launched from 100 feet below the ocean
Booklength: COLD WAR ADVENTURE
American Agent Murdoch's Escape From Russia's Dragnet
Incredible True Ordeal
AFTER 29 DAYS THE CREW ATE PILOT MALMGREN
DO-OR-DIE COMMANDO MISSION
KAYO THE GERMAN LIGHTHOUSE AND SAVE THE ANZIO LANDING

August 1963

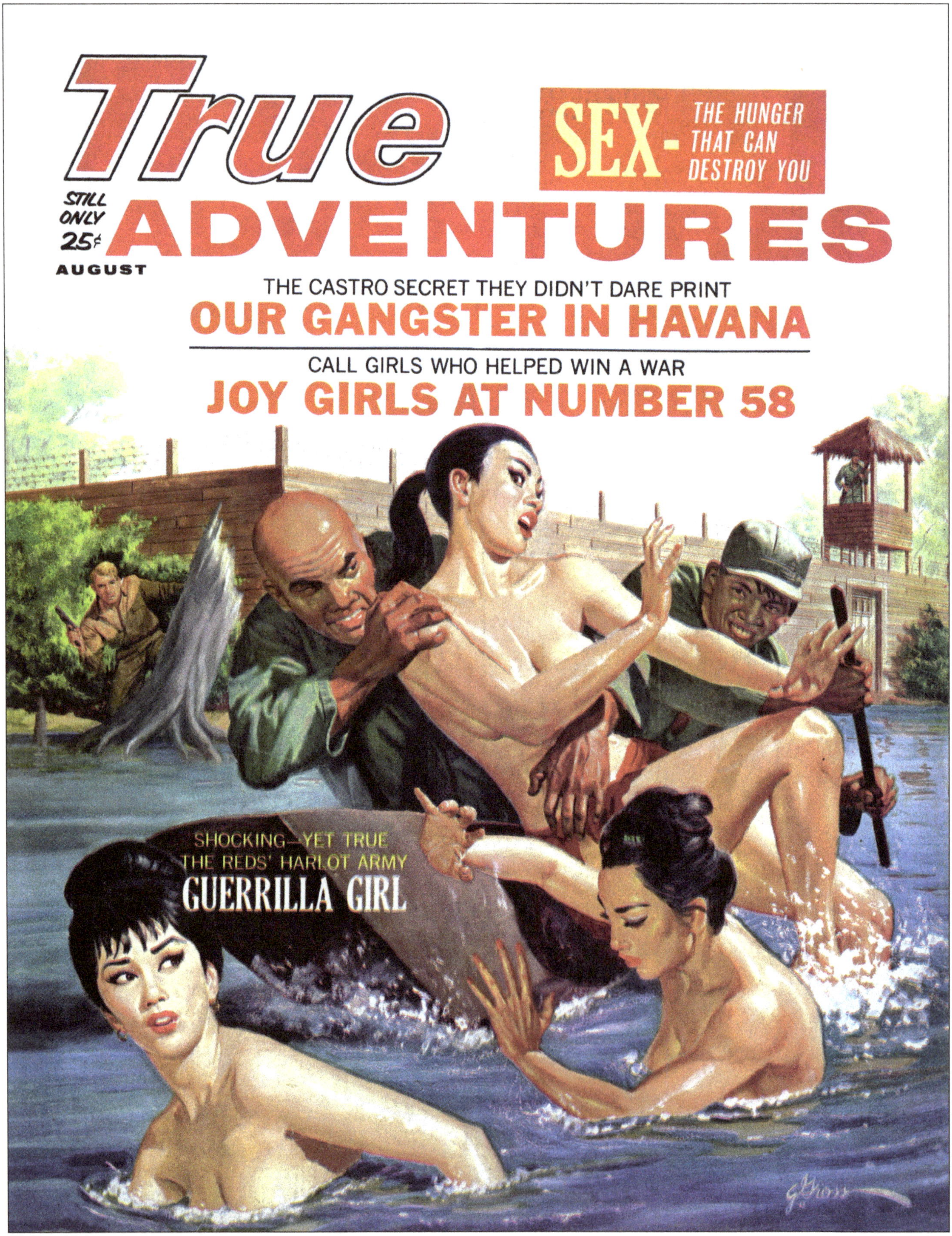

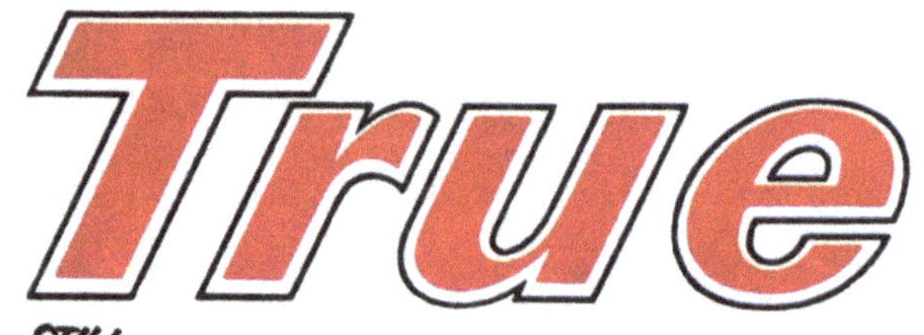
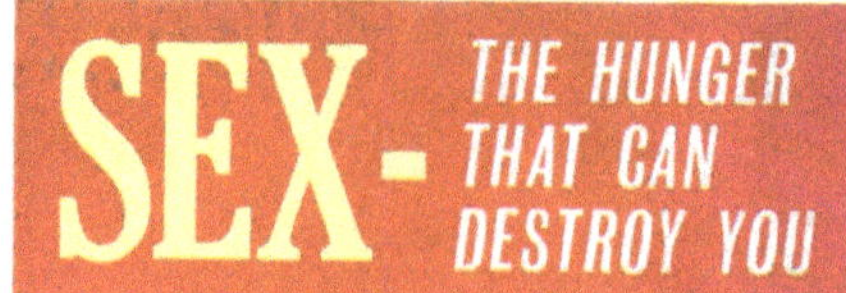

True
STILL ONLY 25¢
AUGUST
ADVENTURES
SEX- THE HUNGER THAT CAN DESTROY YOU
THE CASTRO SECRET THEY DIDN'T DARE PRINT
OUR GANGSTER IN HAVANA
CALL GIRLS WHO HELPED WIN A WAR
JOY GIRLS AT NUMBER 58
SHOCKING—YET TRUE
THE REDS' HARLOT ARMY
GUERRILLA GIRL

August 1963

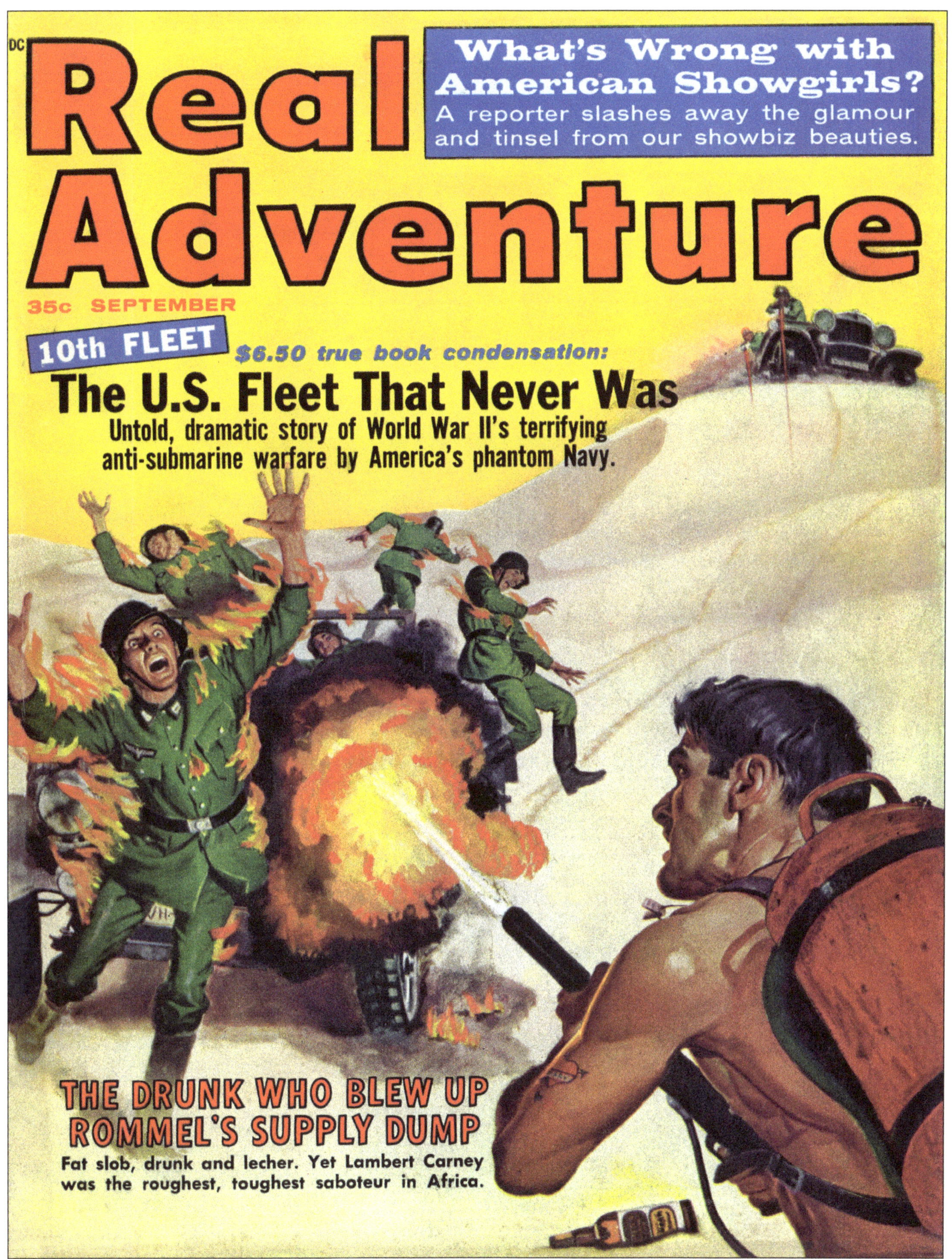

September 1963

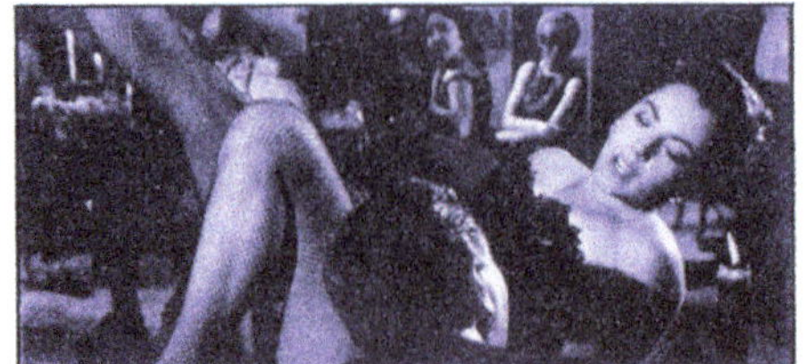

A 3-DAY LOVE DIET TO INCREASE YOUR LOVE POTENTIAL

SEE

THE MAGAZINE FOR MEN

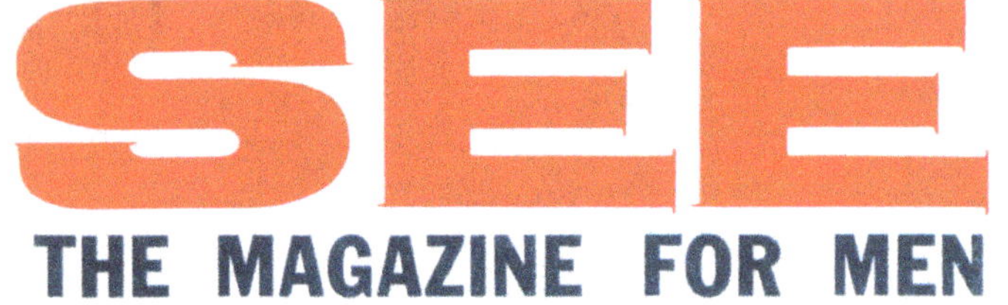

GIRL ROULETTE — THE LATEST INTERNATIONAL PASTIME FOR MEN

THE CULT OF THE MONSTER LOVERS

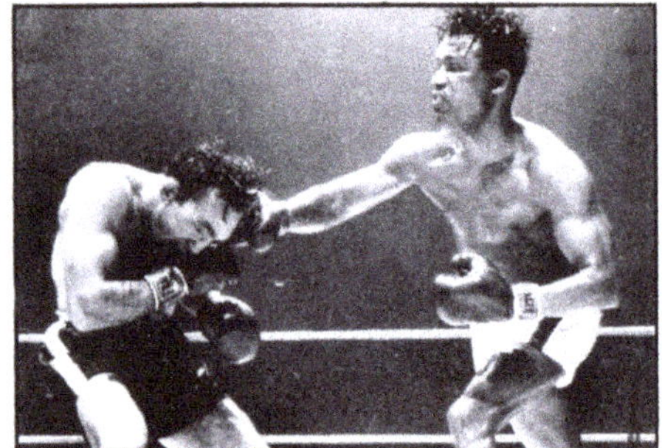

IS THERE A CASE FOR BOXING?

AN OPEN-MINDED, TWO-FISTED ANALYSIS

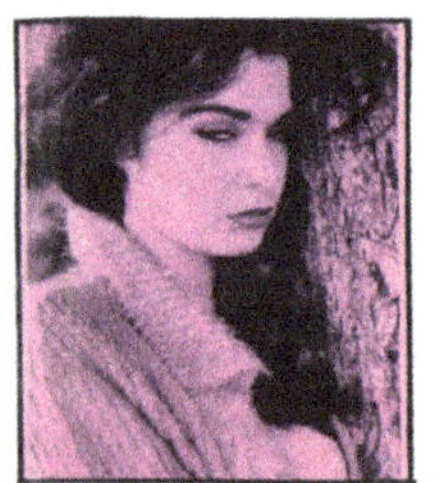
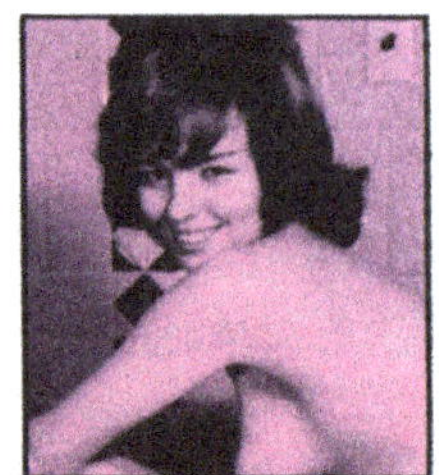

PIN UP MODELS TELL:

WHAT'S WRONG WITH AMERICAN MEN?

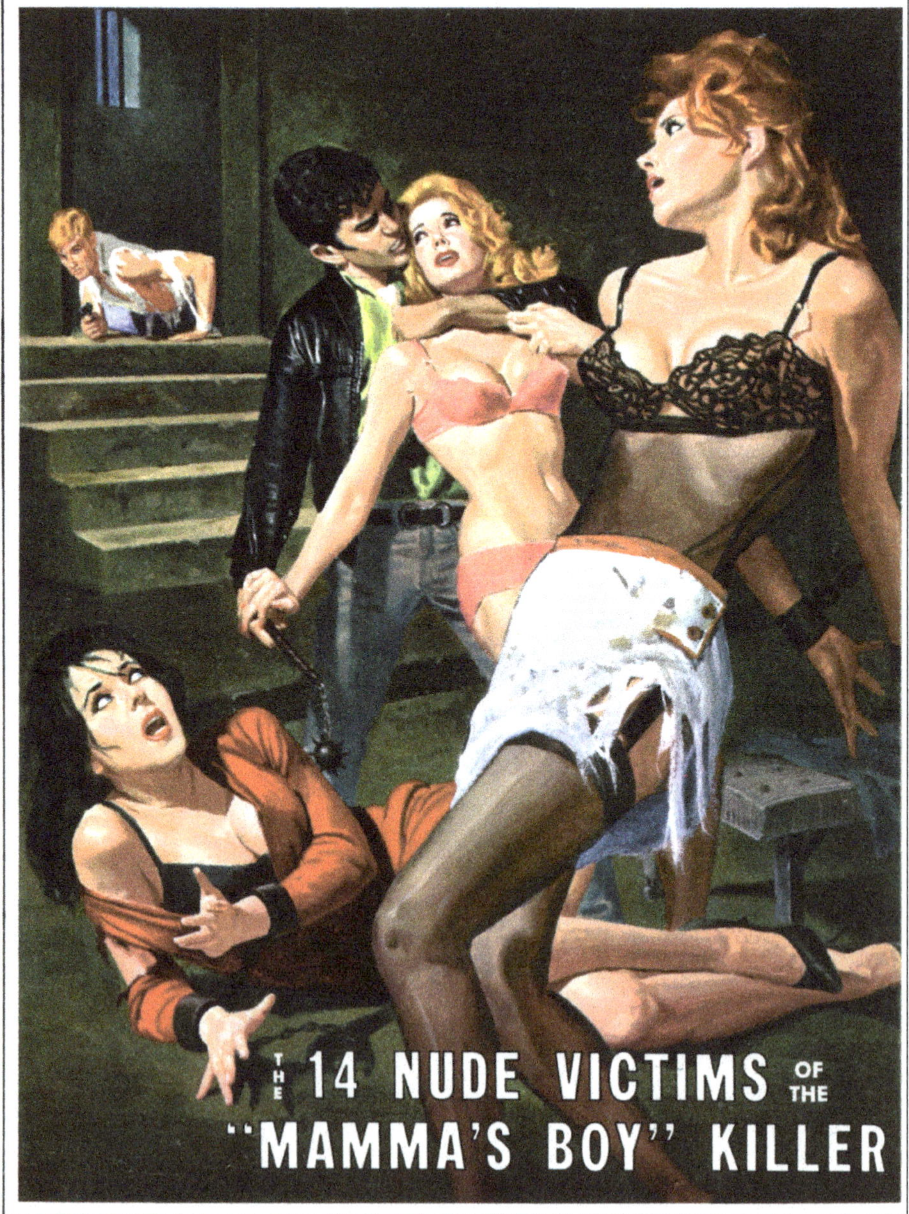

September 1963

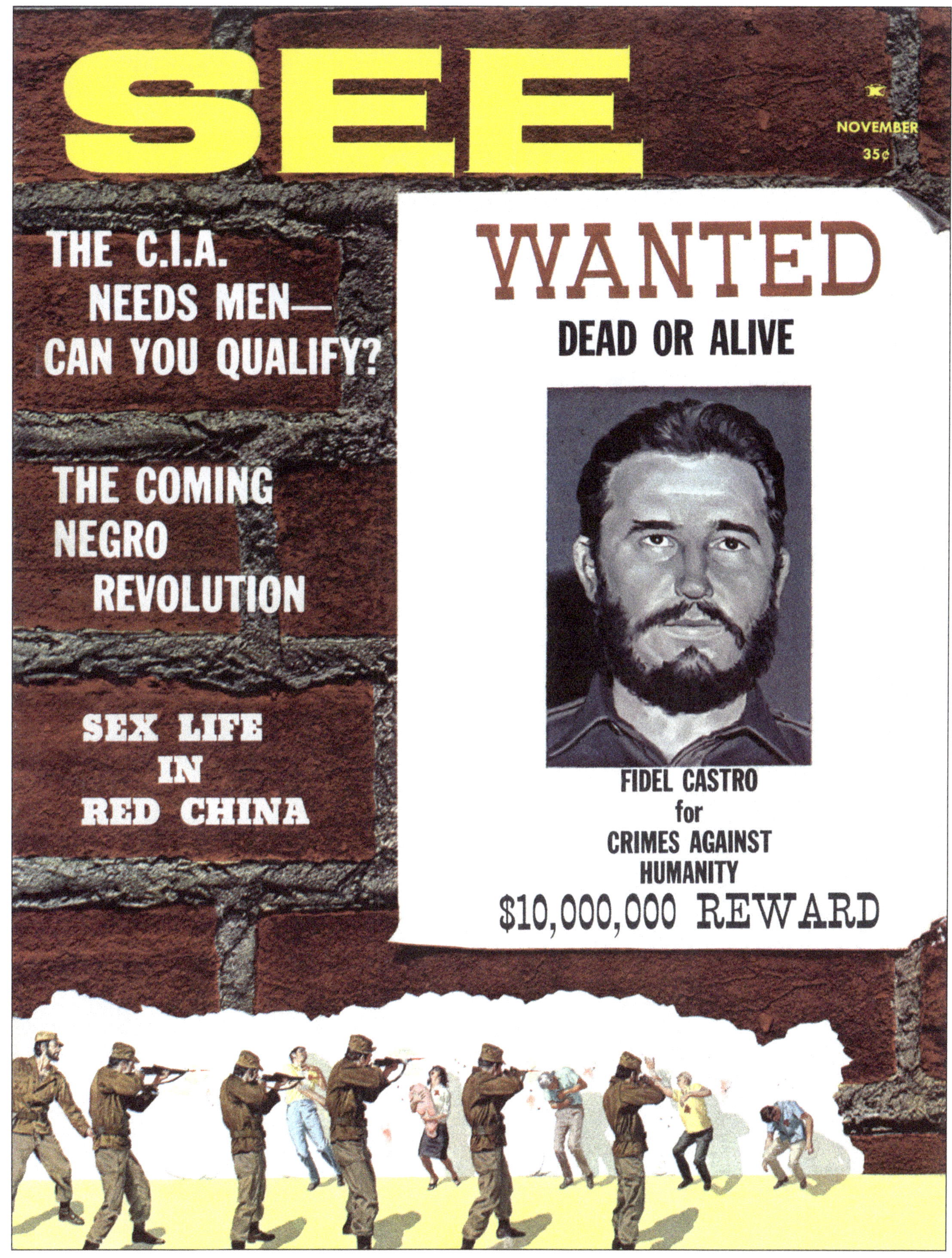

November 1963

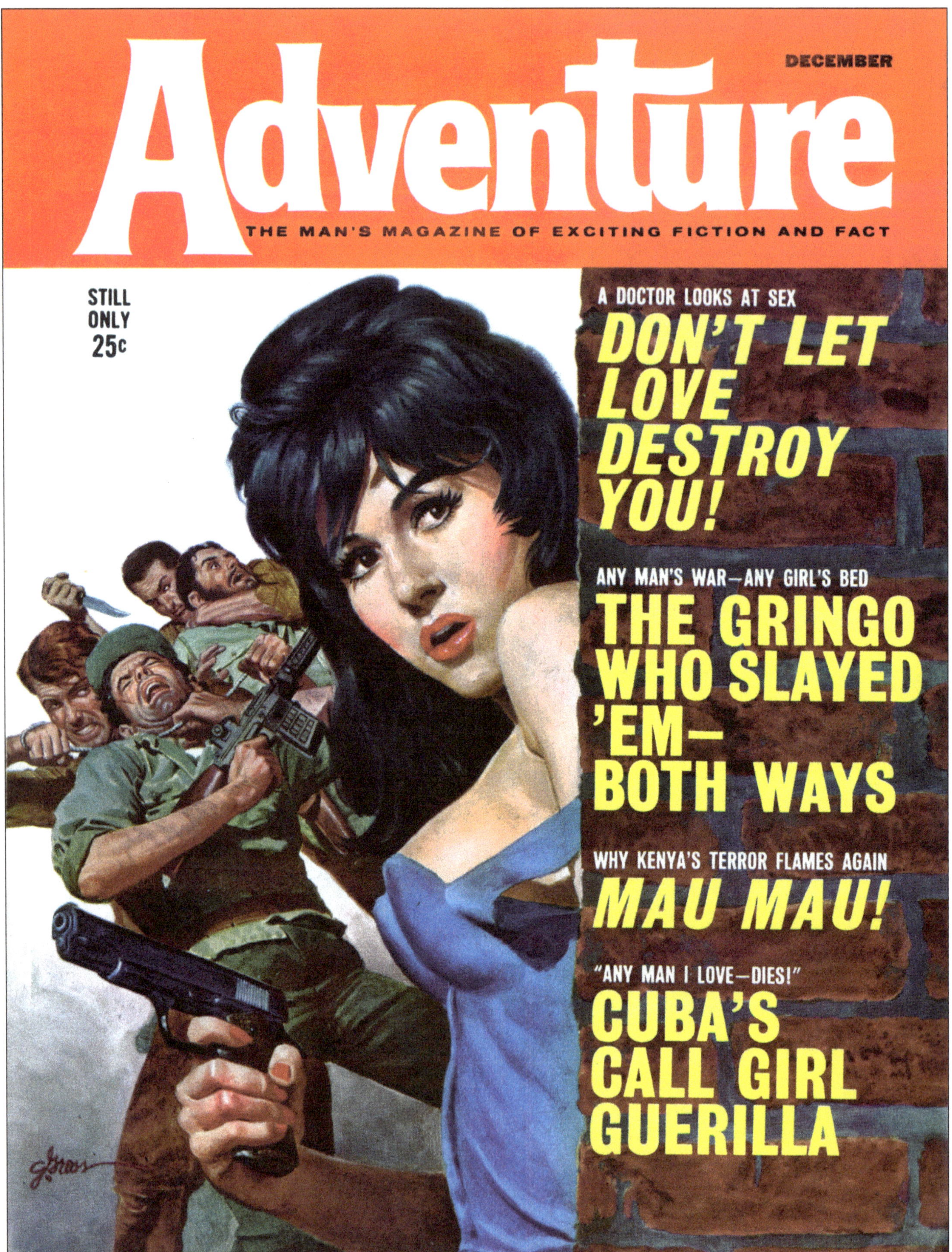

December 1963

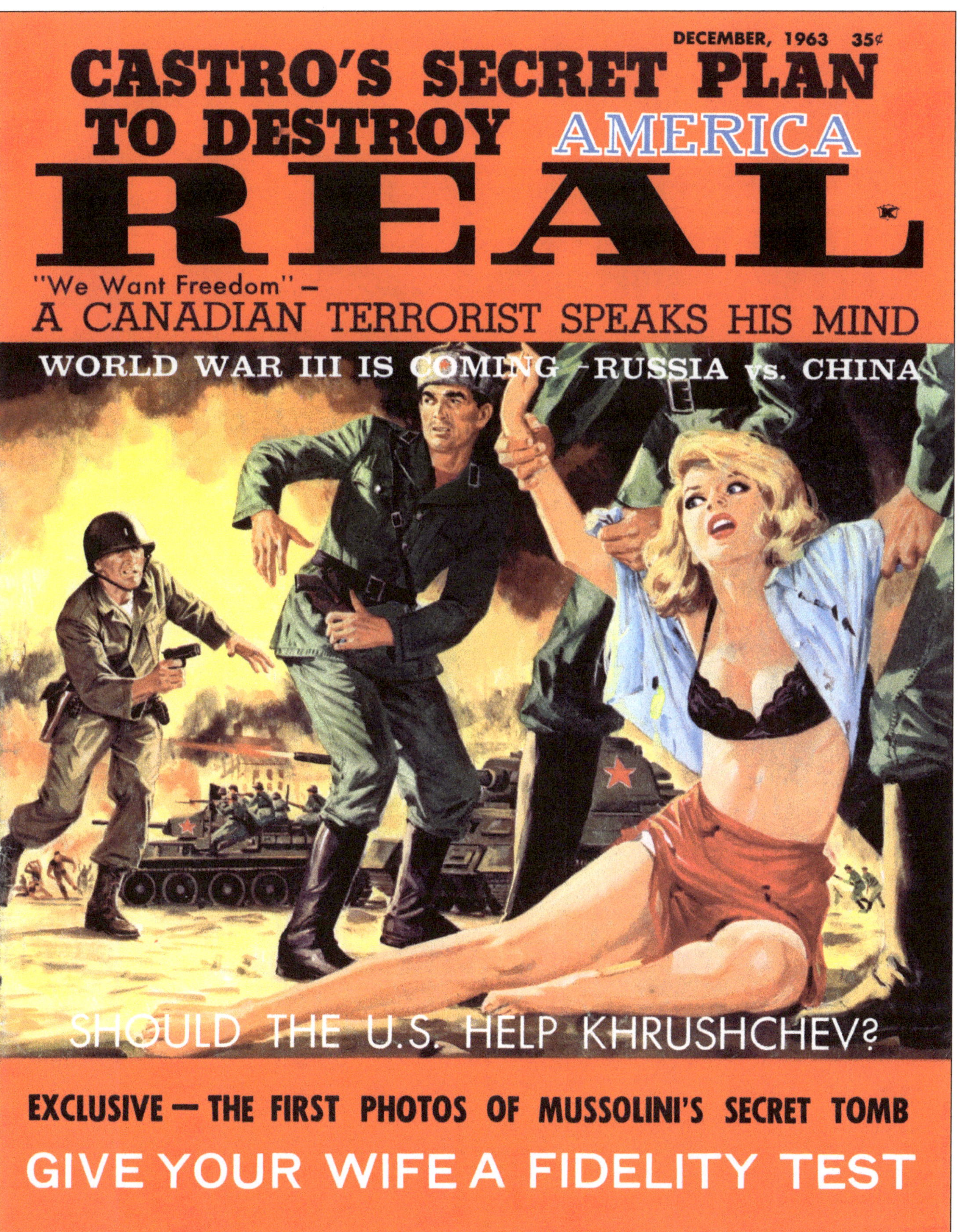

December 1963

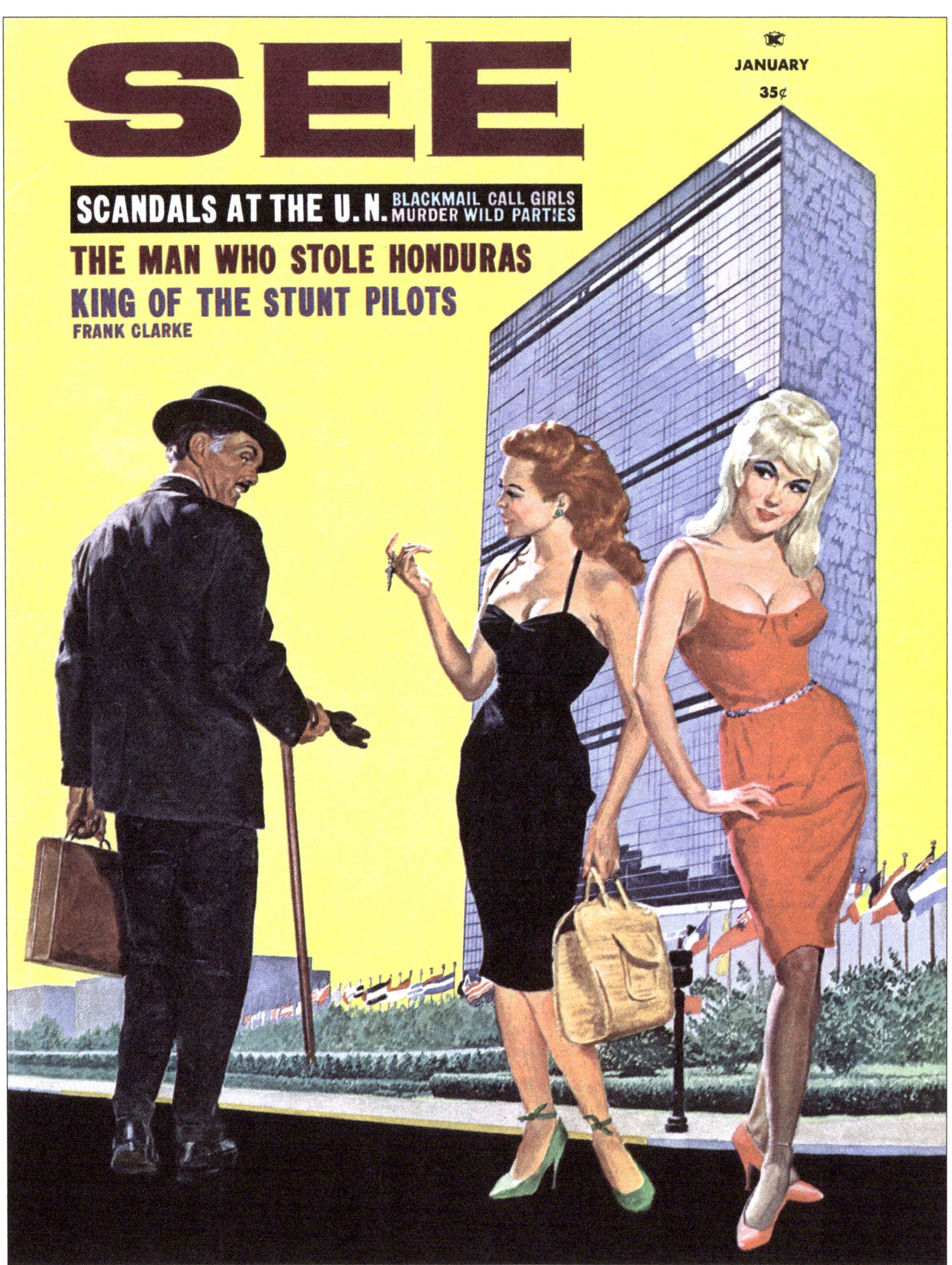

January 1964

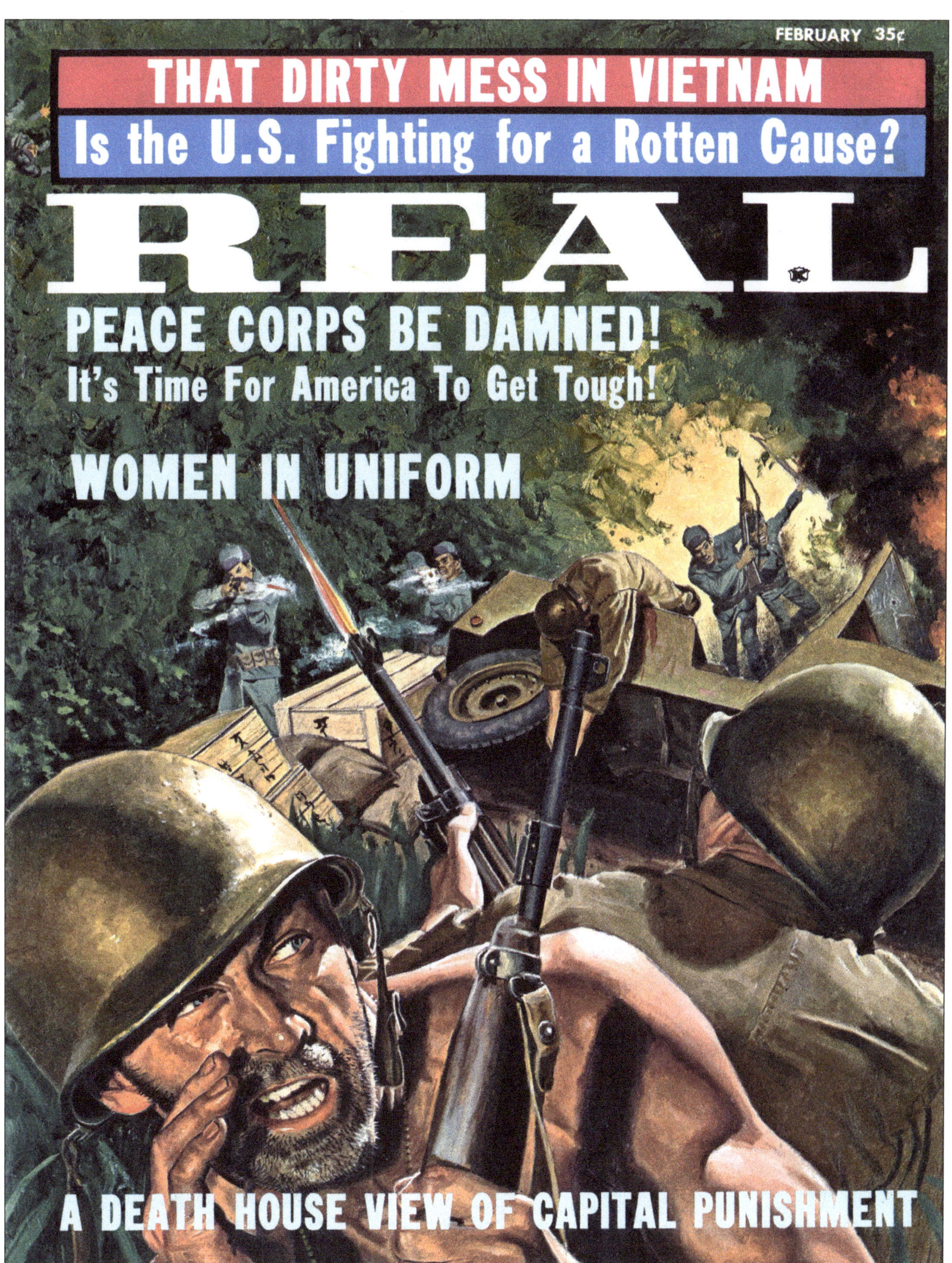

February 1964

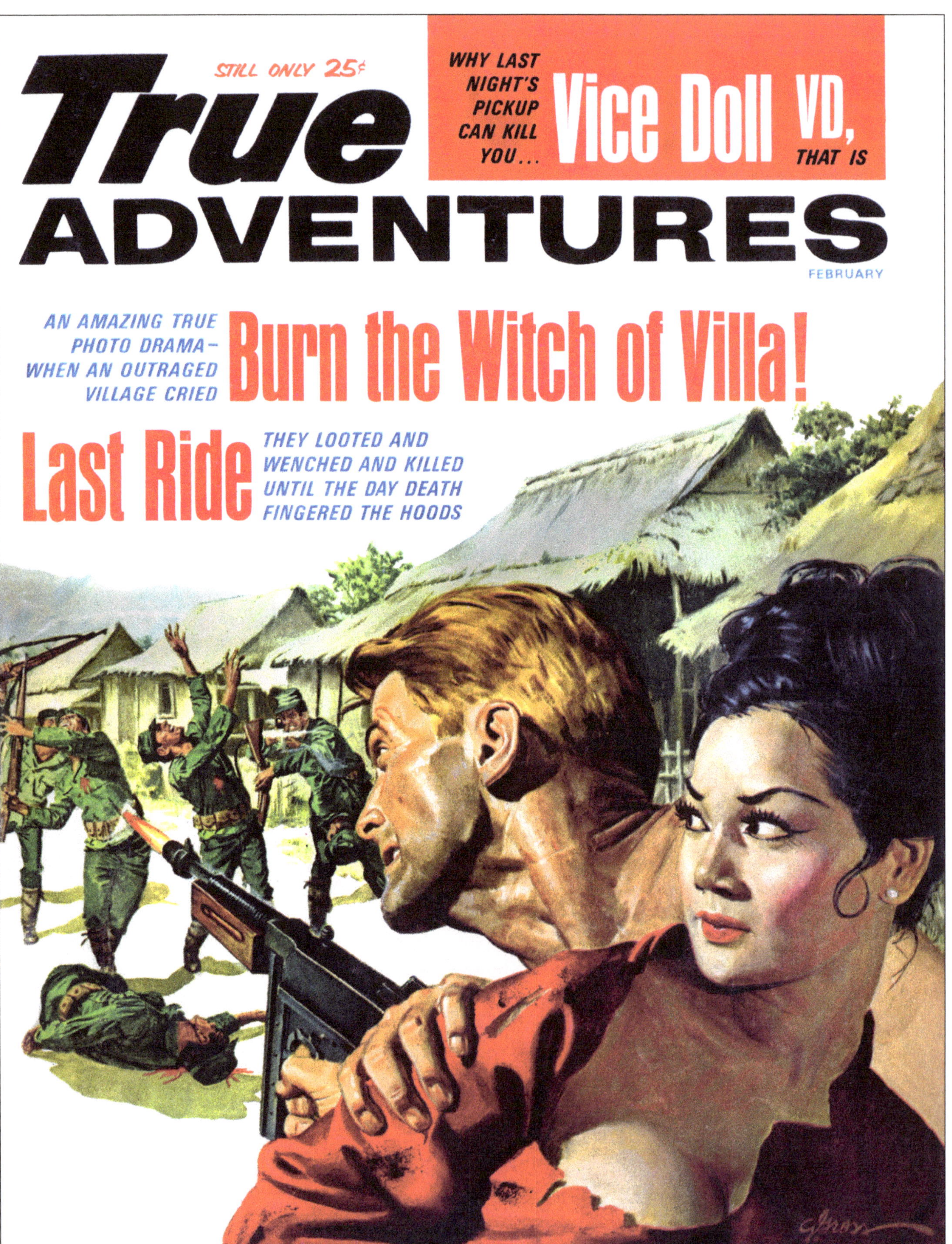

February 1964

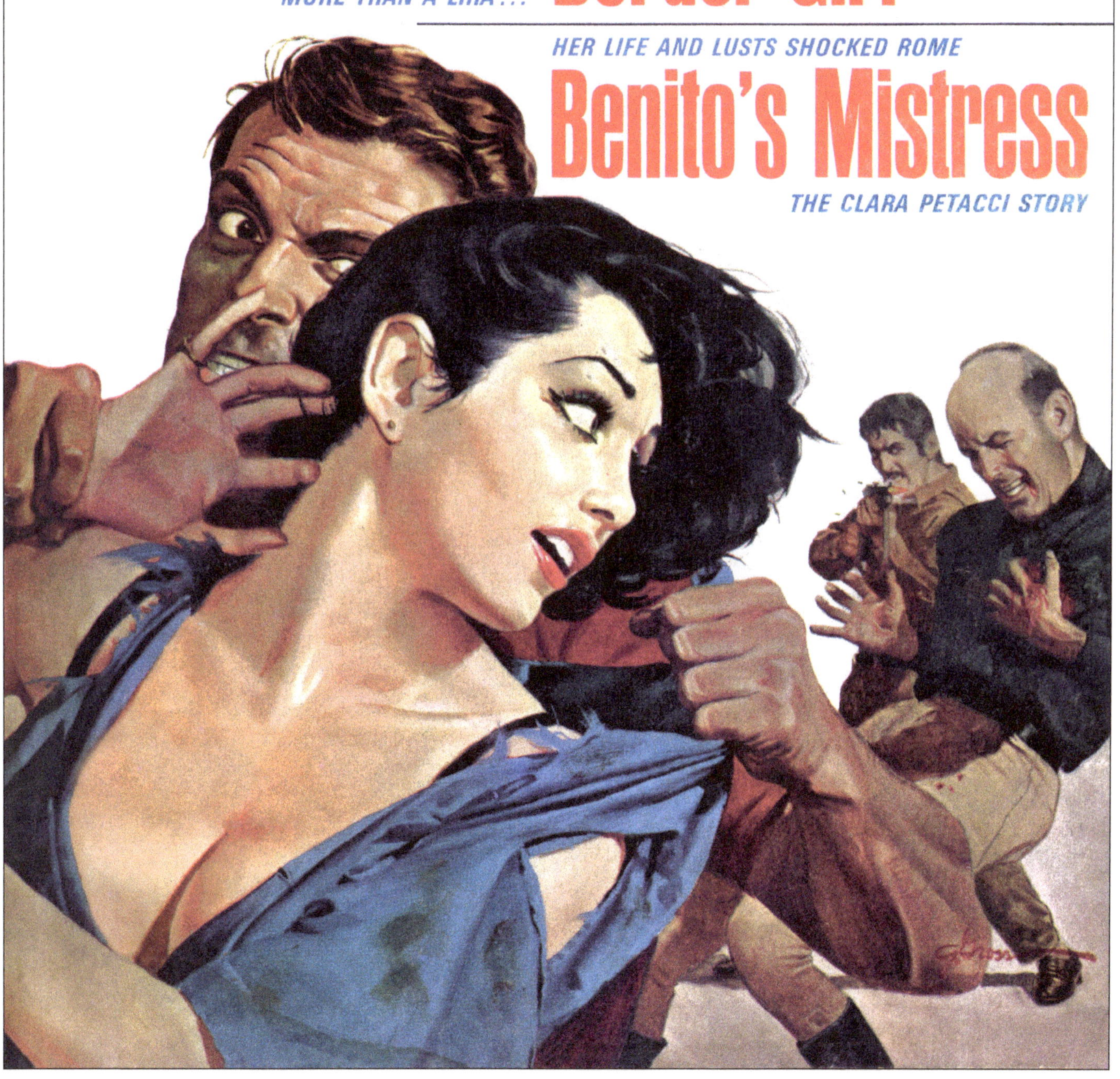

STILL ONLY 25¢

True
ADVENTURES
APRIL

YOUR "DAYDREAMS" CAN HELP
YOU TO A FULLER LOVE LIFE
...OR DESTROY YOU!

"WHERE THE CHICKS
COME A PESO A PARCEL
AND A LEER MEANS
MORE THAN A LIRA..."
Border Girl

HER LIFE AND LUSTS SHOCKED ROME
Benito's Mistress
THE CLARA PETACCI STORY

April 1964

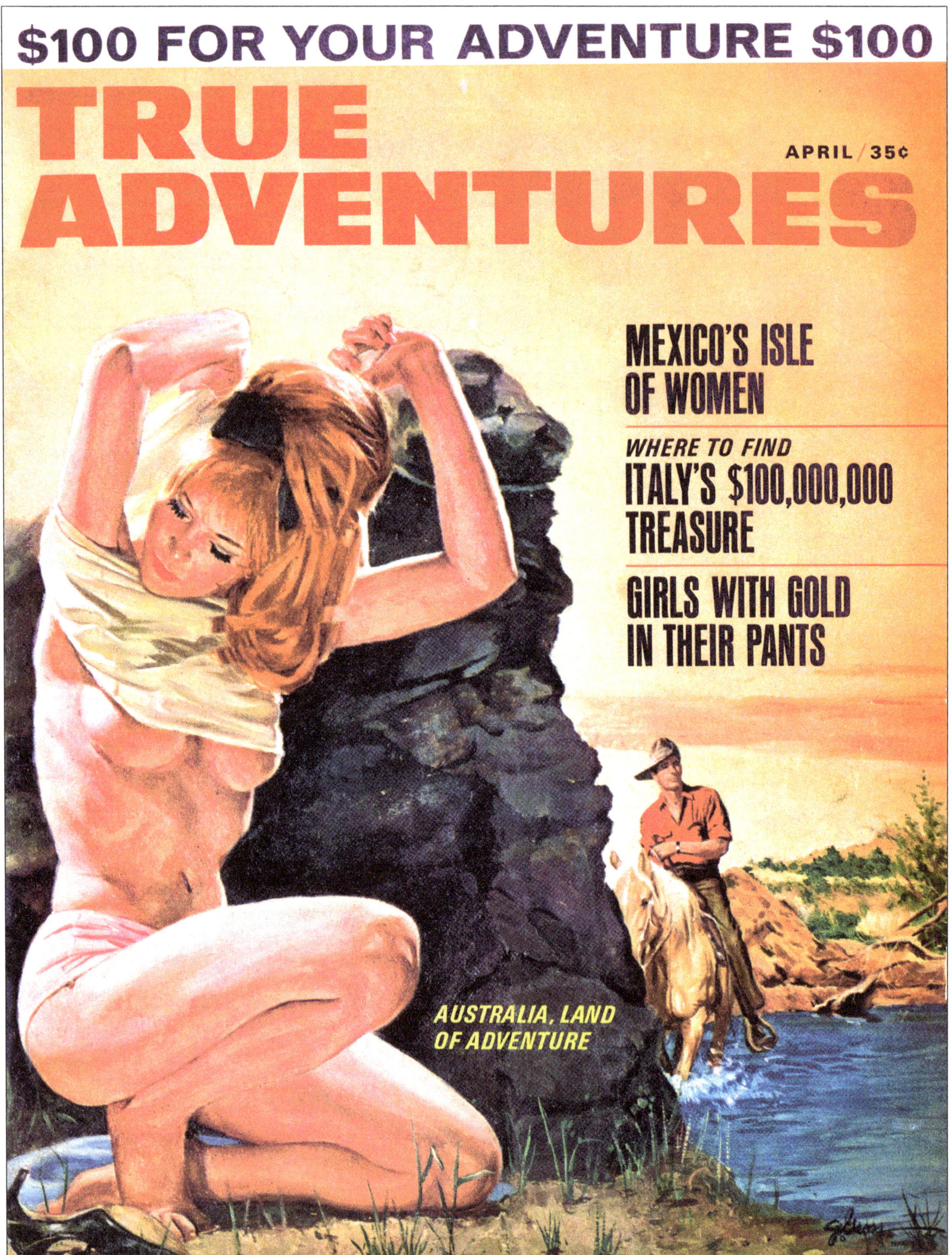

$100 FOR YOUR ADVENTURE $100
TRUE ADVENTURES
APRIL / 35¢
MEXICO'S ISLE OF WOMEN
WHERE TO FIND ITALY'S $100,000,000 TREASURE
GIRLS WITH GOLD IN THEIR PANTS
AUSTRALIA, LAND OF ADVENTURE

April 1965

MAN'S ILLUSTRATED

SEPT. 35c

STERLING

M.I. DISCOVERS
TORRID TONI

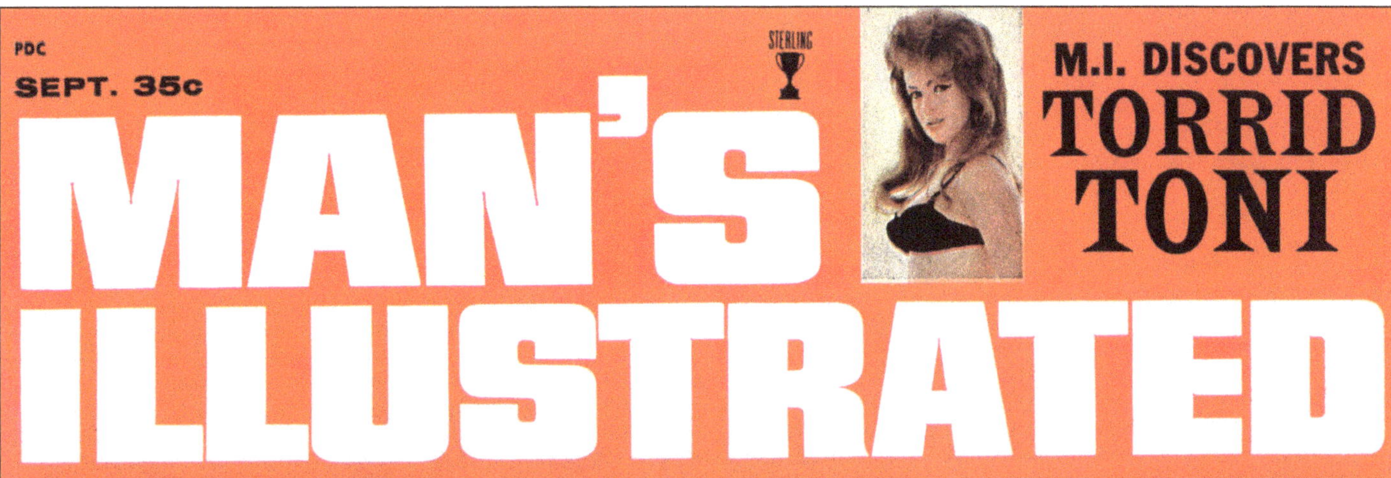

THE MOST VICIOUS TOWN IN THE U.S.

Sizzling expose of our latest vice scandal
PART-TIME CALL GIRLS

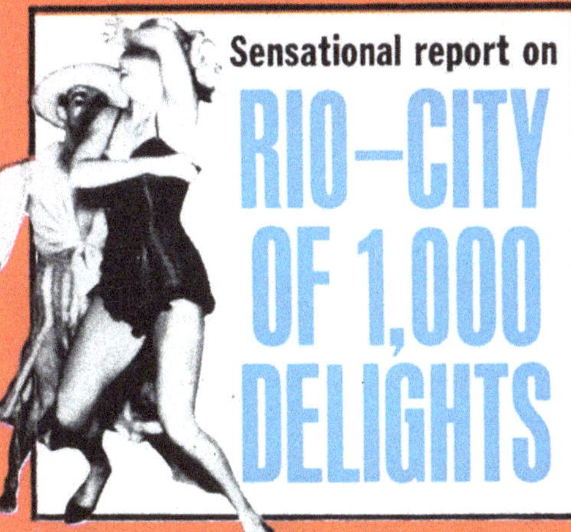

Sensational report on
RIO—CITY OF 1,000 DELIGHTS

SAGA OF THE NAVY'S SUPER-SECRET **S.E.A.L.s**
AMERICA'S TRIPLE-THREAT SPIES

"MY 5-YEAR NIGHTMARE IN A SOVIET SLAVE LABOR CAMP"
True story of an American citizen's ordeal of terror

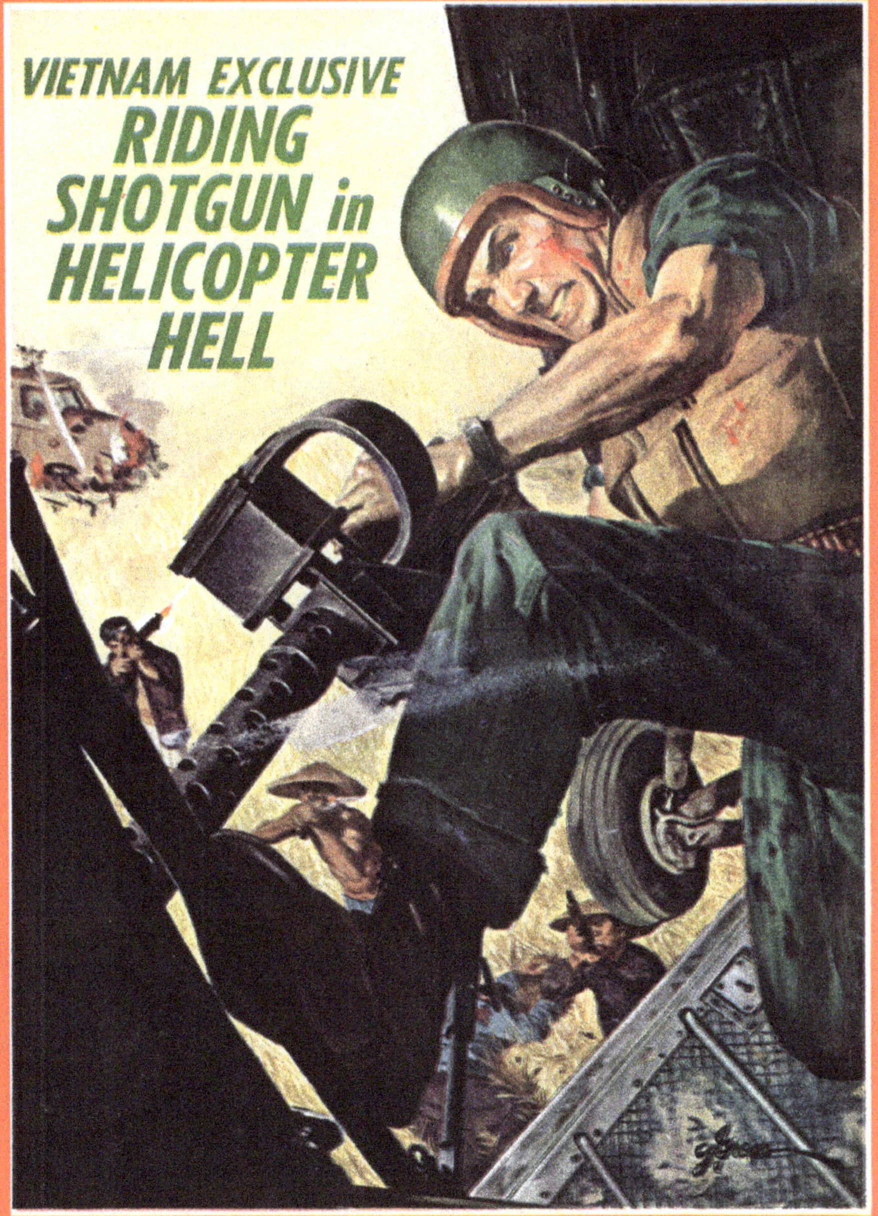

September 1965

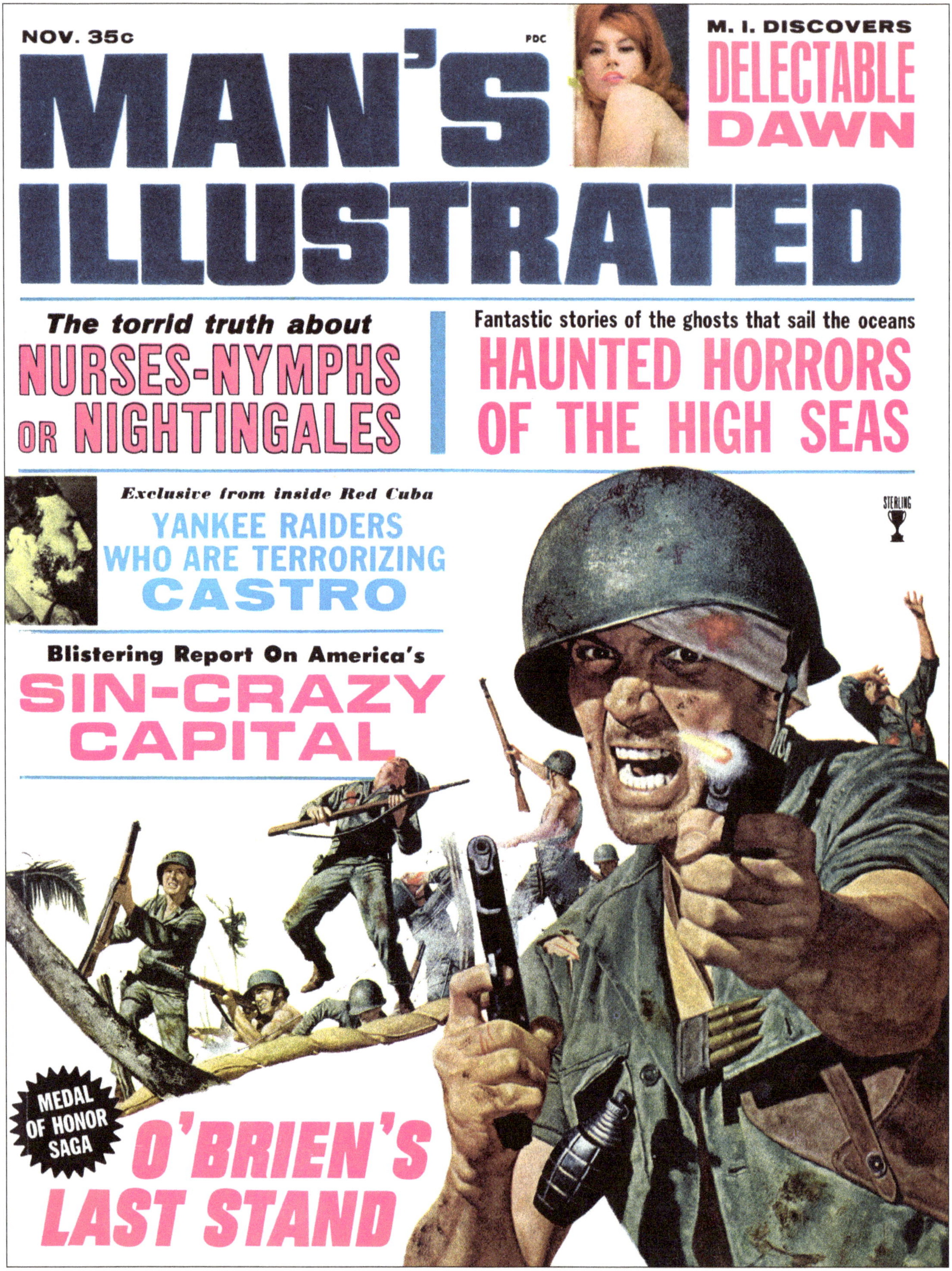

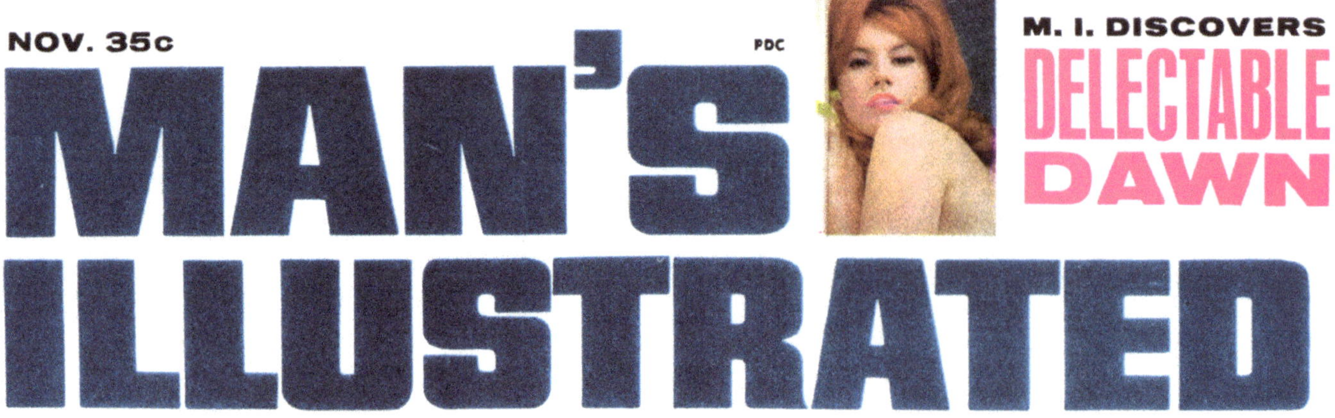

NOV. 35c
PDC
MAN'S ILLUSTRATED
M. I. DISCOVERS
DELECTABLE DAWN
The torrid truth about
NURSES-NYMPHS OR NIGHTINGALES
Fantastic stories of the ghosts that sail the oceans
HAUNTED HORRORS OF THE HIGH SEAS
Exclusive from inside Red Cuba
YANKEE RAIDERS WHO ARE TERRORIZING CASTRO
STERLING
Blistering Report On America's
SIN-CRAZY CAPITAL
MEDAL OF HONOR SAGA
O'BRIEN'S LAST STAND

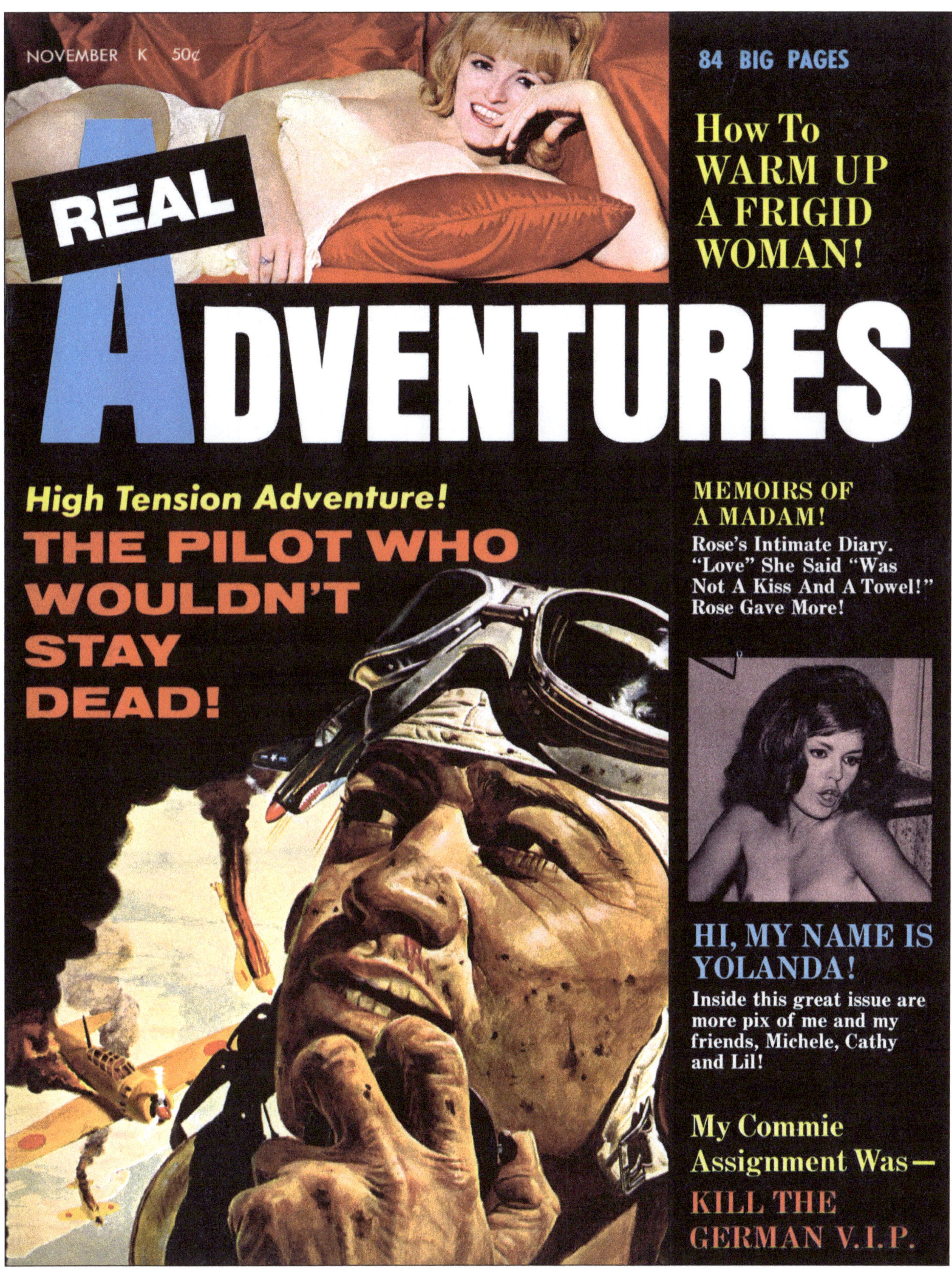

November 1969   *Previously used for* **Cavalcade** January 1961

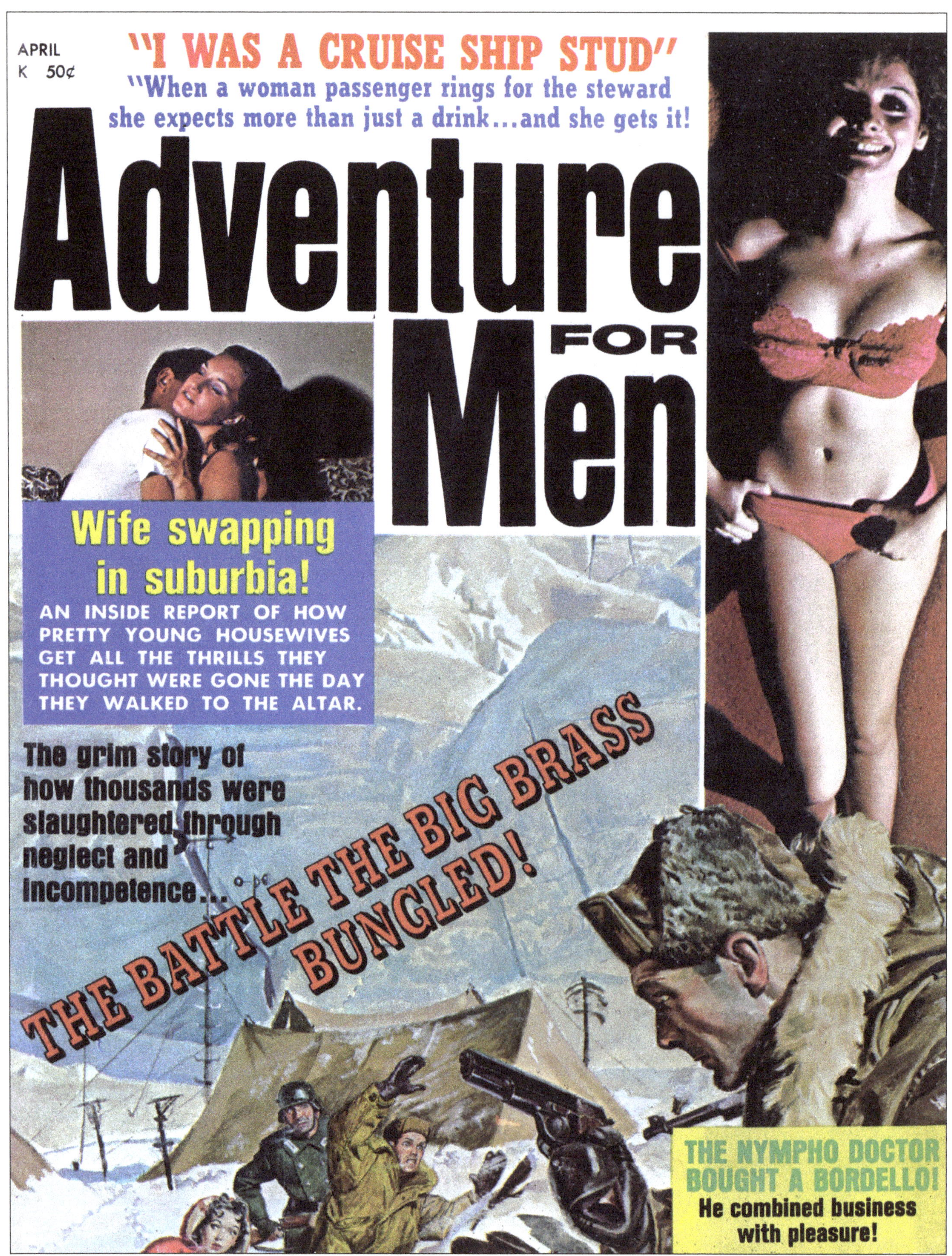

April 1971   *Previously used for* **Real Adventure** May–June 1961

ROBERT DEIS owns one of the world's largest collections of vintage men's adventure magazines (MAMs) published in the 1950s, 1960s, and 1970s. In 2009, he created a popular blog about the genre, **MensPulpMags.com**. A few years later, Bob and Wyatt Doyle of New Texture launched The Men's Adventure Library, a series of books that feature classic MAM pulp fiction stories and artwork. That series now includes nearly 20 lushly illustrated story anthologies and art books. In recent years, Bob and Wyatt have been featured speakers at PulpFest, and Bob was listed in the book *Who's Who In New Pulp*. Starting in 2021, Bob began working with Bill Cunningham, head of Pulp 2.0 Press, to publish a magazine that features MAM stories and artwork, called the *Men's Adventure Quarterly*. He has contributed articles about MAMs to various magazines and fanzines and also writes two blogs about famous quotations, **ThisDayinQuotes.com** and **QuoteCounterquote.com**. Bob lives near Key West, Florida with his wife BJ (who graciously tolerates his fascination with vintage MAMs), their three dogs, and four cats.

WYATT DOYLE is ringmaster of New Texture, and he edits and designs most releases. His own books include *Stop Requested* (illustrated by Stanley J. Zappa), *Dollar Halloween*, *I Need Real Tuxedo and a Top Hat!*, *Buty-Wave Is Now Closed Forever*, and *Jorge Amaya Doesn't Live Here Anymore*. A retrospective of his photography was presented by Gallery 30 South in Pasadena, CA. With Robert Deis, he edits the Men's Adventure Library series, exploring vintage pulp fiction, art, and history. With Jimmy Angelina, he created *The Last Coloring Book* and *The Last Coloring Book on the Left*, as well as *Be Italian*. Together with Hal Glatzer and Norman von Holtzendorff, he produced *Things That Were Made for Love*, collecting the songsheet art of Sydney Leff. He assisted in the publication of Georgina Spelvin's memoir, *The Devil Made Me Do It*, and published Josh Alan Friedman's *Black Cracker* and *Tell the Truth Until They Bleed* via his Wyatt Doyle Books imprint. He administers the creative estate of Rev. Raymond Branch, and curates **RevBranch.com**. His screenplay with Jason Cuadrado, *I'm Here For You*, was produced as *Devil May Call*. A member of The Stanley J. Zappa Quartet, a recording, *The Stanley J. Zappa Quartet Plays for the Society of Women Engineers*, has been released.

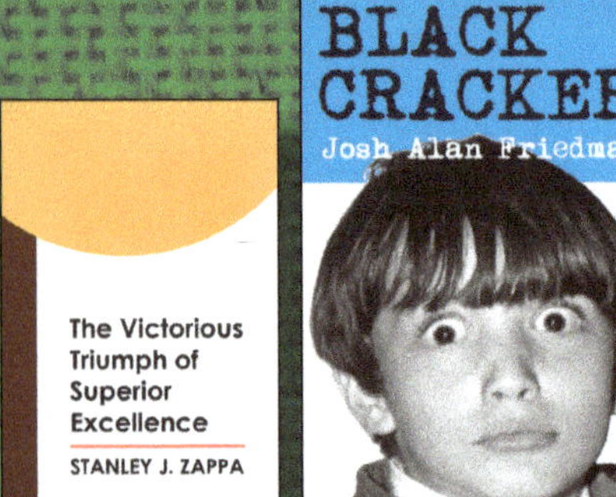
The Victorious
Triumph of
Superior
Excellence
STANLEY J. ZAPPA

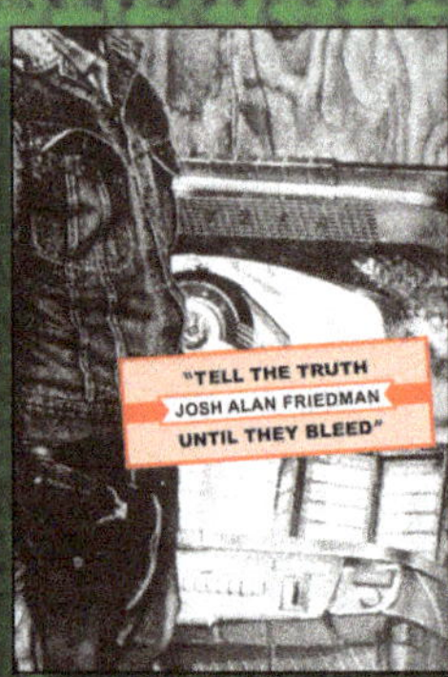
BLACK
CRACKER
Josh Alan Friedman

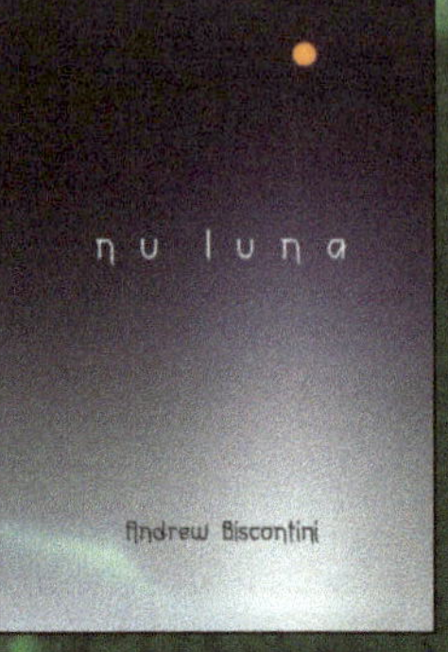
"TELL THE TRUTH
JOSH ALAN FRIEDMAN
UNTIL THEY BLEED"

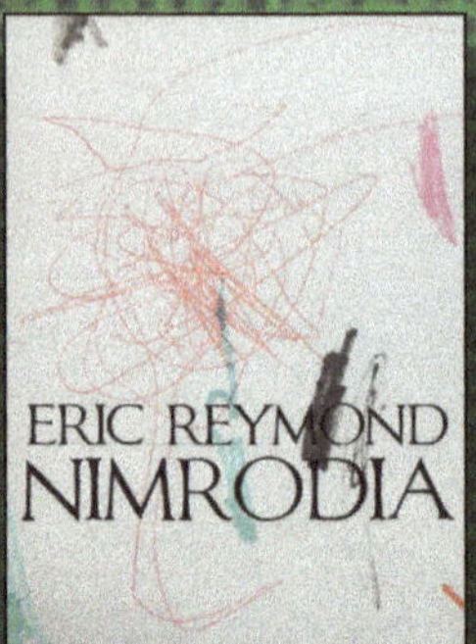
nu luna
Andrew Biscontini

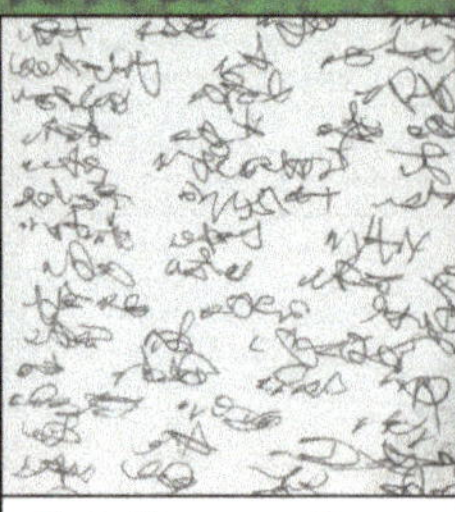
ERIC REYMOND
NIMRODIA

Eric Reymond
Sub-Sub Librarian,
Extracts on a

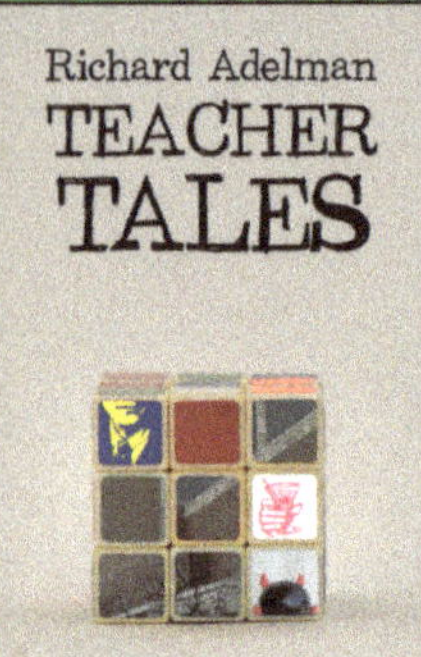
Richard Adelman
TEACHER
TALES

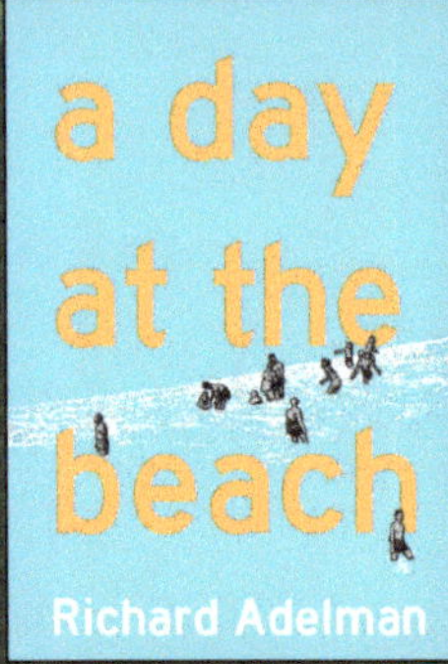
a day
at the
beach
Richard Adelman

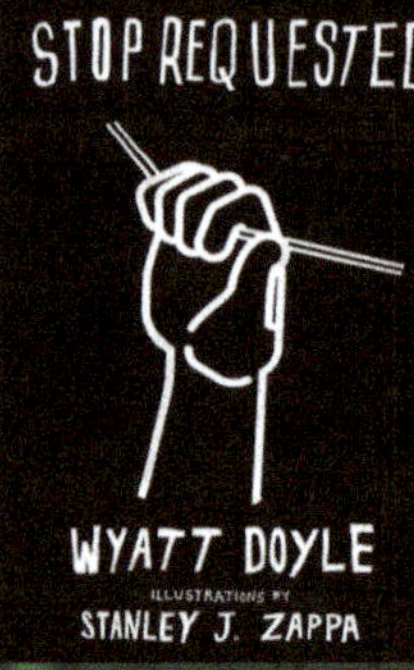
STOP REQUESTED
WYATT DOYLE
ILLUSTRATIONS BY
STANLEY J. ZAPPA

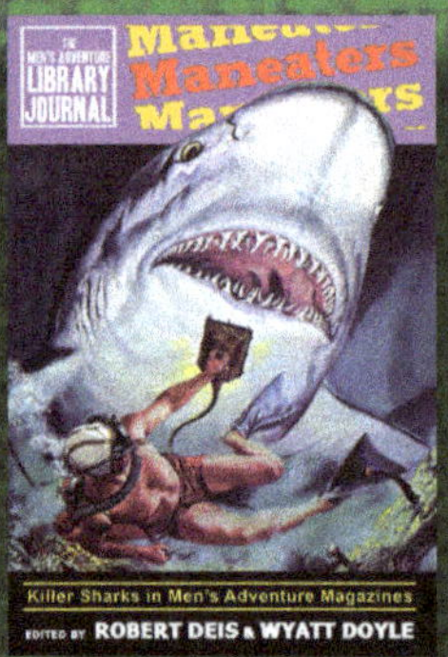
THE MEN'S ADVENTURE
LIBRARY JOURNAL
Maneaters
Maneaters
Maneaters
Killer Sharks in Men's Adventure Magazines
EDITED BY ROBERT DEIS & WYATT DOYLE

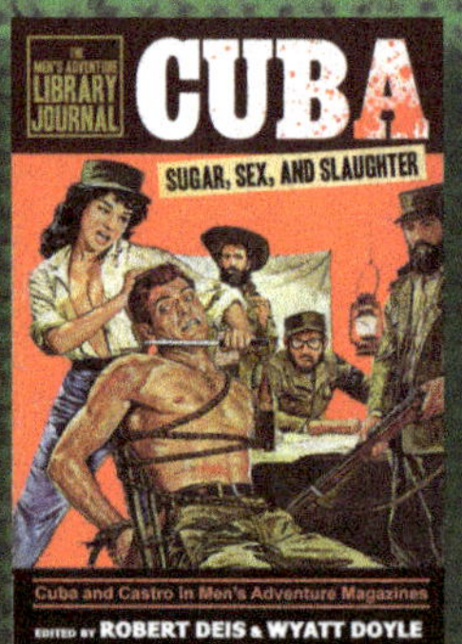
THE MEN'S ADVENTURE
LIBRARY JOURNAL
CUBA
SUGAR, SEX, AND SLAUGHTER
Cuba and Castro in Men's Adventure Magazines
EDITED BY ROBERT DEIS & WYATT DOYLE

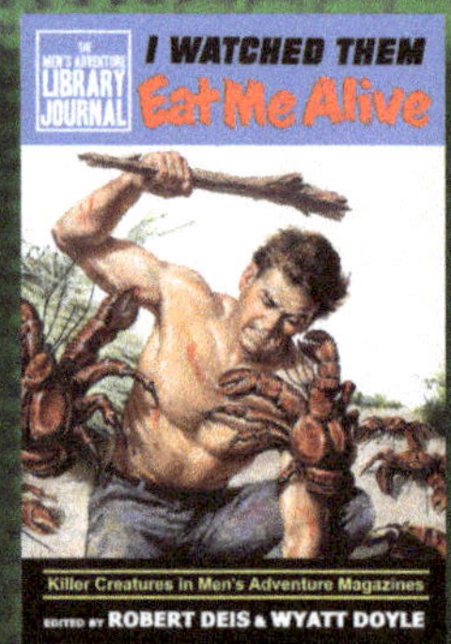
THE MEN'S ADVENTURE
LIBRARY JOURNAL
I WATCHED THEM
Eat Me Alive
Killer Creatures in Men's Adventure Magazines
EDITED BY ROBERT DEIS & WYATT DOYLE

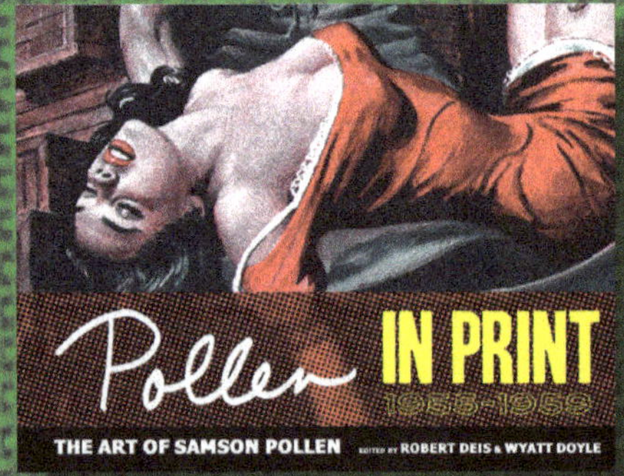
Pollen IN PRINT
THE ART OF SAMSON POLLEN   EDITED BY ROBERT DEIS & WYATT DOYLE

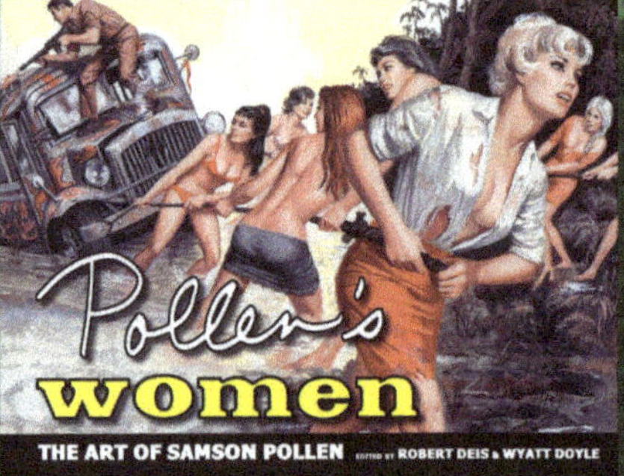
Pollen's
women
THE ART OF SAMSON POLLEN   EDITED BY ROBERT DEIS & WYATT DOYLE

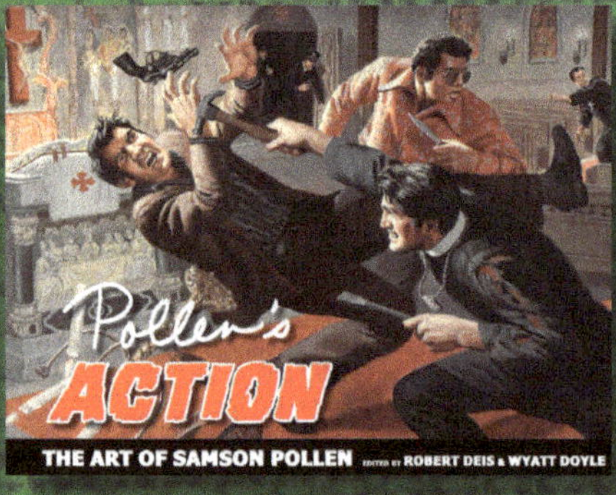
Pollen's
ACTION
THE ART OF SAMSON POLLEN   EDITED BY ROBERT DEIS & WYATT DOYLE

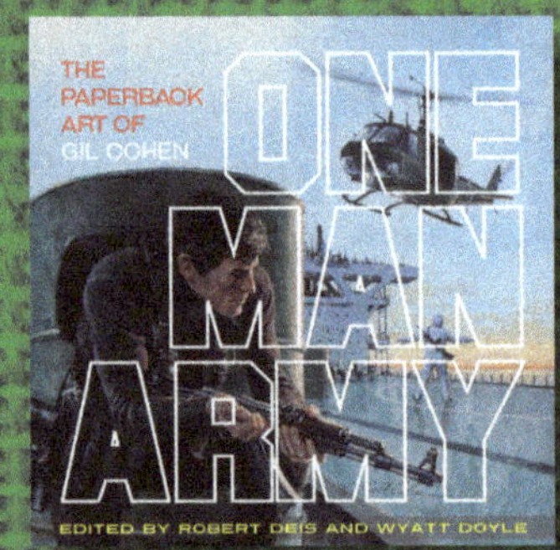
THE PAPERBACK
ART OF GIL COHEN
ONE
MAN
ARMY
EDITED BY ROBERT DEIS AND WYATT DOYLE

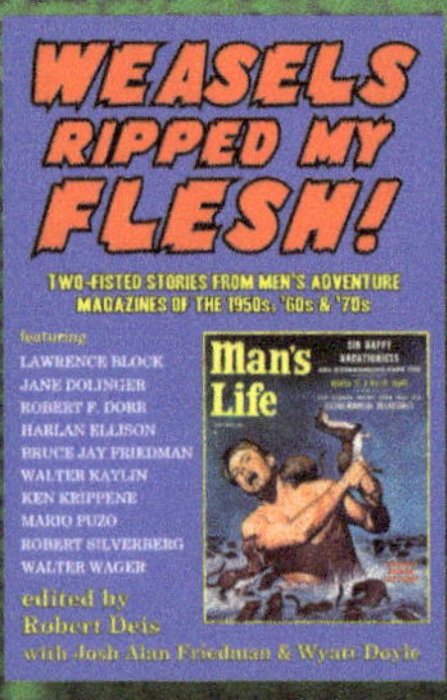
WEASELS
RIPPED MY
FLESH!
TWO-FISTED STORIES FROM MEN'S ADVENTURE
MAGAZINES OF THE 1950s, 60s & 70s
featuring
LAWRENCE BLOCK
JANE DOLINGER
ROBERT F. DORR
HARLAN ELLISON
BRUCE JAY FRIEDMAN
WALTER KAYLIN
KEN KRIPPENE
MARIO PUZO
ROBERT SILVERBERG
WALTER WAGER
edited by
Robert Deis
with Josh Alan Friedman & Wyatt Doyle

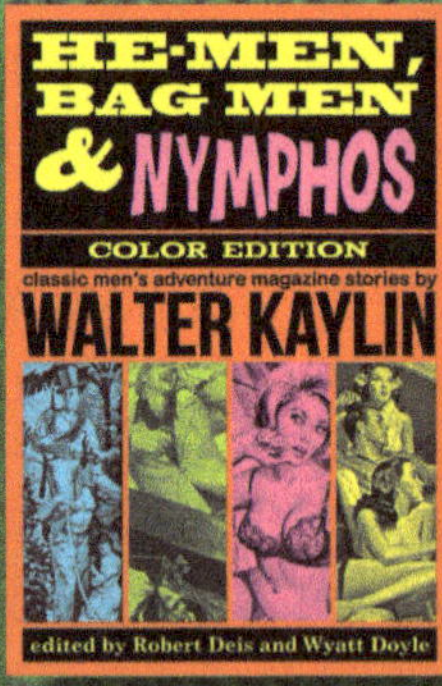
HE-MEN,
BAG MEN
& NYMPHOS
COLOR EDITION
classic men's adventure magazine stories by
WALTER KAYLIN
edited by Robert Deis and Wyatt Doyle

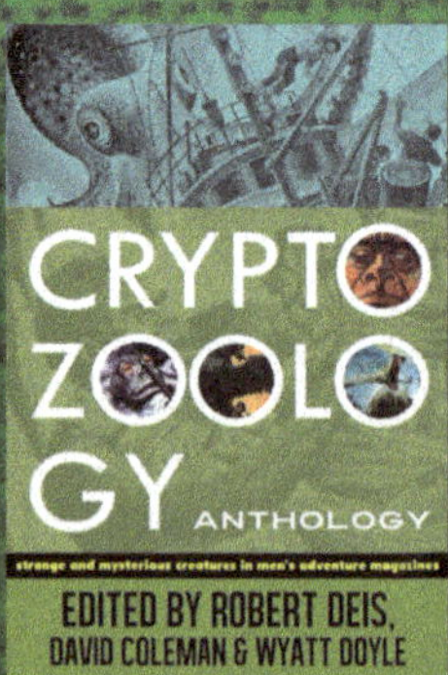
CRYPTO
ZOOLO
GY
ANTHOLOGY
strange and mysterious creatures in men's adventure magazines
EDITED BY ROBERT DEIS,
DAVID COLEMAN & WYATT DOYLE

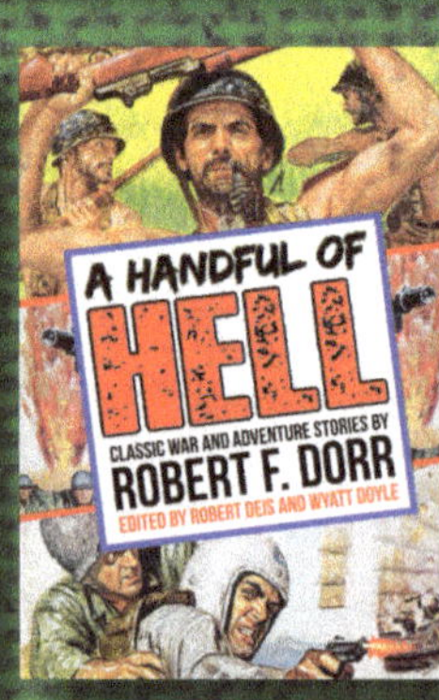
A HANDFUL OF
HELL
CLASSIC WAR AND ADVENTURE STORIES BY
ROBERT F. DORR
EDITED BY ROBERT DEIS & WYATT DOYLE

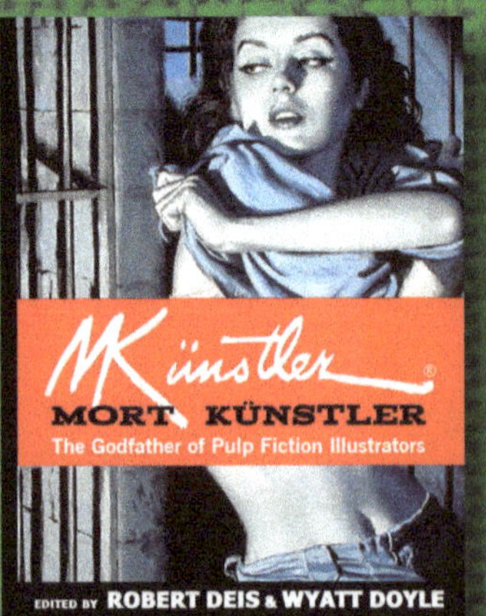
Künstler
MORT KÜNSTLER
The Godfather of Pulp Fiction Illustrators
EDITED BY ROBERT DEIS & WYATT DOYLE

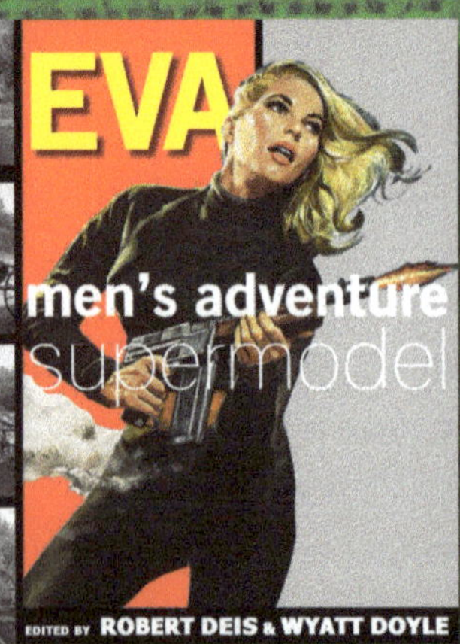
EVA
men's adventure
supermodel
EDITED BY ROBERT DEIS & WYATT DOYLE

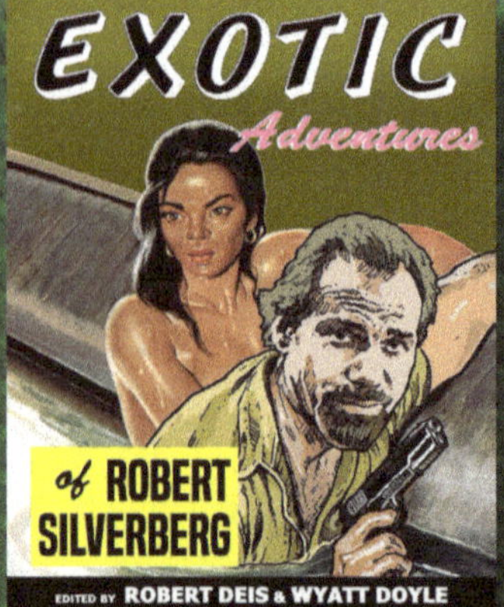
EXOTIC
Adventures
of ROBERT
SILVERBERG
EDITED BY ROBERT DEIS & WYATT DOYLE

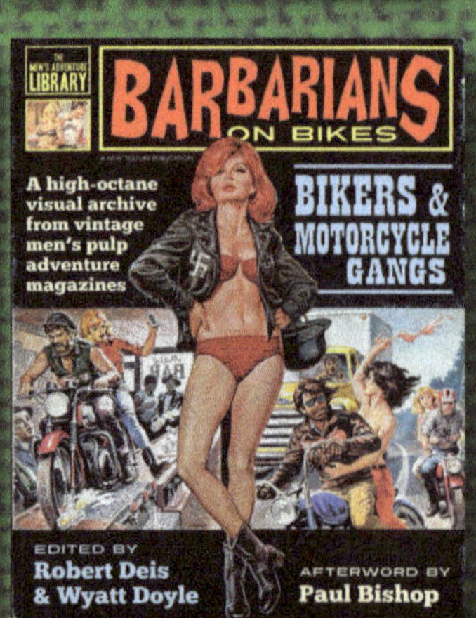
MEN'S ADVENTURE
LIBRARY
BARBARIANS
ON BIKES
A high-octane
visual archive
from vintage
men's pulp
adventure
magazines
BIKERS &
MOTORCYCLE
GANGS
EDITED BY
Robert Deis
& Wyatt Doyle
AFTERWORD BY
Paul Bishop

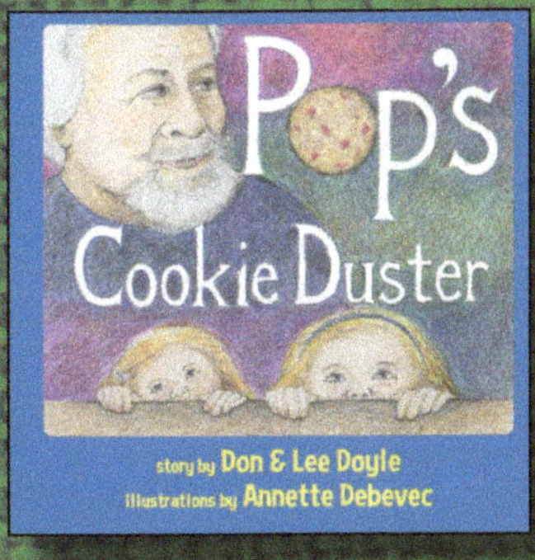

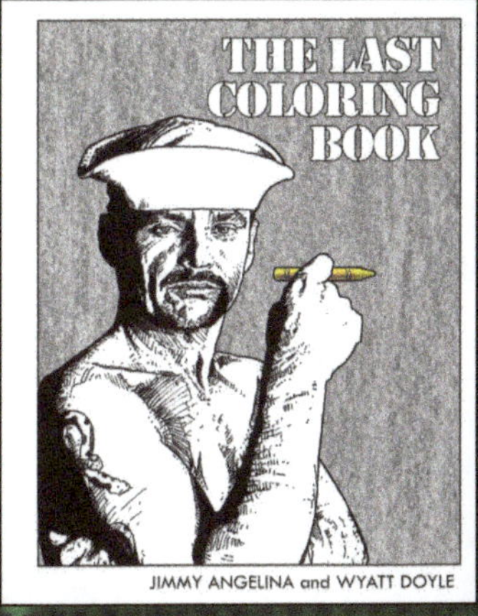

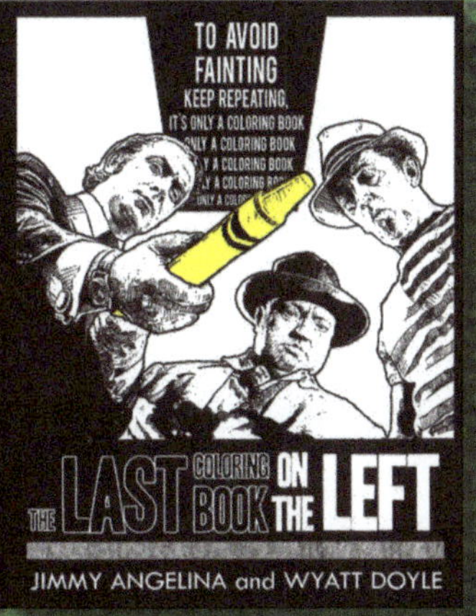

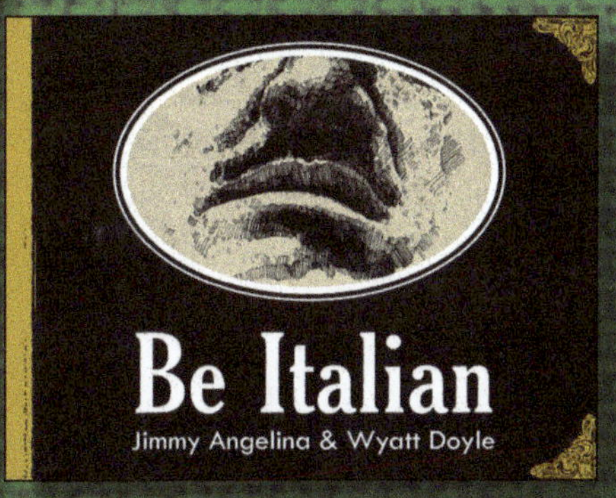

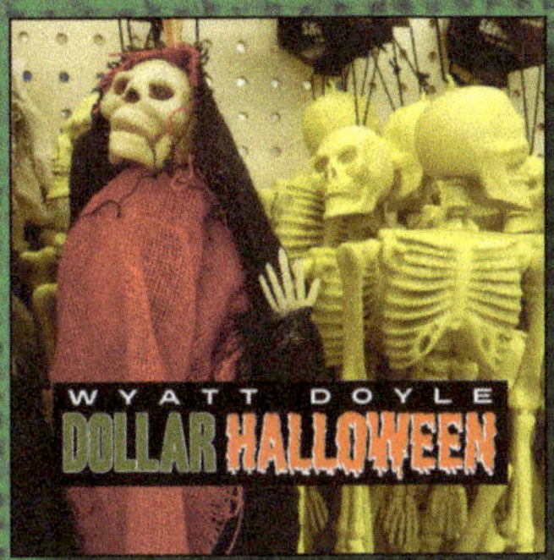

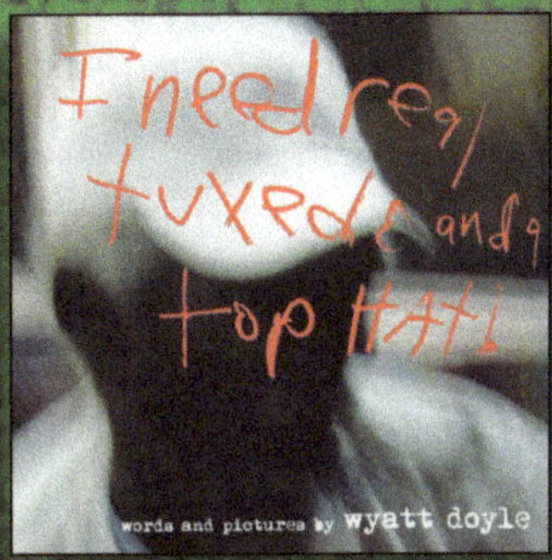

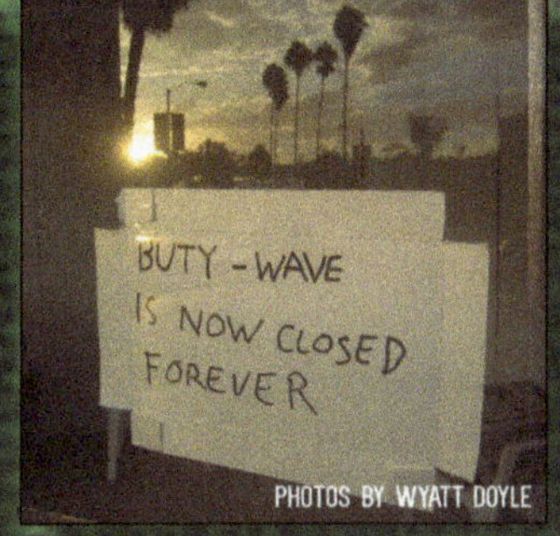

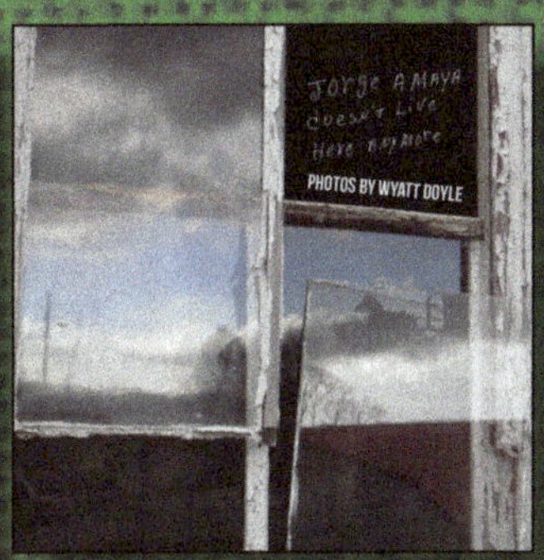

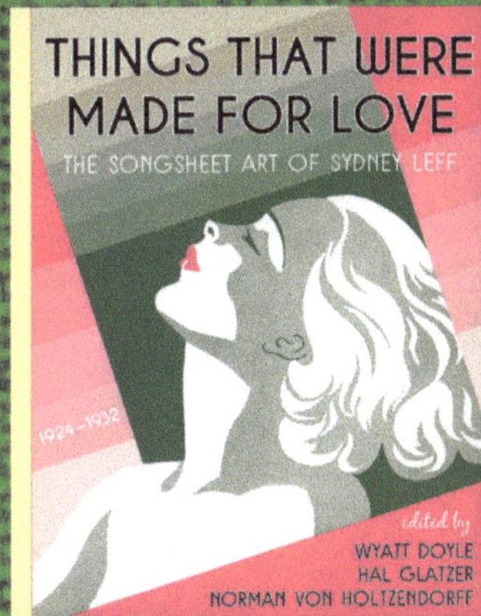

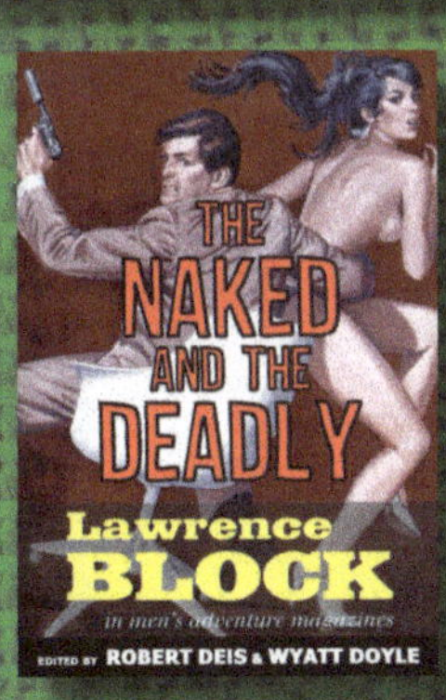

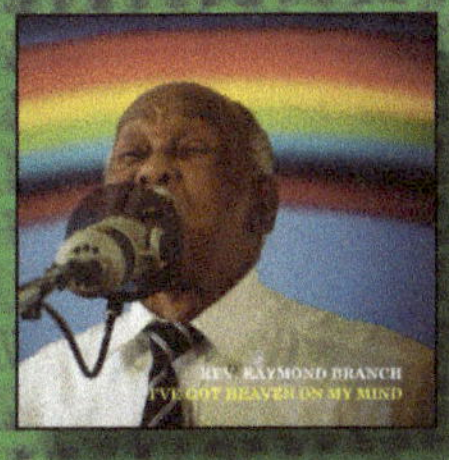

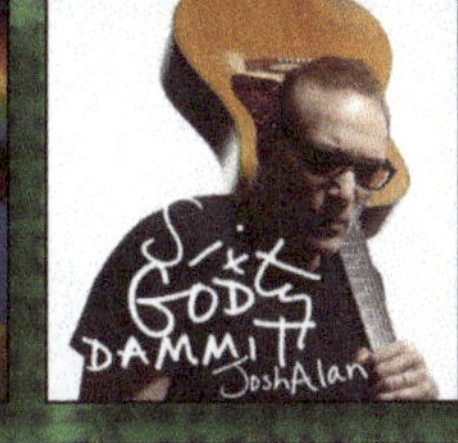

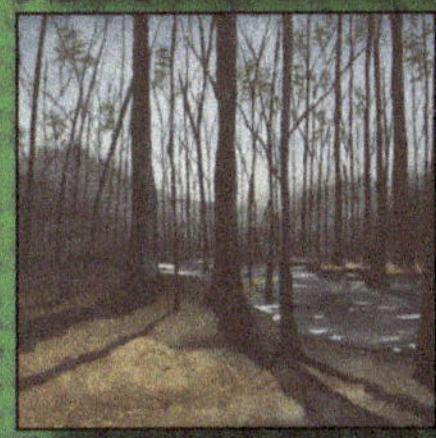

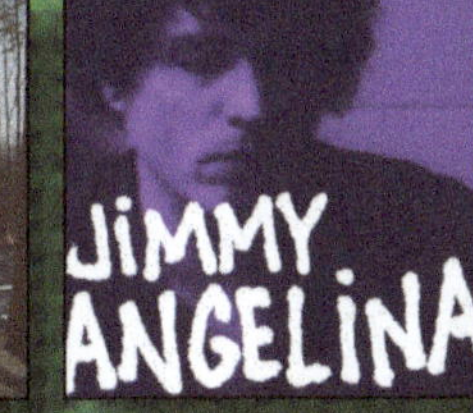

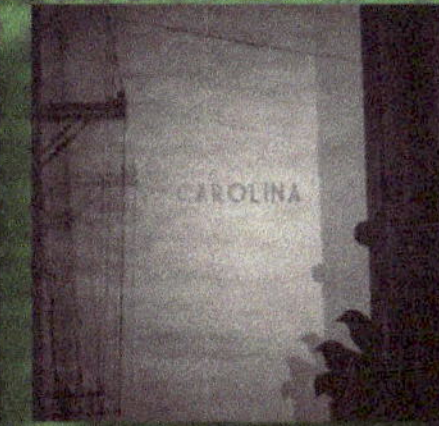

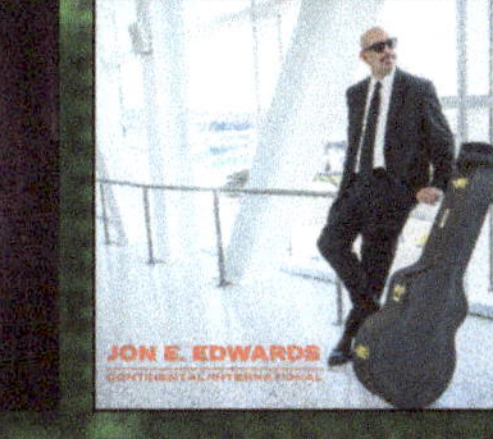

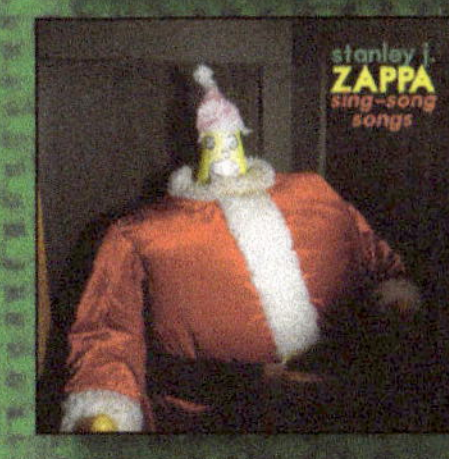

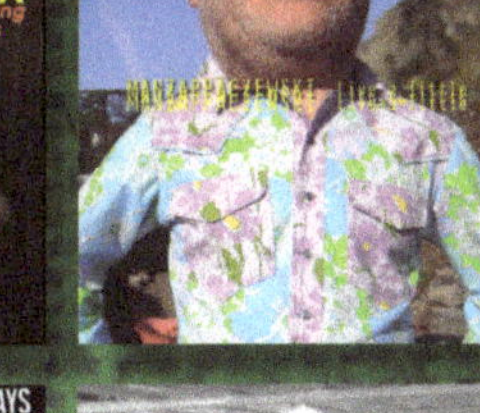

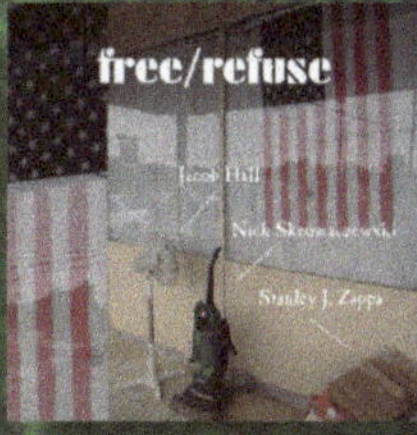

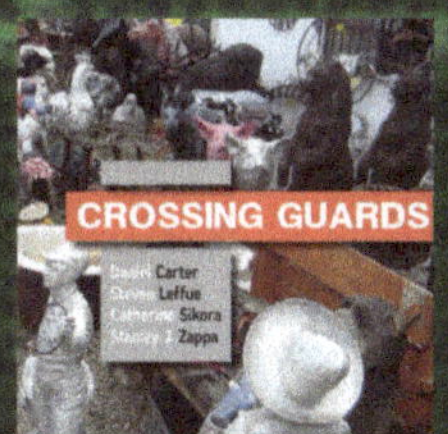

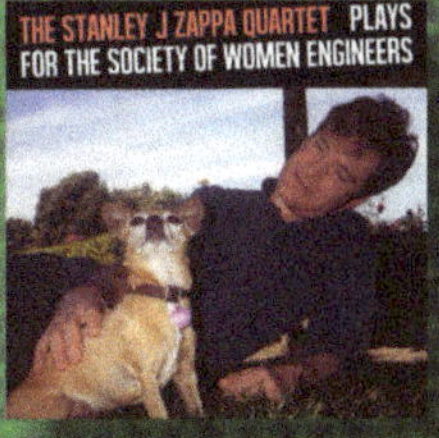

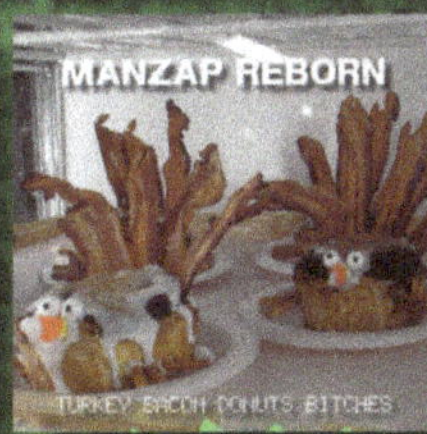

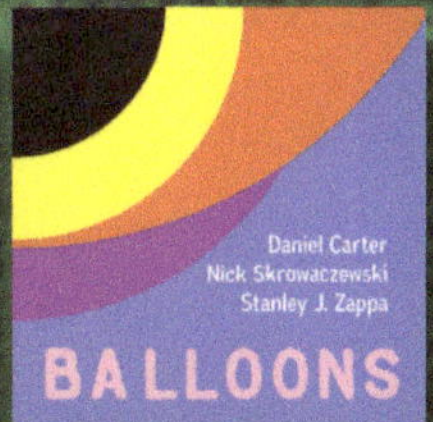

Words and Pictures and Music

new texture

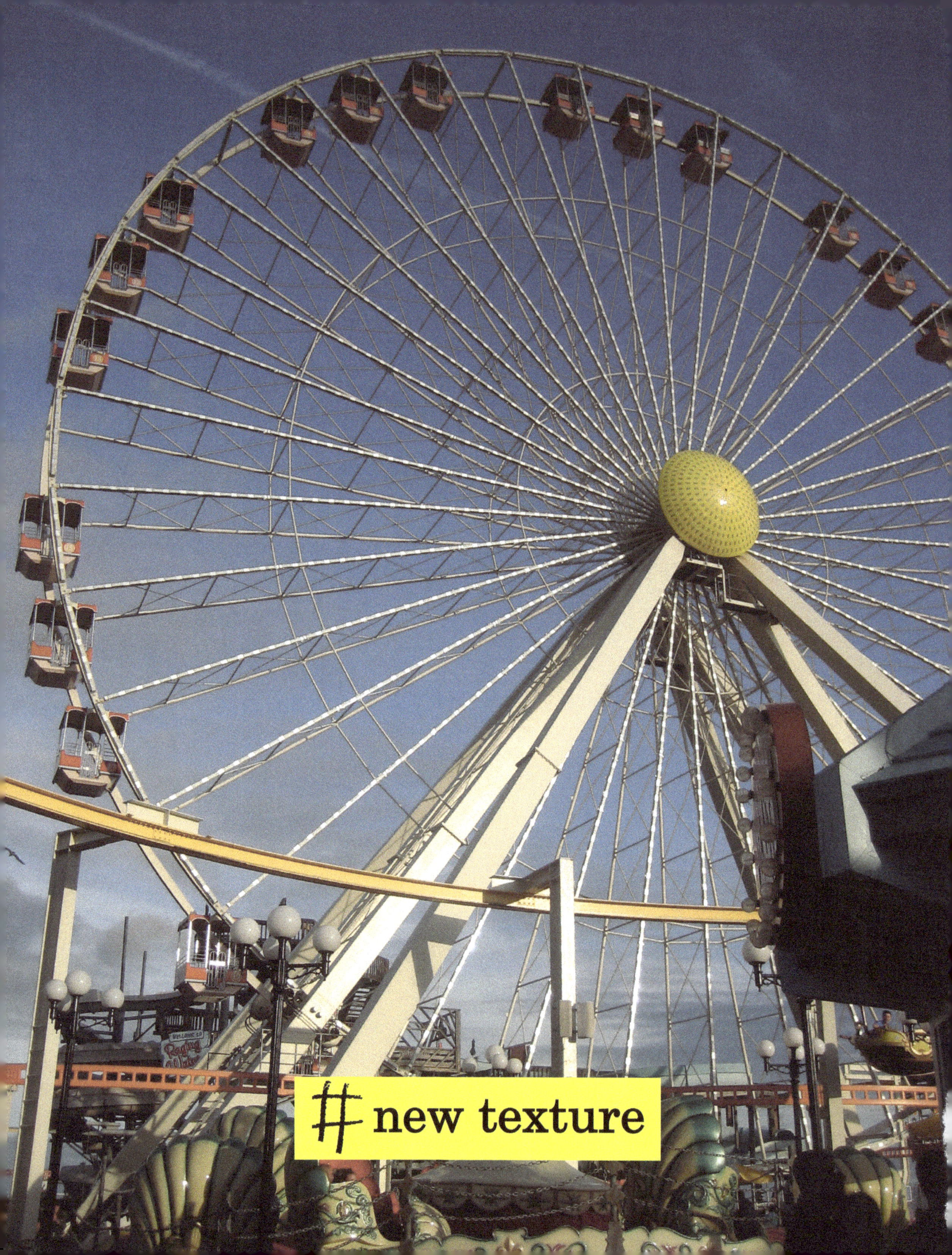

new texture

www.ingramcontent.com/pod-product-compliance
Lightning Source LLC
Chambersburg PA
CBHW042047030726
47599CB00019B/2401